THE HALIFAX EXPLOSION
DECEMBER 6, 1917

THE HALIFAX EXPLOSION
DECEMBER 6, 1917

Compiled and Edited by Graham Metson

Including the complete text of
THE HALIFAX DISASTER
by Archibald MacMechan

McGraw-Hill Ryerson Limited
Toronto   Montreal   New York   St. Louis   San Francisco
Auckland   Beirut   Bogotá   Düsseldorf   Johannesburg
Lisbon   London   Lucerne   Madrid   Mexico   New Delhi
Panama   Paris   San Juan   São Paulo   Singapore
Sydney   Tokyo

Acknowledgments

My first thanks must go to Cheryl Lean for her sustaining encouragement and her research and selection of the photographs in this volume. This book grew out of an exhibition we researched together for the West House Museum of Photography in Halifax. The photo-documentation of the Halifax Explosion was presented to commemorate the sixtieth anniversary of this tragic event and was funded by the National Museums of Canada and the Nova Scotia Department of Recreation.

I should like to thank Linda Price of the City of Toronto Archives, Mrs. Dorothy Cooke of Dalhousie Library, Charles Armour of Dalhousie University Archives, Mrs. S. T. Oslin of the Massachusetts Legislative Library, Scott Robson of the Nova Scotia Museum, Phyllis Blakeley of the Public Archives of Nova Scotia, and Pat Kipping for her sound recordings.

For permission to reproduce material I also acknowledge the Canadian Red Cross (Halifax Chapter), Dartmouth Heritage Museum, Halifax Herald Limited, Kings College Library, Massachusetts State Archives, the Public Archives of Canada, and the Royal Society of Canada.

Research for this book has included numerous primary sources in archival collections, as well as interviews. Among secondary sources, special mention must be made of Michael Bird's THE TOWN THAT DIED, a readable and engrossing account of the whole disaster.

G.M.

ISBN 0-07-082798-2 softcover
ISBN 0-07-082797-4 hardcover

1 2 3 4 5 6 7 8 9 D 7 6 5 4 3 2 1 0 9 8

Printed and bound in Canada

Canadian Cataloguing in Publication Data

Main entry under title:

The Halifax explosion

ISBN 0-07-082797-4 bd. ISBN 0-07-082798-2 pa.

1. Halifax, N.S.—Explosion, 1917. I. MacMechan, Archibald, date. The Halifax disaster.
II. Metson, Graham, date

FC2346.4.H35   971.6'22   C78-001268-2
F1039.5.H17H35

14703

For Cheryl Lean

CONTENTS

Preface

Halifax December 31st, 1977. It is midnight. The Citadel, where I stand, is shrouded in fog and enveloped in sound as the ships in the harbour render their plaintive greeting to a new year. Past time does not vanish into a void. Time is one and eternal; past, present and future are only different aspects, different pressings of perpetual existence. The fog blankets the modern city and through its shrouds I glimpse a past city smouldering in ruins, broken houses collapsed into themselves. The glittering fragments of glass evoke childhood memories, the smells, the noises, voiceless impressions of the London blitz.

How to come close to the experience of an event. We all have the senses in common but the information we receive from them is interpreted by each according to his experience and feelings. Reality is multi-faceted, like a diamond reflecting the infinite possibilities of our inner natures.

The material gathered in this volume forms a quilt of impressions. Some are close to the moment, others have a relationship to the event tempered by the years. Dr. W. B. Moore's vision of the disaster is coloured by legends which are brought into profound perspective by the event. For Archibald MacMechan the object was to ascertain facts and to create an accurate and detailed account of the event; and he brings all his scholarly skills to the work. Another, a survivor, is aware only of the heat from the window on her face, not the thousands of glass particles imbedded in her skin. The threshold of pain once passed forms different sensations. To an eyewitness the first observable phenomenon was leadership, a leadership that arose from the public themselves—social leadership. The photographs present those often painfully formalised frozen moments of time over which the observer pauses. From these interwoven impressions we draw our own personal meaning.

GRAHAM METSON
Canning, Nova Scotia

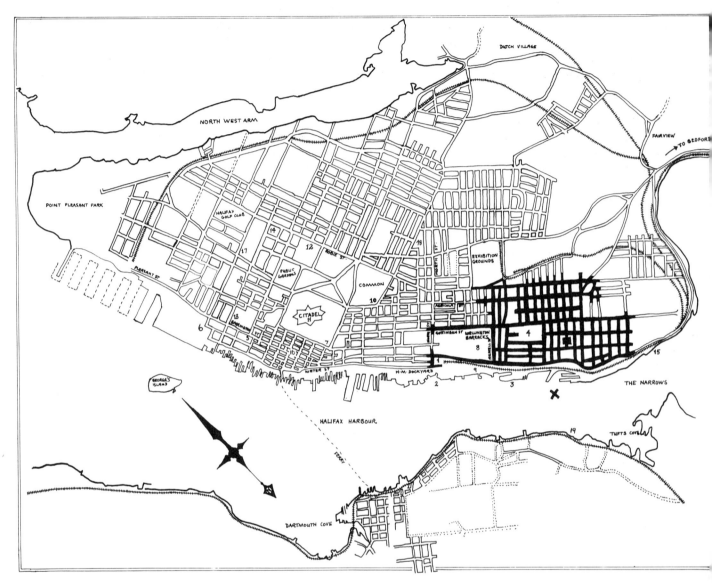

SKETCHMAP of HALIFAX · 1917 ——————————— M78

X EXPLOSION SITE   AREA TOTALLY DESTROYED MARKED BLACK.

1. RICHMOND or NORTH ST. STATION.
2. H·M·S NIOBE DEPOT SHIP.
3. S·S·PICTON AT SUGAR REFINERS
4. FORT NEEDHAM   WHARF.
5. ST. MARYS CATHEDRAL
6. GAS HOLDERS
7. MILITARY HOSPITAL

8. THE MAGAZINE.
9. THE ORDNANCE.
10. ARMOURY.
11. CITADEL.
12. CAMP HILL HOSPITAL.
13. HALIFAX INFIRMARY.
14. DALHOUSIE COLLEGE.

15. Nº 10 TRAIN.
16. CITY HALL.
17. VICTORIA GENERAL.
18. CHEBUCTO SCHOOL MORGUE.
19. IMO BEACHED HERE

The Halifax Disaster
by Archibald MacMechan

Archibald MacMechan was born in Berlin, now Kitchener, Ontario on June 21, 1862. He attended the University of Toronto and completed his academic education at Johns Hopkins University where he received his Doctorate in 1889. He accepted a post at Dalhousie University, to teach English language and literature, where he was to stay until 1931.

MacMechan was a talented and prolific writer in an era when there was little creativity in Canadian literary scholarship. He supplemented his teaching with literary journalism and was a regular contributor to the Montreal Sun. As a critic he wrote numerous articles on American, British and Canadian literature. MacMechan was very impressed by the writings of Melville, publishing an appreciation of *Moby Dick* as early as 1899, many years before the Melville revival. In 1905 he published an article on "The Literature of Nova Scotia" in the *Canadian Magazine*. His interest in both English Canadian and French Canadian literature was to grow until he focused most of his writings and teaching on the subject. His *Headwaters of Canadian Literature,* a study of early Canadian writing, published by McClelland and Stewart in 1924, is his only other writing currently in print.

Some days after the Explosion in 1917 he was asked to prepare an official history of the disaster. "Met Mac-Gillivray in Hollis St. about 11 a.m. He wanted me to 'get busy' about an official history of the disaster. Although not equal to it, I felt I could not refuse." On December 16, "Today I saw Mr. Young, Manager of the Chronicle, at noon and engaged Room 24 for the Halifax Disaster Record Office at $12 per month. Later I engaged John H. Mitchell, my honor student in English, as assistant and Mrs. J. McAloney as another." The quotes are from MacMechan's journal.

All else was laid aside and the Halifax Disaster Record Office began work officially on December 17. MacMechan and his colleagues began the mammoth task of gathering material for a comprehensive history. After much rigorous collecting and selecting, "it has taken me

out of my professional groove and shaken me up generally. Then it is work that is specially congenial—history at its sources." He began this taut and authoritative work.

The report has an astringent quality rare for its time. His realism is touched with a quality of myth that brings the work alive and communicates a powerful sense of the moment. Unable or unwilling to complete a final chapter entitled "The City Heroic," the work was laid aside and never prepared for publication. As we read his powerful document today we realise as he must have that no final chapter is possible to such a history for its repercussions still affect us.

Chapter 1

The Collision

The Atlantic Coast of Nova Scotia is marked about the middle by a deep indentation, which forms a triple harbor. The Indians called it simply Chebucto, or "big," and French explorers *Baie Saine,* or "Safe Harbour." Its bigness and its safeness make it an ideal haven for ships. It has roughly the shape of an hour-glass, with one end broken off towards the sea. The inner harbour is a land-locked sheet of water, twenty miles in circumference, known as Bedford Basin; the hour-glass waist is called the Narrows; then comes the harbour proper, the lower bulb of the hour-glass. The harbour mouth is stopped by a large irregular island called MacNab's, thus forming two channels. The western is the main passage, which affords an ample gateway for ships of all burdens. The eastern passage is narrow, crooked and shallow; it is used only by light fishing craft. Near the mouth of the harbour, a long narrow fissure in the rock runs inland for three miles, forming a shallow picturesque fiord. It is known as the North West Arm, and affords a safe anchorage for small vessels. These three bodies of water formed by the subsidence of the land almost surround a triangular peninsula on the western side of the harbour, the centre of which is a high hill close beside the waterfront.

In the eyes of William Shirley, Governor of Massachusetts, and zealous upholder of British interests in America, this peninsula seemed the natural place for a garrison and naval base which should bridle the Acadian French and counterpoise Louisburg, the French stronghold in Cape Breton. Accordingly, in the year 1749, the year that Goethe was born and *Tom Jones* was published, the city of Halifax was founded. A fleet of thirteen transports convoyed by H.M.S. SPHINX, sloop-of-war, sailed from London and reached Chebucto Harbour in June. That summer the city of Halifax was made a place on the map of the world. The city builder was the Honourable Edward Cornwallis, a British colonel who had served in the same regiment as Wolfe. He was a twin brother of the Archbishop of Canterbury and uncle of the British commander who surrendered at York Town. The settlers were trade-fallen soldiers and sailors who had fought for the rights of Maria Theresa. Of the men who fell in that just war, Collins wrote the noblest of lyric epitaphs:

> How sleep the brave who sink to rest,
> By all their country's wishes blest.

Halifax was built, not for trade or commerce. It was a fiat city, created in a lull between two wars, to meet a military necessity. In a century and a half it outgrew its original boundaries and stretched north and south into a long thin city. Coeval with Halifax is the picturesque town of Dartmouth on the eastern side of the harbour, backed by its cup-like lakes among the hills. The choice of Shirley has been amply justified. In every war since its foundation, Halifax has played an important part. Moreover, in every war it has prospered exceedingly. It never was of greater importance, or more prosperous than on the 6th of December, 1917. Then in an instant of time, it was laid desolate. The town clock, which overlooks the central square still called the Grand Parade, stopped at five minutes past nine.

That December morning will long be remembered for its singular beauty. The air was still and warm, almost like summer. There was no snow on the ground. The sun was a ball of fire as in the season of Indian summer. Nothing in the sky or on the earth portended disaster. The routine of the city was following its usual course. The soldiers in the garrison had been detailed for their regular duties. Laboring men had been at work for an hour, business men were going down town to their offices. The morning trains were coming in at North Street Station. The children of the city were assembling in their various schools. Some Haligonians were at breakfast; some were in bed. There was no warning of the approaching calamity.

Shortly before nine o'clock a French ship, the MONT BLANC, was proceeding up the harbour at a rate of six knots, towards the Narrows. This was a cargo steamer of 2,250 tons, which had been loaded at Gravesend, New York, with high explosives and was coming to Halifax in order to proceed to her destination under convoy. Her cargo consisted chiefly of picric acid, of which she carried 2,300 tons, including moist and dry. Sixty-one tons of gun-cotton were stowed forward, and 225 tons of T.N.T. abaft the engineroom. Its money value was three million dollars. The MONT BLANC also carried a deckload of benzine in drums. Such a cargo was, of course, dangerous, but in wartime, when high explosives are vital, and every cubic foot of shipping capacity is invaluable, dangers must be risked. Every precaution seems to have been taken against the risk of fire. The dangerous materials were most carefully stowed. The boards of the bulkheads were fastened with copper nails instead of iron, men were not allowed matches on deck; and there was no liquor on board. The certificated Halifax pilot, Mackey, was in charge of the MONT BLANC. He did not understand French and testified at the Court of Inquiry, which was held later, that "demi-tasse" was French for "half-speed."

As the MONT BLANC was proceeding inward towards the Basin, a Belgian Relief ship, the IMO, left her anchorage in Bedford Basin and proceeded towards the Narrows, outward bound across the Atlantic. She had been searched by the Naval authorities for contraband and had complied with all the regulations of the port. She, too, was in charge of a Halifax pilot, William Hayes. Her course was not altogether clear. Preceding the MONT BLANC all the way to the Narrows was an American tramp steamer, which, desiring to anchor on the western side of the Basin, turned to the left instead of to the right, and forced the IMO towards the eastern, or Dartmouth shore. Hardly had the IMO passed this vessel, when she encountered the STELLA MARIS, a local tug 120 feet long, towing behind her two barges. This was equivalent to a ship 400 feet long. The STELLA MARIS followed in the wake of the American tramp and met the IMO in the Narrows, forcing her out of her course still farther towards the Dartmouth shore. In order to avoid a collision on the one hand and to escape grounding on the other, the IMO stopped her engine and reversed it. The manoeuvre tended to swing her head round the stern of the last barge. She did not start her engines again, but continued to drift. By this time the MONT BLANC was close upon her, signalling according to the established rules of the road that she would keep to the right. At the last moment, the MONT BLANC turned out of her course, directly across the bows of the IMO. Why she did so can perhaps never be known. One plausible theory is that the pilot's order at the critical moment was misunderstood, owing to the difference between the French and English words of command. The stem of the IMO came without great violence against the starboard bow of the MONT BLANC and crushed in the plating to the depth of ten feet. The ships separated almost at once, the IMO drifted towards the Dartmouth shore, while the head of the MONT BLANC continued to move slowly towards the Halifax shore. The collision occurred about seventeen minutes to nine.

Almost at once the MONT BLANC was observed to be on fire. According to the expert testimony, it was caused by the sparks resulting from steel grating against steel. Dense clouds of smoke rose into the still morning air, shot through with flashes of fierce red flame. The spectacle drew all eyes. Women in the North End went to their windows to look, or came outside their houses into the street. Men stopped their work to gaze. To most who thought about the matter at all, the burning MONT BLANC looked like an oil tanker on fire. There were observers on the Halifax and on the Dartmouth side, and on the ferry boat which plies across the harbour. Soon after the fire broke out, the crew of the MONT BLANC were observed to lower two boats and row as hard as they could to the Dartmouth shore.

The abandoned ship continued to drift head on towards the Halifax shore, close to the piers at Richmond, where deals are loaded from the long strings of freight cars into the square-rigged ships which sail for the United Kingdom. The danger of a burning ship drifting into wharves piled with lumber was evident to not a few. Constant Upham, who kept a large store in Campbell Road, went to the telephone and gave the alarm to the various fire stations. In response, the fire bells rang; the Chief of the Fire Department and his assistant started

in his car to the scene of danger. The "Patricia," the fire department's new chemical engine, and the hose-wagon from the Isleville station hurried to the threatened section of the city, as did also the chemical engine from Quinpool Road. The danger of the burning vessel was most apparent to the practised eyes of sailors. Assistance came from the NIOBE and a whaler from H.M.S. HIGHFLYER, which was lying at anchor in full view of the collision.

The fire was also observed by Vincent Coleman, train-dispatcher in the Richmond Station. He called up the station at Truro and gave this message, "Munition ship on fire, making for Pier 6. Goodbye." J. R. Ronayne, reporter for the *Echo,* residing in North Street, saw the fire and called up the office to say that he would be late, as a burning steamer was coming up the harbour. He would see what happened. It was his last assignment. The STELLA MARIS anchored her two barges and turned back to the MONT BLANC's aid. At five minutes past nine, the MONT BLANC, which had drifted close into Pier 6, blew up with a report that was heard two hundred miles away.

Chapter 2

The Explosion

The theory of explosion is not very well understood by scientific men. From the chemist's point of view it is an extremely rapid burning, the explosive material being converted into gas in a fraction of a second. The fiery gas expands rapidly in all directions, driving the projectile out of the cannon, or tearing to pieces the receptacle which contains it. In the case of the MONT BLANC the grinding of steel on steel created a stream of sparks which ignited the picric acid and this in turn set fire to the drums of benzine above it. Watchers on shore saw burst after burst of flame through a cloud of smoke, apparently due to the ignition of separate drums of benzine. One woman compared it to fire works at the Exhibition. An artist on the Dartmouth Ferry noted the picturesque effect and counted four separate sheets of flame. It was observed as a "pinkish" light from Connaught Battery. When the fire had raged a certain time between decks in that confined space, the whole twenty-six hundred tons of picric acid, gun-cotton and T.N.T. was converted in a split second into a hemisphere of intensely hot gas which sprang up into the air for possibly a cubic mile. The sight was observed by Captain Campbell off Chebucto Head, approaching Halifax in the steamer ACADIEN. With his

The numbers in the margins refer to the map on page 10.

sextant he shot the angle and calculated the height of the column of smoke and fire to be about two miles.

The physics of explosion is not so well understood, because experiment and opportunities for measurement and observation must necessarily be almost impossible. Those who have calculated the amount of gas produced by the explosives in the MONT BLANC's hold differ widely as to the quantity produced. They also differ as to the nature of the energy so released. The difference is between the pressure theory and the blow theory. It hardly seems possible that pressure of the air, a sort of push, in fact, could break in window glass fifteen or even two miles away. On the other hand, if the energy created by the instantaneous conversion of solid explosives into fiery gas springs out in all directions and drives the air before it, is this the air nearest to the hemisphere of gas, or is it the air nearest to the object smashed or overturned? The lower calculation of the volume of gas also makes it difficult to account for the extraordinary destructive force exerted over such a wide radius.* One feature of the explosion would seem to be the setting up of small whirlwinds or cyclones, because heavy solid bodies were completely reversed without being carried from their original positions, noticeably the boiler of the tug HILFORD; and there are numerous well authenticated cases of persons being carried through the air by the force of the explosion and set down without injury.

A party of Haligonians at Lawrencetown, thirteen miles away, had a curious experience. They were sitting at breakfast and expecting every moment the arrival of a motor which was to take them back to the city. As they sat at table they heard a sound which they took to be the noise of the motor coming along the road. It died away. They were then called out by their host to see a strange column of smoke in the direction of Halifax. As they faced it they all felt something like a blow in the face and then a sort of recoil or pull back in the opposite direction. The narrator illustrated by holding his hand in front of his face, moving it towards his face, and then backwards. This incident, together with what may be inferred from the condition of damaged buildings, would seem to confirm the blow or wave theory of the explosion. Another curious phenomenon was the condition of a spruce wood on the Dartmouth shore, directly opposite the scene of the explosion. The trees have been thrown down in a semicircle, the tops pointing outward away from the explosion. A little further on, beside open fields, trees lining the road have been thrown down but in the opposite direction, pointing toward the explosion. The cautious scientist refuses to dogmatize and will not say just what form was taken by the energy which the explosion released. As to its effects there can be no dispute.

* See page 129, "Some Notes on the Halifax Explosion" by Howard L. Bronson, a contemporary analysis read to the R.S.C., May 1918.

The sound of the explosion has been compared to the awful subterranean rumble of an earthquake, to "all thunders rolled in one", to the Trump of Doom, as indeed it was to well-nigh two thousand souls. At some distance two reports were heard, but in reality there was only one. The sound travelled through the earth more quickly than through the air. Many, of course, heard nothing at all. Some thought the noise local, due to some accident in the house, such as a bursting boiler. One driver of a motor thought only of a blown-out tire and got out of his car to examine the damage. Some thought it a blast at the Terminals, only heavier than usual. One deaf lady thought it was her son's practice with heavy artillery. The heart-shaking underground rumble was followed a few seconds later by the terrifying crash of breaking glass and splintering wood all over the city, as windows were shattered and doors forced by the terrific air-blast. The first thought in many minds was "the Germans, at last!" They were shelling the city from the harbour, or dropping bombs from the air, and everyone thought that his house was the only one hit.

For ten minutes after the explosion a "black rain" was observed to fall from the sky. This was an oily soot, the unconsumed carbon of the explosives. It blackened clothing almost like liquid tar, ruining housewives' linen. It blackened the faces and bodies of all it fell on, in some cases making it impossible to distinguish white persons from negroes. It penetrated clothing to the skin and coated the ruins of the houses, until the snow and the rain storms washed it away.

The first effect of the explosion was to blow the MONT BLANC to atoms. The vessel was resolved into a spray of metallic fragments, which were hurled in all directions, with the deadly swiftness of shells from a cannon's mouth. These missiles rained all over the surrounding scene. Masses splashed into the harbor. The rivets showered like shrapnel. One gun was hurled three and a half miles, and was afterwards found buried in the earth near Albro Lake. Another was found in the grounds of Armdale, near the head of the Arm. Part of an anchor crashed through the Exhibition Building. Richmond and the North End generally were bombarded with bits of the ill-fated steamer.

The drifting IMO was caught in the storm of scrap-iron and riddled. The two men on the forecastle head were killed. Hayes, the pilot, was found dead, crouching down under a boat on the bridge. By a miracle the helmsman, Johansen, escaped with a badly injured leg. Below, the cabins were wrecked and all was in confusion. Another survivor was a dog, whose unearthly howls shook the nerves of men exploring the confusion between decks in the dark on the night of the fatal 6th. The creature refused to leave the cabin, threatened all who approached and finally had to be shot. The vessel itself was flung aground on the Dartmouth shore, a wreck, all her superstructure being demolished, and the ironical legend

19

GAUVIN & GENTZEL PHOTO, PUBLIC ARCHIVES OF NOVA SCOTIA

''Belgian Relief'' still on her side in huge red letters, her bow still pointed hopelessly seaward.

The destruction of the shipping near at hand in the harbour was very great. A certain portion of the force of the explosion was taken up by the water and caused a wave which played a part also in destroying life and wrecking property. This wave swept up the bank across the open space known as Mulgrave Park. Tokens of its progress were found far up Roome Street. In this district several persons were swept away and drowned. The boat from the NIOBE had actually reached the MONT BLANC and the boatswain had mounted the deck, when the ship disappeared in flame. All but one in the whaler from the HIGHFLYER were killed or drowned. The survivor was a sailor named William Becker, who, though badly injured, succeeded in swimming to the Dartmouth side. He has since been awarded the Albert medal for gallantry in saving life at sea. The same honour was awarded posthumously to Acting Commander T. K. Triggs, R.N., the officer in command. The whole crew

S.S. IMO with armed guard. The 5043-ton vessel was seized and torn, stripped of her superstructure by the blast of the explosion, and thrown across the channel where she beached on the shingle of the Dartmouth shore. (See 19 on map.) After four months the IMO was refloated and arrived in New York on July 28th for repairs. Rechristened GUVERNÖREN, she went to sea again as a whale-oil tanker. In 1921 on a voyage from Norway to the Antarctic she struck a rock. Her crew were taken off, and, as salvage was impossible, she was abandoned to the sea on December 3rd.

knew the danger they were running, as appears from the official report.

The STELLA MARIS was nearly swamped by the explosion wave and was flung up on the shore near Pier 6. H.M.S. HIGHFLYER was anchored only three hundred yards away from the scene of the collision. Warships are built to withstand sudden and violent shocks. Though her hull and superstructure were damaged, almost as if she had been in action, and, though she lost three ratings killed and fifteen injured, she was able to perform all the duties required of her soon after.

H.M.C.S. NIOBE, her cruises over, had long been lying moored at the Dockyard as a depot ship. To accommodate hundreds of men in training, her decks had been built up with wooden houses until she resembled the Noah's Ark of the nursery. The air-blast shook down one of her funnels, and part of her wooden superstructure, smashing in the glass of the skylights, while the wave wrenched her forcibly from her moorings. The iron of the huge links of the cables which fastened her to the shore, was two and one half inches in diameter, yet some of them parted under the strain. In one case, the cable did not part, but the anchor at the end was torn out of the solid concrete in which it was imbedded. Naturally, there was some confusion, the newer hands being not completely disciplined, but the old hands rallied to meet the unexpected situation with the traditional coolness and steadiness of the British sailor. The first thought of the officer in charge was that the magazine had gone up, and, as the immediate consequence of such a disaster, the flames sweeping through the ship. He had seen many a ship go up. He at once took measures to fight fire. Four leading stokers with a hundred men each, were swiftly sent to their fire stations. The electric wires were cut, the injured were cared for, damages were repaired and order was restored.

Merchant ships lying alongside various wharves were damaged and members of the crew killed. At Brookfield's sugar refinery wharf the steamer PICTON was lying. This was a freighter of 6,000 tons which, in coming to Halifax, had run ashore and damaged her stern post and rudder. A large force of longshoremen was engaged that morning in removing her general cargo, so that when sufficiently lightened the damages might be repaired. A great part of her lading had been removed; the longshoremen had got down as far as the 1,500 tons of fused shells stowed below the water-line. The air-blast slew nearly all on board and stripped them mother-naked. The black rain discoloured the bodies. The superstructure of the ship was wrecked and the deck beams buckled; in particular, the smoke-screen apparatus was knocked to pieces. This consists, in part, of chemical cartridges, into the composition of which phosphorus enters. They can be ignited by mere friction, and produce almost instantaneously a thick black smoke. These cartridges, or parts of them, were scattered about the deck and were a fruitful cause of alarm and distress, not only on the 6th of December, but weeks afterward. Other ships were driven from their moorings and injured more or less by the explosion wave and the air-blast. The explosion covered the harbour with wreckage and confusion.

Devastation. The IMO can be seen on the far shore.

THE JAMES COLLECTION, CITY OF TORONTO ARCHIVES

Chapter 3

The Destruction

The munition ship MONT BLANC drifting in towards Pier 6 that December morning was in reality a floating bomb charged with more than two thousand tons of high explosives, attacking the City of Halifax. The detonation released destructive energy which smote and tore and overthrew everything it encountered within a wide radius of devastation. It was like the fury of some convulsion in Nature, comparable to the ravages of volcano, tornado, and earthquake. The three wharves nearest simply vanished into loose rafts of floating timber or piled heaps of gigantic spillikens. The long strings of cars and locomotives standing on the rails beside them were smashed and broken to pieces. The huge fabric of the Sugar Refinery toppled down into a heap of brick rubble. Two-thirds of the long roof of iron and glass forming a shelter for the trains at North Street station blew up and then collapsed; but thirteen trusses in the centre remained intact. All had to be pulled down. The whole structure was wrecked and the railway departments housed there were disorganized; but only five persons were actually killed within it. The escapes here, as everywhere, were miraculous. Superintendent J. T. Hallisey of the Canadian Government Railways was in his official car at North Street: he was severely cut about the head. Mr. George Graham, General Manager of the Dominion Atlantic Railway, was breakfasting with his wife and daughter in his car when the roof crashed down. All three escaped uninjured. Leaving his wife and daughter to make their way to the south, Mr. Graham started for Rockingham on foot walking and running. From Rockingham he sent the following message to Kentville: "Organize a relief train and send word to Wolfville and Windsor to round up all doctors, nurses, and Red Cross supplies possible to obtain. No time to explain details but list of casualties is enormous." The line itself was impassable by reason of the wrecked rolling stock, smashed girders, broken glass and twisted rails.

From the water, the ground rises rather steeply to a height crowned by an old *point d'appui* known as Fort Needham. This hillside was covered with the houses of the industrial class, employees in the railway, the Dockyard, the various factories and wharves. Some undoubtedly lived in very poor conditions, but in the main these wage-earners were thrifty, industrious, self-respecting. The schools and churches of this district were thriving and well-frequented. Roman Catholics predominated; but there were strong Anglican, Methodist and Presbyterian congregations. Many of these people were paying for their dwellings by degrees, and some had completed their payments and owned their homes. The buildings were, as a rule, of wood and cheaply constructed. What the explosion did to this whole Richmond district was to lay practically every house in it flat in an instant of time. All that the inmates would hear would be an unearthly roar, and at the same moment the house would be falling on their heads. The plaster of ceiling and walls would come down in a bruising, blinding storm. The windows would drive in like a rain of sharp daggers. The furniture would be hurled about. The roof would collapse on the second storey; the second storey would come down on the first; the first would drop into the cellar. Before one could take two breaths, their friendly shelters had fallen upon the living, sentient beings within and condemned them to all kinds of horrible death. Sick and sound, grandparents and infants in arms, were overwhelmed in their own homes and buried beneath the wreckage. In all conceivable ways was this poor human frame rent and broken and shredded and cut. Whole families were killed at once. Men, women and children were slain instantly by the concussion, or were flung yards away from their homes.

Nor was this the worst. In every house the stove was upset, and soon each individual house was on fire. Under the wreckage of Richmond that morning there were hundreds of human beings injured, but in some cases unhurt, who were to die by fire. The mind refuses to dwell upon the horrors of that morning, men and women like ourselves, broken, bruised, bleeding, half conscious, or, worse still, uninjured but imprisoned in the wreckage and the inexorable flames coming swiftly nearer. The pity of it . . . to see your own perish in torment before your eyes and being impotent to help. To see their faces, to hear their words, and to be forced away from helping them. All that morning a tall silvery column of smoke rose to the sky above the burning North End.

The scenes presented in the streets of Richmond that morning immediately after the explosion can be but faintly imagined and cannot be described. The whole quarter had been laid flat as with the blast of a tornado. By a single stroke of evil magic the whole place had been transformed. All dwellings had been swept away, and the streets were filled with the strangest apparitions: men, women and children with their faces streaming with blood from head wounds dealt by flying glass, faces chalk-white with terror and streaked with red, faces black with the "black rain" and smeared with blood. The dead, the dying and the severely injured lay about the streets, amid ghastly, bleeding fragments of what had been human beings' heads and limbs. Here was a man with his side torn open and his entrails exposed. There was a woman cut in two and gasping her last. One woman was seen walking dazed with pain and terror with her eyes turned up to heaven. She was naked and bathed in blood. Her left breast had been cut off but for a shred of flesh, and as she walked unconscious, she held it up with her hand. The immediate impulse in most was to

The glass roof of North Street or Richmond, the city's only railway station, collapsed upon the platforms and tracks. The whole terminus, its sidings and marshalling yards were a mass of shattered railway cars and debris.

find a place of safety, where their injuries could be dressed. Blinded persons were seen feeling their way with sticks; their goals were chemists' shops, doctors' offices, hospitals. Some were dazed and semi-conscious from the shock. Some were uttering shrieks of pain and terror. Some fell to prayers, thinking the Last Day had come. Some were helping injured people away, or struggling to extricate them from the ruin of their houses. There was no order or direction, but the tendency was to flee from the scene of horror. Confusion without example was the rule. Parents were searching for children, children for parents. Husbands and fathers who had been in various employs came racing back to their homes to find what had become of their wives and children; all the time the separate houses were burning, and the smoke stood up over each pyre.

In the central section or business section of the City, stretching from North Street to the Academy of Music, the chief damage done by the explosion was to shatter the glass in all the windows of shops, warehouses, banks, churches, institutions. Here, again, hundreds of persons were injured about the head and face by the flying glass. Here, too, the population took to the street, although no buildings were demolished. Most did not know what had happened, and thought chiefly of having wounds dressed, or repairing damages. The streets were full of broken glass, for the air-blast and its reaction drove this deadly stuff both ways, in and out. One observer in this part of the city described the sound of the broken glass on the pavement as a musical jingle, as if some giant were throwing strings of sleigh bells on the pavement. A clergyman racing from one dismantled druggist shop to another to find aid for an injured friend was afraid he would cut his feet through the leather of his boots. The shock was felt here much less severely than in Richmond, and not a few business men proceeded coolly to their offices and their work, as if nothing out of the way had happened.

In St. Mary's Cathedral, Father Driscoll was saying Mass when the explosion destroyed the stained glass windows on both sides of the church. No one was injured. Father Driscoll ended the service and walked calmly to the sacristy. It was noted that the one window which escaped was the Pelican window. A moment after the explosion, St. Mary's looked like an old Gothic ruin.

5

The curate of St. Joseph's in the ruins of the church. Identified as Monseigneur T. J. Buchanan, retired and living in Amherst, Nova Scotia.

Richmond, January 10th, 1918. Gauvin & Gentzel operated a highly respected portrait studio in Halifax beginning in the last nineteenth century. Little is known of them, but many of their works display sensitivity and fine composition.

The South End, or residential portion of the city escaped most lightly. Here again glass was broken and doors forced in, but very few people were cut or injured. One notable fact was the strange hush that immediately followed the heart-shaking roar of the explosion and the crashing splintering sound of broken wood and glass in each dwelling. No wheel turned, there was no traffic, no out-cry. The silence was uncanny.

The damage done to a dwelling house by the instantaneous removal of all windows is not slight. It leaves the inmate practically without shelter from the weather. In Government House, the stately Colonial mansion now more than a century old, nine hundred panes of glass were broken. Such damages could not be quickly repaired. Lieutenant-Governor Grant and his family were forced to live in the basement, and in the bitter weather which followed on this day of unnatural calm, underwent not discomfort merely but actual hardship. This case is typical. Every householder or tenant found it necessary to make what repairs he could as soon as possible. Windows were stopped with boards, curtains, rugs, pasteboard, any material that could be fastened into gaps to keep out the bad weather which was so soon to afflict the desolated town. All through that still morning the sound of tapping hammers might be heard throughout the South End; making repairs was not a work that could be postponed.

The western section of the city suffered in like manner and underwent the same experience. In addition to the houses actually destroyed within Richmond itself by the force of the explosion, many others outside the devastated area were made uninhabitable. Not only were the windows gone, but the chimneys were demolished, sides kicked in or torn aside as if by a giant, the interiors one confusion of broken furniture and fallen plaster. The buildings might stand, but they could not be lived in. It is no exaggeration to say that the explosion rendered at least fifteen thousand people destitute and shelterless.

And this calamity fell upon the city, without warning, in a moment of time.

What happened in Halifax, happened to a less extent in Dartmouth. The northern part of the town suffered most severely. Houses were blown down or partially wrecked, but there was no wholesale loss of life. Many hundreds were cut by glass and some lost their eyesight, but the number of killed was only twenty-five. There were no fires in Dartmouth, and no repetition of the worst of the Halifax horror. The Micmac reserve at Tuft's Cove was destroyed. This was nearest to the scene of the collision. Towards the south the effects were less and less in proportion to the distance.

The disorganization of the city, one would say, was complete. All the usual services came to an abrupt stop. Halifax was like a man suddenly smitten with blindness and paralysis. The trams ceased to run in the streets for cars were wrecked or so damaged as to be useless, and

employees were killed or wounded, or were aiding in the rescue work, or looking for the missing. There were not hands enough to keep the tracks clear of the snow which fell so heavily on the Friday and the Monday following. For days the only way the ordinary citizen could get about was on his feet.

Telephone communication was also disorganized. The central building was wrecked, a number of the employees injured, and others were called away by the needs of their families. Many instruments in private houses were rendered useless by the explosion and could not be repaired for weeks, because the claims of public buildings came first, and many additional telephones were urgently needed in the buildings appropriated for the work of relief. The telephone cable connecting Halifax with Dartmouth was shifted five hundred yards and the connection broken. With a smaller staff, there was a very much larger number of insistent calls which must be attended to. The overtaxed employees worked under great disadvantages, and some to the point of exhaustion.

The gas system suffered like the rest. Many houses in Halifax are dependent on gas for light, or heat, or both. The pipes and fixtures in many cases were broken or disconnected. Some of the crown plates on the huge gas holder in the South End were sheared off and 200,000 feet of gas were lost. Fortunately, there was no light or fire near at the time to ignite the escaping gas, or a second explosion might have wrecked the South End as badly as the North. It cost three days and three nights of hard work to repair the damage. The company took the wise precaution of cutting off the mains entering the devastated area; and those who used gas for cooking and light had to find some substitute. A thorough inspection of all houses using gas was made and repairs were effected as speedily as possible. Until this was done, much hardship was endured.

A single illustration will suffice. A widow lady was living with her two daughters in a flat near one of the hospitals. The windows and doors were driven in, the kitchen chinaware was smashed to bits, and she herself was badly cut in the arm by the flying glass. There was no help available to stop up the windows or make the necessary repairs. The gas stove was useless; all the meals had to be cooked over one tiny grate. A patient was brought in from the hospital nearby, who could not be turned away, a critical eye case, demanding hourly attention of doctor or nurse. Needless to add, this doubled their burdens. Then the patient's father and mother came from a distance to take charge of their son. He could not be moved for some time; and his parents remained in the flat. The family gave up their bedrooms to the visitors and the patient, and slept where they could. The incident shows the hardships endured by the people of Halifax, but it also shows their ready self-sacrifice.

The delivery of goods of all kinds, milk, bread, groceries, except those used for relief also came to an abrupt standstill. Every vehicle in the city was requisitioned for other uses. Anything that had wheels could be employed to good purpose by the Transportation Committee.

Very soon after the explosion, the shop fronts all along the business streets were boarded up with fresh tongued-and-grooved planking. This not only rendered the unlighted streets more dark, but induced a special feeling of gloom in all hearts. It seemed as if Halifax as a city had put up the shutters for good and all, as if the boarded fronts meant *finis*, and as if all business traffic and life had come to an end. Towards Christmas, openings began to be cut in the middle of these plank screens and little windows inserted which were lighted at night. It was a poor makeshift for the huge panes of plate-glass but it was a token of reviving energy and purpose and tended to dissipate the spiritual as well as physical gloom.

The local newspapers have most modern equipment, but they are dependent on linotype or monotype machines, and these in turn are dependent upon gas. The offices were damaged, the gas was off, and the presses could not run. Nevertheless, by recourse to job printing firms, the papers came out. The *Chronicle* of December 7th had the headline "Halifax in Ruins," and the phrase was exact. Damage was done to the city as a whole. No part of it escaped. At once efforts were made to compute the material damage. Some estimates were excessive; and a careful survey of the whole city by competent appraisers reduced the earlier figures to accuracy. In the first report of the Halifax Relief Commission, dated March 1st, 1918, the appraisement on the damaged property in the city of Halifax and town of Dartmouth and portions of the surrounding municipal district amounted to $16,026,000.*

This included dwelling-houses destroyed and damaged, their contents, schools, churches, charitable and other public institutions, business properties and merchandise, municipal and public buildings, manufacturing plants, and special cases.

It is possible to sum up the material damage, but to compute the totals of human suffering endured that day, the grief of wounds, the agonies of death, the torture of fear, of anxiety, of suspense, of bereavement, is beyond all human arithmetic.

---

* This preliminary estimate did not include the damage to government property and shipping in the harbour. Later computations by the Relief Commission showed the damages had been underestimated, and that, on the same basis the damage would amount to at least $20,000,000. Including the government and shipping losses and the allowance of about $7,500,000 for emergency and temporary relief and provision for pensions, the direct loss would probably amount to thirty-five million dollars.

Chapter 4

The Dockyard

The Dockyard of Halifax was established in the midst of the Seven Years' War. A pillar of the gate still bears the figures 1758. At first it was like a separate little town to the north of Halifax proper, walled and defended by three redoubts. Gradually the city crept up to it, and the new invention of the railroad ran alongside. The *enceinte* contains officers' quarters, barracks, workshops, repair shops, stores, etc. From the beginning of this war it had been a scene of activity, without example since the days of the great French wars of a century ago. The force of the explosion smote this complex of buildings with terrific violence, modified somewhat by the fact that the tall brick structure of the Sugar Refinery intervened between it and the MONT BLANC. This fabric bore the brunt of the air-blast. Its fifteen stories were shaken down into a heap of rubble on the heads of the workers inside. The syrup-soaked timbers immediately caught fire and blazed up fiercely. In the Dockyard just south of it the various buildings were broken down and broken in. Men were killed or badly wounded by the fragments of the ship or by the falling buildings. One man was completely beheaded. The new Y.M.C.A. hut, just erected for the benefit of sailors, was smashed into a heap of kindling wood, the officers' quarters were broken open, and the interiors ravaged as if by a tornado. The staircases were demolished. Only the heavy old chimneys, each containing brick enough to build a modern house, saved the quarters from being laid level with the ground.

In one house an officer's wife was giving her two children breakfast while the baby was asleep in its cot upstairs. When the inexplicable shock was past, she found herself on the only clear spot where heavy furniture had not been thrown down. None of the three was injured, but the whole house was one chaos of lath and plaster, the staircase was broken, and the distracted mother could not tell the fate of the baby upstairs. She called the first blue-jacket she saw to her aid. He ventured boldly up the ruins of the house to the second storey and found the baby still in his cradle, safe and sound. He had been protected from falling timber and plaster by a closet door which had been flung across his little bed. In illustration of the confusion which followed throughout the whole city, the baby so rescued and his nurses became separated from the mother and the other children. They were taken to a hospital, and not discovered till many hours after. In the meantime, her husband was lying in the Naval college, unconscious, with severe injuries to his head and face. Neither husband nor wife knew what had befallen the other.

A large number of the hands employed at the Dockyard were married, men with homes and families in the

North End. Many of them came rushing up to the Dockyard gates to find out what had happened in their homes. They got leave and hurried off, in many cases to find those they had left alive and well but an hour before, now dead, dying, mangled, suffering or missing.

One of those who found his home wrecked and his family missing was John T. Gammon, master-at-arms on the NIOBE. For weeks he had been superintending the building of a concrete foundation for a crane beside the wharf. It was laid under the water by divers. The first diver had just gone down and the second was preparing to follow him down the ladder. One of the men was passing a board which the first diver was going to nail in position. What follows is best told in Gammon's own words.

"A few minutes past nine, a terrible explosion occurred. I was blown on my stomach, and on regaining my feet I saw the buildings collapsing and shrapnel falling. To my horror the house in which the pump was secured was demolished, the men all blown away from the vicinity by concussion, and the pump was stopped. I first thought we were being bombarded by a German submarine which had crept through the gates and was shelling the Dockyard. My next thoughts were the divers. I sprang to the ladder where they would have to ascend and noticed that the water had receded eight or ten feet. I saw no men in sight, but noticed that the diving pump was intact. At that moment a man picked himself up about twenty yards away. I shouted to him to man the pump. He did so single-handed, holding the roof of the building with one hand and turning the handle of the pump with the other.

"On getting close to the bottom of the ladder I got the diver, took his glass off and pushed him up the ladder. I grasped the air pipe and breast rope of No. 2 Diver and pulled him back to the ladder, but unfortunately the air pipe got entangled and with one hand I had to haul down the slack from above and pull the other. I thank God I was able to get him to the ladder and took his glass off and assisted him up the ladder, and he fell exhausted. This took several seconds and I was expecting any moment for the water to return and drown us both."

Gammon's promptness had saved two lives. From his account it is evident that the so-called tidal wave had drawn the water from other parts of the harbour. The divers were rescued just in time. What the submerged diver felt was a sudden and tremendous increase of pressure from the water. He thought the crane had fallen on his head.

Only after he had done the duty that lay nearest did he think of his own family. He hurried from the Dockyard along Campbell Road to his own house. "I saw the burning houses and women and children shrieking. Some were terribly injured. I turned up Russell St. The heat from the burning houses on each side was so intense that I had to put the hood of my coat over my face. After a great struggle I reached my own street."

The officer in charge of the Dockyard was Captain Pasco, during the absence of Captain Martin. He was so severely injured by the flying glass that the command devolved on Captain Hose, R.N. This officer was in charge of the Patrol Service, but, being on the ground, was given command, and was thenceforth responsible for all measures taken within the Dockyard.

Those of the staff who were not hurt or who suffered lesser wounds rendered first aid as far as possible, tearing up clothes and household linen to provide bandages.

Standing with its gable towards the Sugar Refinery was a long narrow brick building. This was the old Naval Hospital, which had been turned into temporary quarters for the Royal Naval College of Canada. Across the northern end a T-shaped brick addition had recently been made, in order to provide further classroom accommodation. At the time of the explosion, the cadets, thirty-five in number, were waiting for "Divisions". The two senior terms were in the senior gunroom, which looks out upon the harbour, and while waiting and brushing, stared idly at what they thought was the burning oil tanker. The junior term were in the junior gunroom on the opposite side of the building, also awaiting orders. When the MONT BLANC blew up, the window glass of the senior gunroom was driven in pelting showers into the watching faces. The plaster came down, the building rocked, the crash of wood and glass was deafening, and for a moment confusion prevailed. Cadet-Captain Kingsley, who was standing in the door, shouted "All out of here," and those who could get out of the room at once only to find themselves in a dim atmosphere made by the falling plaster, and their way blocked by fallen debris. Engineer-Commander Howley shouted "Clear this away," and in a very few seconds cadets were outside on the western side of the College. Cadet Brett, who is six feet tall, carried out Cadet Orde. The latter was blinded and bleeding. He spent many hours of unrelieved pain in a corridor of Camp Hill Hospital, before he received any attention and had his injured eye removed. In the senior gunroom, at the time of the accident was Mr. King, Chief Petty Officer. Glass was driven into his eyes, totally depriving him of sight. Cadet-Captain MacKenzie who also had both eyes filled with broken glass, heard King crying out for water, and somehow got him over to a corner of the room where there was a basin and a tap. King is a full grown man, MacKenzie is sturdily built, but an undersized boy of eighteen. In his efforts to relieve King, he tore down the roller-towel above the basin, and, with the intention of getting the helpless man out of the building, drove his left fist through a remaining pane of the window nearby, cutting his forearm and hand. Then both fainted.

The head of the College, Commander E. A. E. Nixon, R.N., was driven through the door of the small

12

room he was in, his forehead was laid open by a long gash, his cheek was also cut severely and his eyes injured. He lay outside the room, stunned and bleeding. Mr. William Robinson, instructor in Mathematics, heard the roar of the explosion, a crash of wood and glass and plaster within the Naval College, looked out the window of the bathroom he was occupying and saw, in his own words ''everything falling.'' He dashed out into the open, heard that Commander Nixon was still inside the building. He dashed back into what for all he knew was a collapsing ruin and carried his friend outside, laying him on the bank beside the entrance. Commander Nixon had by this time somewhat recovered consciousness, and refused to be moved further, until he was assured that all the cadets were out of the building. He retained command and despatched a cadet to tell his wife he was not badly hurt. He thought the magazine just north of the Naval College had exploded and that this building was the only one affected.

Engineer-Commander Howley is a man with a record. He wears a medal for services rendered in the wrecked city of Messina after the earthquake of 1908. He was penned down in the engineroom of the IRRESISTIBLE when she was torpedoed in the Dardanelles, March 1916, and succeeded in escaping to the deck, only to have a case of shrapnel burst behind him and inflict a hundred separate wounds. He escaped from death by a miracle; and was sent far away from scenes of war to be wounded again in this explosion. He must bear a charmed life. At the time of the accident there were three char-women in the building, two of whom were badly hurt. Howley went back into the building and assisted in getting them out. The cadets in the junior gunroom escaped serious injury. Two lively youngsters, who at the time were dancing on a table, were blown through the open window and landed unhurt on the bank outside. Hall, the porter, a typical old sailor, was heard to exclaim devoutly, ''The Lord preserveth the righteous.'' He was not hurt in any way and did yeoman service all that long trying day.

Then occurred a little scene which deserves commemoration by some Canadian historical painter of the future: Howley ''fell in'' the cadets on the gravel path facing the College, where they paraded for service on Sunday. Except two or three, who were lying, unable to move on the grass, all sprang to attention in their usual order. All were capless, almost every one was cut and bleeding freely about the head and face, but their expression was quiet, confident, smiling; in the words of their officer, they were ''ready for anything.'' Their orders were to ''carry on,'' the less injured helping the worse hurt to the Naval Hospital, as their own sick quarters within the Dockyard enceinte were demolished. All this occupied not more than four or five minutes. The cadets set off in a body to the Naval Hospital, found it so injured by the explosion as to be useless, ''carried on'' to the Military Hospital at Cogswell St., found that already congested, and ''carried on'' once more to the great catch-basin of injured that day, the newly built hospital for convalescent soldiers at Camp Hill.

Circumstances separated the cadets, but they followed out their orders in the spirit and the letter. Cadet-Captain Kingsley had charge of Cadet Holms, probably the most seriously injured of all the Cadets. Some constitutional defect made it almost impossible to staunch his wounds. He was about the last to recover, and a very difficult operation was necessary to prevent the worst gash in his face from reopening. Kingsley supported him along the street to Camp Hill, although his strength was failing fast. Probably not more than fifteen minutes was occupied in this tragic journey from the Naval College to Camp Hill. There Kingsley found MacKenzie bandaged and blinded. Even at that early hour the fearful congestion at this hospital had begun, and Kingsley was asked if MacKenzie had not friends in the city who would take him in. Kingsley at once got permission from an officer standing by to use his car, which was driven by an orderly. He whirled MacKenzie off to his friend's house and then procured medical assistance, returning in a short time with a doctor. This little incident is typical. It illustrates the initiative and spirit of comradeship manifested that day by the cadets of the Royal Naval College. Canada may well be proud of these, her young sons.

Within fifteen minutes after the explosion, Mr. Robinson was at work in Russell St. rescuing injured people from the scattered burning houses. He worked until he found himself faint from a cut artery in his breast. Commander Nixon was taken off in an ambulance to Camp Hill. Engineer-Commander Howley carrying his great-coat over his arm, with his wounds unstaunched, made his way to a dressing station on the Common, saw the long queue of injured waiting for treatment, decided to look elsewhere for relief. He was taken in a motor-car, still protesting and somewhat dazed, to Pine Hill, the home of the Halifax Theological College, which had been turned into a convalescent hospital for returned soldiers. This too was congested and he was taken thence to his own home in Le Marchant St. which he reached almost fainting from loss of blood. His wounds were dressed only just in time, and before he could recover strength, he and his wife were hurried out into the grounds of Dalhousie University by the alarm of a second explosion.

The director of studies, Mr. B. S. Hartley, escaped injury entirely. He too was watching what he thought was a burning oil ship, through the window of his office, which faces the harbour. With a presentiment of what was coming, he stepped outside just in time and stood under the clock in the hall, the safest place in the building. He escaped without a scratch and was rendering first-aid in the Dockyard, when the alarm of the second explosion reached him. Then, with the injured persons

25

he was dressing he made for the open spaces.

The story of Mr. King is the strangest of all. When he was brought out, he was thought to be dead, and was removed, not to a hospital but to an improvised morgue in Chebucto School. Here he lay semi-conscious for many hours, knowing that persons were moving by, removing the cloth from his face and trying to identify him. At last he recovered sufficient strength to seize a passer-by, a soldier, whose horror at being grasped by a dead man can be readily figured. King recovered, although his sight is completely destroyed, and relates his experience with gusto.

It was at the Dockyard that the people of the United States first manifested that prompt and efficient aid, and that brotherly sympathy will ever endear the name American to the City of Halifax and to the Canadian people. The American hospital ship OLD COLONY was lying alongside the wharf, and, within fifteen minutes of the explosion, had two working parties with surgeons and all appliances, giving first aid to the injured and bringing comfort to the suffering. Bad cases were transferred to the sick bay of the OLD COLONY, where they received every attention, and later in the day, patients were transferred from the overflowing hospitals in Halifax to the care of this generous ship.

Chapter 5

The Picton

Sir Thomas Picton was a British General who fought not without glory throughout the Peninsular War, and fell at Waterloo. The memory of this hero was carried on by good patriots who named towns in Ontario, New Zealand, and Australia in his honour. On the day of the explosion, a big freighter was lying in Halifax Harbour, which testifies in her christening to the same tradition. This PICTON, while on her way to Halifax, grounded and damaged her rudder and stern-post. She had been berthed alongside the Sugar Refinery wharf in order that her cargo might be discharged sufficiently to make the needed repairs. A force of eighty men was working about this steamer, discharging the cargo which consisted chiefly of bags of flour and oats, cases of baked beans, and other food-stuffs. It was well known that a large quantity of dangerous explosive composed part of the cargo. The captain and officers of the ship kept strict watch over the stevedores to prevent them smoking. The superintendent foreman was named Frank Carew, and his two assistants were Alonzo Bezanson and James Leahy.

At ten minutes to nine, Carew heard of the collision between the IMO and the MONT BLANC, and that fire had broken out on the French ship. His first thought was not for his own safety but the safety of the people of Halifax. The burning MONT BLANC was only some three hundred yards away from the PICTON and no one could tell what the outcome of the fire might be. Carew was a man of much experience and well acquainted with the nature of explosions. He could not possibly know that the MONT BLANC was a floating mine, but he was well aware of the nature of the cargo under his feet and the consequences of fire reaching it. He and his men put on the hatch covers and took every other precaution possible against fire occurring on board the PICTON and so exploding the ammunition in her hold. They were still engaged in their unselfish task when the MONT BLANC blew up. Carew, Leahy, and sixty-eight of the men at work were killed; six seriously injured and four escaped with slight hurts. These devoted men lost their lives in the performance of their duty like so many others on that day of terror and heroism.

Shortly after the explosion, the PICTON was boarded by a party of blue-jackets from a warship in the harbour, and the few survivors were taken off to a hospital. Apparently Carew had sent most of his men ashore, for later in the day an eye witness saw only three or four dead men on her deck. The PICTON herself was judged to be in no danger and the Naval men paid no further attention to her. Nonetheless, she was a source of serious anxiety to one man among the distracted crowds in Halifax that morning. This was Captain James W. Harrison, Marine Superintendent of the Furness Withy Co., the agents of the vessel. He knew that one item in her manifest was fifteen hundred tons of Field Artillery fused shells. He knew also that the removal of the general cargo would leave open hatches and all the deadly stuff exposed. He knew furthermore that the Sugar Refinery, beside which the PICTON was lying, was blazing, and that there was the greatest danger that she would catch fire and blow up like the MONT BLANC. He was at Furness Withy's when the explosion occurred, and after trying to find out by telephone what steamer had blown up, and failing to do so, because the whole telephone system of the city was out of commission, he started for the PICTON on foot. He was making his way to the north end when he met his son, Lieut. Leslie Harrison, in his car who had already made two trips to the north end and conveyed injured people to the hospitals. As he was proceeding along Water St. on his third trip, he met his father who stepped into the car and gave the brief order, "Drive me north," vouchsafing no reason or explanation of his action. Capt. Harrison is a typical British master mariner formed in the hard school of the mercantile marine. He is a man of middle size, spare, athletic, with the steady, wide-open eyes of a sailor. His hair and mustaches are white, but he has all the quickness and energy of a very much younger man. He is no talker or seeker after popularity. His vast practical experience makes him invaluable to his firm.

The Harrisons, father and son, proceeded in their car as far as North St. when they were turned back by the cordon of police and soldiers who warned them that there was danger of a second explosion of the powder magazine. They turned back along Barrington St. and both men kept shouting to the crowd, ''Go south. All go south.'' At Jacob St., Capt. Harrison got out and went back to the Furness Withy wharf. Foiled in his efforts to reach the PICTON by land, he decided to make the attempt by water though he did not speak of his intention to his son. Young Harrison continued his work of transferring injured people to the various hospitals till eleven o'clock that night. Some time elapsed before Capt. Harrison could get any conveyance on the water, but at last Hendry's tug, WEATHERSPOON, came alongside. He got on board and ordered the captain to take him to the PICTON.

The little WEATHERSPOON in charge of her master, Thomas Ormiston, had had her own experiences already that morning. By telephone, Ormiston had been directed by his employers, Hendry's Ltd. to tow a schooner away from Pier 6 because there was a fire nearby. The WEATHERSPOON steamed towards the pier and had just come abreast of H.M.S. HIGHFLYER, that is within 300 yards of the MONT BLANC, when the explosion occured. The WEATHERSPOON suffered not a little from the shock. Some of her steam joints were started, but her injuries were not sufficient to prevent her rendering most effective service that morning. Ormiston the master at the wheel, was thrown down, cut about the head, and badly dazed, but he soon recovered himself and got the tug, which was running wild, once more under control. There was no longer any question of towing the schooner. That vessel disappeared with Pier 6. It was reported as one of the freaks of the explosion that her anchor chain was found coiled round and round a box car in the railway yard. Damaged as she was, and her crew badly knocked about, the WEATHERSPOON began rescue work at once. She took five or six wounded men off the DOUGLAS THOMAS, no easy task, and put them ashore at Pickford & Black's wharf. She then returned and got ''a second bunch'' of seven or eight off the MIDLAND CASTLE and put them on board a three-masted schooner lying at the Furness Withy Wharf.

About fifteen minutes after commandeering the WEATHERSPOON, Capt. Harrison was on board the PICTON. There was some hesitation on the part of Ormiston in laying his boat alongside, for steam and smoke were visible coming from the after part of the bridge. Two of the WEATHERSPOON's crew, John Benoit, the cook, and Robert Edwards, a deck hand, volunteered to go on board with Capt. Harrison. Capt. Harrison's report states: ''Two men from the tow boat followed me.'' The

deck was a scene of desolation. The superstructure had been wrecked by the force of the explosion and the hatches had been blown open. In the report which he was asked to make by his firm, Capt. Harrison states: ''For some time I was unable to find out where the smoke was coming from, but eventually found out that it was coming from burning debris that had evidently blown on board or found its way on board when the burning sheds fell. The PICTON's bow was within a few yards of the burning pier. Her hatches had been all blown off and the explosive matter in the holds was all exposed. I examined the hold to see if there were any burning embers, and at the same time, to see if there were any injured men. I found nothing and came up again.''

In order to understand what follows, it must be stated that vessels coming into the Sugar Refinery Wharf, drop an anchor and then swing around to be moored. The PICTON was so anchored with her bow pointed south, and also moored at the bow and stern by wire and manilla hawsers. Capt. Harrison states: ''I ordered the tow boat to make a rope fast anywhere they could near the bow of the PICTON, at the same time the two men and I got to work and cut the moorings''. This was a long hard job, hacking at steel wire with a dull axe. The WEATHERSPOON had passed a line as directed, and kept up a strain upon it to assist this operation. It was at least an hour before this work was done. The fire on the wharf was particularly fierce and there was no guarantee that the PICTON would not at any time share the fate of the MONT BLANC. When the various cables were finally severed, the plight of the PICTON was little better than it was before; her anchor was still down, and as there was no steam up it was impossible to lift it. What was done was to pay out the cable, the little WEATHERSPOON dragging at the huge mass of the freighter with but little effect. Capt. Harrison's statement is: ''Eventually, I hailed two more tow boats, and it took the whole three of them to haul the PICTON from amongst the wreckage of the wharves. When we got the steamer well clear of the range of fire, I had another anchor dropped down so as to hold her . . . The ship was at this time in my opinion, safe.'' In other words, the PICTON was ''in the stream,'' riding by two anchors, one alongside the wharf, and the other at a considerable distance from it. It was four o'clock before the job was done. But the work of the WEATHERSPOON was not over. The business of a tow boat is to tow. There was plenty of work for her to do that day. In addition to the PICTON she towed off the MIDLAND CASTLE and the MACKEY, and her crew did not get ashore until dark.

The adventures of the PICTON on the other hand, were by no means at an end. Indeed, they were only beginning. The weather* on Friday was bad enough on shore. Its effect on the shipping in the harbour may be

* See Weather Reports, December 6th—12th, page 92.

27

imagined. In the blizzard, various vessels lying inside the submarine nets dragged their anchors and went careering about the narrow limits of the harbour in the dark. All were more or less damaged and short-handed. The shorelights were gone. Collisions and groundings were only narrowly avoided by marvellous combinations of good luck and good seamanship, but the work that was done by the sailors in that black night of storm must remain an unwritten chapter.

On Saturday, the Furness Withy people were notified by the Admiralty as to the vagaries of their vessel, and received instructions to take her from her position off the Dockyard and beach her in the Eastern Passage some three or four miles away. Under the direction of Capt. Harrison this was done. The PICTON could hardly be called a lucky ship. As she was passing the gates, she only just escaped colliding with an incoming steamer. Thanks to Capt. Harrison, she reached her destination, and, as all must have hoped, a place of safety. Capt. Harrison's own words are: "We . . . left her hard and fast on the beach. She was afterwards pulled off by the Admiralty tugs and moored with one anchor, but she had not sufficient cable chain out, and was dragging around the harbour. The Admiralty seeing this, ordered us to procure another anchor. We did this as early as possible with the help of the Admiralty's tow boat. The steamer now lies where we left her." (Jan. 2nd, 1918).

Before this date, however, the PICTON had caused great alarm in her new berth. It is a question whether the "rubbish" which Capt. Harrison threw overboard was set on fire from the shore. The PICTON carried a smoke screen apparatus for protection against submarine attacks. It is installed upon the deck and consists of chemically composed cartridges which can be readily ignited and produce a thick cloud of black smoke. This apparatus was knocked to pieces by the explosion and the cartridges were scattered about the deck. To step on one of these cartridges is sufficient to ignite it. When the PICTON was beached, a patrol vessel was anchored nearby and a guard of the 63rd Halifax Rifles was placed at Crow's Point, the object in both cases being to prevent unauthorized persons from going on board. But the wrecker instinct is not unknown along the coast, and apparently some unauthorized persons not only approached the derelict, but got on board, for later some youths were arrested for attempting to pilfer from her. It must have been such occurrence which set the chemical cartridges in operation once more, for on Sunday morning, the inhabitants of Eastern Passage awoke to see the dreaded ammunition ship on fire. Flames were spurting from the ship, and smoke went up in thick black clouds from a fire close to the after hatch. The people of Eastern Passage had suffered from the explosion. Their windows had been broken, and some of them had been hurt. They knew that the PICTON carried munitions and they fled from their homes in the pouring rain.

Sergeant Zwicker, in charge of the guard, had observed the fire and with the three riflemen, Beaver, Kennedy, and Rafuse, put off in a boat to the steamer. They saw a man on board, who had apparently been left there by the patrol boat. In answer to his cries for assistance, they swarmed on board. They attacked the fire, throwing the burning rubbish overboard, or smothering it with the slushy snow. For all they knew there might be an explosion at any minute. They expected, in their own words, "to hear it crack." It took them about twenty minutes to extinguish the fire. Zwicker went ashore and reported what had occurred to his regimental headquarters. An officer was sent at once to Crow's Point, but by the time he arrived the Naval authorities were in charge of the PICTON. She was towed out into the stream and was anchored with a heavy anchor. While this was being done, fire broke out once more. The efficacy of the smoke-screen apparatus to produce smoke rapidly and in quantity would seem to be beyond doubt or question.

Zwicker and Rafuse (Rehfuss) are well-known names in Lunenburg, which was settled, one hundred and fifty years ago by Protestant emigrants from the Palatinate. Sergeant Zwicker told his story with Teutonic phlegm. After the fire was out, he satisfied himself that ammunition really was on board. The party went below and "busted a box open." All four were included in the official report, receiving "special mention . . . as having rendered noteworthy services." The official statement runs: "They immediately boarded the steamer knowing she was loaded with munitions, and at the risk of their lives, remained on board until the fire was completely extinguished. They even went down the hold of the vessel and put out a fire which had started in the straw in which the munitions were packed."

After this, the PICTON faded from the local consciousness until the end of January. On Tuesday the 29th, she was lying alongside the pier at the Ocean Terminals to be unloaded. The ammunition was being taken out and inspected case by case. As a case was being dragged across a bench, it caught fire. A small blaze flared up causing some little panic, but it was speedily extinguished. Once more the fault lay with the disorganized smoke screen apparatus. Fragments of the chemical cartridges had been mixed with cordite, and the friction of the heavy case being pulled across the bench had set them ablaze. The news of the fire had spread rapidly, and the alarm was communicated to the whole neighbourhood. Many people in the South End left their houses, and the children were ordered out of the schools. The public nerves were raw and readily excited. The alarm caused no little suffering and mental distress. Public opinion would be satisfied, apparently, with nothing short of the sinking of the unlucky vessel, and dire punishment of the "authorities" responsible, but at last the excitement died down.

Capt. Harrison's exploit was very widely noticed in

the newspapers. The tendency of journalism, especially where the facts are not accurately known, is to exaggerate; and in some cases, too much was said. To Capt. Harrison on December 6th, the situation was simple enough. The ship he was personally responsible for was in dangerous position and it was his duty to get her out. Danger is part and parcel of the sailor's daily life. It is never far away, and must be disregarded if the sailor's work is to be done. For all he knew, as long as he was on board, the ship might have blown up at any minute, but he was taking the most energetic measures to prevent such an occurrence. Again, if all the ammunition had exploded, it would have meant death to all on board and loss of life in the immediate neighbourhood, but it could not have caused any such destruction as that wrought by the MONT BLANC. It would have been like a string of firecrackers each a six-inch shell. Capt. Harrison is a man of deeds not words. He did not talk about the affair himself and discouraged talk about it in others. The first account in a local paper was very general. It did not mention his name or the name of his firm, but the facts gradually became known to the public. The Canadian National Council of the British and Foreign Sailors' Society awarded him the Nelson salver of copper "for heroism," for he saved the PICTON and her cargo of ammunition "at the greatest possible personal risk . . . and probably averted a second explosion."

Chapter 6

The Magazine

Wellington Barracks is a complex of brick buildings, standing on the hill immediately above the Dockyard. It is of the familiar pattern, various buildings grouped about a gravelled square where the forces are drilled, exercised and paraded.

On the morning of the sixth of December, a small group of officers belonging to the Composite Battalion, stationed at Wellington, was standing at the northern end of the officers' quarters, watching the burning MONT BLANC. They had been roused by the fire bells and the engines tearing along Barrington. "It was the best fire I ever saw in my life," one eyewitness reported. A tall column of dense black smoke was rising up into the sky, like the genie in "The Arabian Nights", then through it would come a rush of flame clear up to the top. This they considered was due to oil barrels vapourizing. "Then she went up." The officers were flung to the ground.

They did not see or hear anything. Lieutenant C. A. McLennan, of the 76th Regiment, threw himself at once into the nearby moat, an excavation directly in front of the officers' quarters. His idea was to get under cover, and he did so "before the steel began to arrive."

As soon as the explosion was over, he clambered out of the moat and found his friends lying in a heap. Two were not injured, but Lieutenant H. C. Balcom, orderly officer for the day, was unable to rise. His right thigh had been shattered by a fragment of the MONT BLANC. Curiously enough, though his clothing was torn, his flesh was not. McLennan doubled into the middle of the square, where a hundred men had been drawn up for guard mount a moment before, together with a number of the Army Medical Corps attached to the Composite Battalion for quarters. All had been thrown to the ground; many were injured; confusion reigned. He got a Sergeant-Major from the Army Service Corps and a stretcher for his injured friend. He put Balcom in the stretcher to be removed to hospital, and then proceeded to "fall in" B Company. There was no bugler to give the customary signal, so he ordered men to shout the command "Fall in, B Company." In this way he got together some fifteen or sixteen men. Everything was in confusion. Men rallied to him covered with blood, but he selected for his work only such as were uninjured.

His first idea was to extinguish fire. Beginning at the southwest corner of the officers' quarters, he worked northwards systematically round the building and ended at the southeast corner, making a complete circuit. The window panes were all shattered. His method was to look in, drop off a man to put out the fire, and then go on with what remained to the next room. When he completed the circuit of the building he saw that the magazine down the hill at the gate of the barracks, was, in his own phrase, "shot to pieces." The explosion had shaken down the wooden portico, broken in the door and injured the roof. McLennan doubled down the hill with his three remaining men, placed them on guard, though they had no rifles, only their natural weapons. Then he raced back to the square in order to report the situation to his Commanding Officer. In the square, he found that the orderly sergeant had collected about eight more men of B Company. McLennan "grabbed them" and hurried back to the magazine.

In view of the fires now universal in the North End and the dismantled exterior of the magazine, this young officer's idea was to make it perfectly secure. On the second visit, he was able to make some hasty inspection of the damage done. He found that a fragment of the MONT BLANC's plating, about seven feet long and eighteen inches broad, and weighing, perhaps, six or seven hundred pounds, had wrapped itself round the top of the iron picket fence surrounding the magazine and smashed a hole in it large enough to let a man through. The magazine itself appeared to be uninjured, but the

8

heavy wooden doors at the side of the portico were smashed inward and the "duck-boards" on the floor were broken to bits. McLennan went inside. It was pitch dark. He had to learn the condition of everything by the feel. "I had sense enough not to light a match." All was in confusion. He could feel with his hands that things were upset and smashed up and the floor covered with "kindling wood." He moved some of the "kindling wood," and then rushed back to the barrack square in search of more men to help him. He saw there a naval officer with about twenty blue-jackets. He asked for a detail, got it, and went back with the men to the magazine. His orders to the working party were, "Get this kindling wood out of that, and light no matches." They went in and got to work, while McLennan examined for the first time the heater-house.

This was a small erection attached to the magazine on the eastern side. In it was a furnace, similar to that used to warm an ordinary house. Its purpose was, of course, to keep up the temperature of the magazine in order to prevent the explosives from deteriorating through damp. He found the doors blown open and the roof smashed in. The furnace was not upset, but the live coals were scattered about and an "honest-to-God" fire was raging. An open wooden four-foot duct led from the heater-house into the magazine to convey the hot air, a sufficiently alarming spectacle in the glare of the fire. In reality the hot air passes through iron pipes running from the furnace through the duct and round the walls of the interior magazine. McLennan seized one of the two chemical fire extinguishers in place, for just such an emergency, and began to play it on the fire. It raised a huge amount of smoke and steam in and about the magazine, which looked most alarming. In a few seconds, the danger was over. The next thing McLennan knew, his working party had stampeded through the hole in the picket fence made by the fragment of the MONT BLANC. According to his own account, the only reason he did not follow them, was because the hole was blocked by hurrying men. His thought was that they had discovered a fire inside the magazine, and it would only be seconds before the whole thing would "go up." The check gave him the necessary moment to think and he reflected that it was no use running away and he manfully stood his ground. "It was an hour before I breathed normally."

Being outside, he saw that the roof of the magazine was damaged and scrambled up, having a fear that there was still fire somewhere in the interior. From this coign of vantage, he saw that the crowd on the street had vanished. One moment the thoroughfare was crowded, the next moment it was as "empty as the sea." One other man did not run. This was the sentry he had posted, Private W. Eisnor. He was only a boy, a new recruit, with little experience of military life. Knowing well the risk he was running, he turned from his post at the East Gate and went straight to the magazine, got the second fire extinguisher and aided his officer in putting out the fire. It was the victory of mind over matter, for a couple of hours later, he collapsed with what may be called shell-shock. He was unable to control his hands or even his facial muscles. Officer and private worked together, taking out the kindling wood and quenching the embers of the fire. It was, in McLennan's own phrase, "a most trying time."

Reinforcements began to arrive. One was a small working party of sailors under the command of Engineer-Lieutenant Bannatyne. This officer had been acting as orderly to Captain Hose, conveying orders from point to point and making reports. The working party that left the magazine through the picket fence, crossed the road and the bridge, and had got inside the Dockyard gates. Here they were halted by Captain Hose in person, fallen in on the exercise-ground and told off to various tasks. When Bannatyne arrived on the scene he saw what he took to be a burning magazine which might explode at any moment. The sentry and the officer on the roof were the only persons about. Recognizing the danger, Bannatyne raced back to the Dockyard, collected a small working party, broke into a store, obtained buckets, filled them with salt water and brought them back to the still doubtful magazine. To Lieutenant McLennan, M.C., the apparition of Bannatyne with his buckets, "was like an act of Providence," for now the immediate danger was over.

It was about this time that General Benson, the officer commanding the fortress of Halifax, with several members of his staff walked down the hill from Wellington Barracks and caught Lieutenant McLennan in *flagrante delicto*. The General approved of the junior proceeding and gave him general permission to "carry on." Thinking that the General's orders were valid, McLennan went out into the street, which was beginning to fill again, and "grabbed" men in uniform, wherever he could get them. In this hasty levy were two men in the 72nd Battery C.E.F. and a British recruit. With the help of these and other men, he established a fire picket and was fully occupied until two o'clock that afternoon in clearing away the broken woodwork and getting the place into something like order. McLennan was not relieved until eleven o'clock the next morning. During the night, he improvised a shelter for himself and his guard in what remained of the lantern house, the small shed between the magazine and the street. It illustrates the pressure under which all capable men worked at this trying time, that, after being relieved from his guard on the powder magazine, McLennan was detailed to guide a party of engineers from an American ship to the Barracks; and when that duty was performed he was set to compiling casualty lists.

The official report states boldly that this officer performed "meritorious work" immediately following the explosion. His action and work are considered most commendable. The sentry Private W. Eisnor of the 75th regiment, No. 1583, has had his "action and work highly commended by the officer in charge of the party at the magazine." These two names head the official list of recommendations.

Chapter 7

At Wellington

During the days which followed the disaster, it was a commonplace on the lips of returned soldiers that Richmond looked like a battlefield in France. If the whole district had been attacked by heavy artillery and bombarded at point blank range from the Dartmouth side, the destruction would hardly have been more complete. Wellington Barracks were, so to speak, on the edge of the storm. The chief buildings are two plain, solid structures of red brick running north and south, parallel to each other. The men's quarters face on Gottingen Street and contain accommodation for eight hundred men. The officers' quarters, overlooking the harbour, are outwardly the duplicate of the men's. Between these two buildings to the north of the square, were the married quarters, five blocks of dwelling houses occupied by married soldiers and their families. On the opposite side were the usual guardrooms, medical offices, canteen and recreation rooms, etc., which are necessary for the well-being of the modern soldier. At the time of the disaster, Wellington was occupied by the Composite Battalion, about eight hundred strong; but not many were actually in barracks. About forty per cent of the strength were disposed at various points about the fortress on different guards. Most of the remainder were outside the buildings.

The scene in the barracks square that morning at five minutes past nine was a familiar one. About one hundred and fifty armed men were paraded on the gravel, waiting for inspection at a quarter past nine, before marching off to the day's duty. The Composite Battalion enjoyed the luxury of two bands; the brass band was playing in the archway as the troops waited. In the farther corner of the square nearest to the MONT BLANC, Lieut. H. C. Balcom watched the burning ship with three other officers. There were a few seconds allotted to several gazers in which to realize the coming catastrophe. Some brief interval of time elapsed between the actual explosion and the "arrival of the steel," as

one officer put it. He had time to throw himself into the "moat," while another took cover behind a tree and escaped injury. The next instant the whole parade were flung to the ground like the troops in front of the Armouries. Before they could recover themselves, the square was bombarded from the sky by a rain of rivets, bolts, and larger fragments of the disintegrated ship. The packs were torn off the men's backs; rifles were broken by the impact of these missiles. It was as if the square had been sprayed with shrapnel. The gravelled rectangle, which, a moment before, presented the spectacle of military order, was littered with prostrate forms bleeding and torn. For some time confusion reigned; then discipline reasserted itself and all who were able sprang to do the obvious task nearest to hand. The marvel was that so few were actually killed in and about the barracks.

All the buildings at Wellington suffered severely from the shock of the explosion. The brick fabrics, of course, offered more resistance than the wooden buildings and came off better. The roofs were broken in both the men's and the officers' quarters, particularly at the northern end nearest to Pier 6. Inside partitions were moved or shaken, stoves were upset, furniture thrown about, and all the windows shattered. The buildings were likewise battered by fragments of the ship. Portions of her plating which had been flung to an immense height, crashed through the roof and all through the floors to the very basement. In a room occupied by the bandsmen, one man was instantly killed by this means, and the band instruments were demolished. A curious freak of the explosion was that while the outer walls of the building remained intact, the dividing partition inside was thrown down. The sleeping rooms for the men on the upper floors were completely wrecked. Lieut. Banks was in a room in the attic of the men's quarters. He had just stepped inside the door and was standing at one side of it, against the wall, when the explosion occurred. When he recovered himself the man he was talking to had disappeared. He was found under the door, which had been blown across the room and covered with a pile of bricks.

The officers' quarters being nearer to the explosion, suffered more severely than the building opposite, but it broke the force of the blow. Prompt action on the part of Lieut. McLennan saved this building from fire, and Lieut. Ray Colwell performed the same service in the men's quarters. On his own initiative he collected men and buckets of water and put out the dangerous fires from the overturned stoves. Then he had the fire engine at work; carried the hose over the high barrack wall on Gottingen St., and played it on the blazing shop just opposite the gate, which threatened the rest of the city with destruction. He was engaged in this work when Controller Hines came up with the city firemen. The married quarters also were badly damaged in roofs, doors, windows, partitions, etc. About two hundred women and children had their homes in them. Many were cut by the glass and otherwise injured, and some were imprisoned in the ruins. The wooden buildings were shaken to the ground, caught fire, and were soon destroyed. The material damage was bad enough, but more serious was the physical damage.

The uninjured soldiers had their hands full. There were wounded comrades to bandage and get off to hospital. Hurt and frightened women and children came pouring out of the married quarters needing medical attention at once, and others remained inside in need of rescue. The wooden buildings which had been thrown down caught fire. The two chief needs were "first aid" and firemen. As for fire, the Battalion had an organization of its own and appliances to meet such emergencies. At once, they set to work to extinguish the fires with the local engine; and this task occupied a number for a large part of the morning.

One episode must be chronicled. Attached to the Composite Battalion, was No. 6 Special Company. Special service means that men who have enlisted in good faith may be found upon further trial and examination to be in some way unfit for the hardest parts of the soldier's task. Such men are not discharged, but are retained as competent to perform lighter duties which may be found for them. At Wellington, the staff of No. 6 Special Service Company occupied the Royal School of Infantry, a long low wooden building divided up into many rooms, each of which was warmed by means of a stove. It collapsed in a heap and almost immediately took fire. All got out except Capt. Jesse Turner, Q.R.N.R., who was in imminent danger of being burned to death. He had broken his hip and was pinned down in the wreckage. The fire had made great headway and a report flew about that ammunition was stored in the building that it might blow up at any moment. Undeterred by all these dangers, real or imaginary, two sergeants of the Company, Horace Basil Crosscup and Charles Edward Hamilton, made their way into the burning building and, at the greatest personal risk, succeeded in dragging their officer out to safety. The bald statement of the official report is the highest praise, "They did not hesitate to do their duty." This rescue would seem to demonstrate the value of Special Service companies.

The other crying need was for first aid and medical attendants. The need brought forth the men, who proved themselves to be equal to the occasion. They were not surgeons or military doctors, but a corporal and a private, namely, John Hogbin and M. C. Drysdale, Medical Orderlies. Hogbin is an old R.C.R. man and wears the South African ribbon. At the time of the explosion, they were in the Medical Inspection room. Immediately there was a rush of all who were injured within the barracks, men, women, and children, to this room which became forthwith a dressing station. The two proceeded to render first aid to all who needed their attention within

the barracks, and continued until this part of their task was complete. By one o'clock they had completed their good work. Then, as they were no longer needed in Wellington, they moved their medical supplies out into Gottingen Street by the barrack gate, and established a dressing station there. They had a pile of blankets to wrap round the injured when taken away to hospital. All that afternoon, they dressed and bandaged wounds, rendering invaluable aid to all who needed it, until they came absolutely to the end of their supplies about 6 o'clock in the evening. They stopped only because they had nothing more to work with. They had been at their humane task without a minute's break for nine hours. Their names were included in the official list of recommendations, "for noteworthy services."

The losses in the Composite Battalion that day were ten killed and three hundred and seventy-seven wounded. Of the latter, one hundred and eighty-seven are classed as serious. These figures include the men who were on guard at North Ordnance, the Dry Dock, and Pier 8, in the immediate neighbourhood of the explosion, twenty-nine in number, all of whom were killed or seriously injured. In the midst of the confusion in the guards' barracks one of the guards at Pier 8 reported himself. All were much impressed by the fact that he came with all his equipment, even to his bayonet, "present and correct." But these figures do not tell the whole story. Altogether, one hundred and fifty-two non-commissioned officers and men lived with their families in Richmond, out of barracks. Many of them lost their wives and children.

Chapter 8

At Headquarters

At the foot of Spring Garden Road is an old-fashioned wooden dwelling house, once the home of a wealthy Halifax merchant, which has been used as the Headquarters of the military establishment in Halifax for many years. The only outward sign of its purpose is the Royal Arms carved and brightly painted over the entrance. The accommodation it afforded was quite inadequate, and since December 6th, the offices have been transferred to a more modern building elsewhere; but on that date it was still the central ganglion of the entire military system for Halifax and its environs.

The Assistant Adjutant-General for the fortress was Colonel W. E. Thompson. Before the war, he was by profession a lawyer, but he had always taken a warm interest in soldiering and was major of the P.L.F. He is a college graduate and ex-football player of the type usually described as "burly" or "bull-dog." On the morning of the 6th he was in his office at the time of the explosion, and never budged from it for many days except to eat and sleep. It was his duty to sit at his desk and keep things moving, to direct and organize the military forces available, to meet the new unforeseen emergency. His first impression was, "At last the war has come to us. I'm glad. People will know that we are in it." He went out into the street, and looking north, could see the silvery column of smoke standing high above city roofs, and soon learned from flying rumours that a munition ship had exploded, that Richmond had been levelled to the ground, that hundreds had been killed and injured and that the district was on fire. He received no official information of the disaster, and no orders as to what he should do. On him devolved the whole responsibility of grappling with the situation, but "Ernie" Thompson is not the sort of man who fears responsibility or lacks initiative. He is the kind of man who gets things done.

Halifax is a first-class fortress which has been called the Gibraltar of America. The city Cornwallis founded on a peninsula was defended against the French and Indians by forts actually upon it. But with the growth of long-range artillery, the system of defenses has been extended miles away from the original centre, on the islands that stop the harbour mouth, and the high cliffs that look down on the Atlantic. Soldiers of various regiments were distributed among these points, and had to be recalled, transported to the city, equipped and set to work. This was done by means of three duty boats, small steamers which ply up and down the harbour.

"My duty," said Colonel Thompson, "was to get the troops at McNab's and York on the scene as soon as possible, to see that transport from men and supplies was ready, by land and sea, and ordnance in a state to move necessary supplies such as boots, blankets, picks and shovels." Orders flew about, and the available staff rallied at once to meet the needs of the hour. The ordnance and engineers are supposed, in the army, to be more or less hampered by red tape, unwilling to act without written orders, and all the machinery of requisitions, receipts, indents, etc., but in this case they proved to be quite human and rose nobly to the occasion. Colonel Thompson really assumed direction of the forces, making plans, the details of which were worked out by members of his staff, particularly Major R. B. Willis. A detail of the 63rd P.L.F. was the first to arrive. They were ordered to proceed north, calling at the Ordnance in Water St., the old-fashioned stone buildings at the Gun Wharf. Each man was to receive and take with him a blanket for the protection of those who were injured or without clothing. Half an hour after the explosion, the Ordnance were conveying blankets to the North End for

wrapping round the wounded who were being taken to the hospitals. This much abused department issued practically everything that was required for the work of rescue, etc., beginning with hospital equipment and later such things as shovels, picks, coal-oil, stoves, lanterns, forks, wash-basins, and pails. "By twelve o'clock we had all our troops out and working, that is, they were carrying dead and wounded to vehicles of all kinds to be taken to hospital, or digging out bodies from the ruins, in a systematic and orderly way under the orders of their officers." An army is an organization which is designed to meet difficulties in a systematic way. Part of Headquarters duty that day was to allay excitement caused by the second alarm and keep the citizens cool. It was a centre of great activity all that day.

"Commandeering" was a word much in vogue that day. Perhaps the most urgent need was transportation. With many of the sufferers, rapid transit to the hospital, or dressing station, was a matter of life and death. A rumor flew about that all vehicles had been commandeered by military orders. Colonel Thompson's general instructions were, "Wherever you want a car or a team, stop and take it." Cars were appropriated under the owner's nose, and many a car was worn out that day by unskilful and too zealous drivers.

Headquarters had many visitors. Officers dashing in for orders or to make reports, civilians to consult or to be told what to do. Some errands were futile enough, others showed headwork and were for the benefit of all. Futile or not, visitors showed a universal disposition to help in every way possible. Their hearts were in the right place. Colonel Thompson was particularly impressed by the visit of Mr. A. O. Saunderson, the local manager of a tar-paper manufacturing concern. Since the whole city was windowless, in winter weather, tar-paper and roofing materials would be at a premium; and there was great danger of the whole supply being cornered by some unscrupulous dealer, who would reap exorbitant profits from the necessities of his fellow citizens. If the military authorities commandeered it, it could be given out in small quantities to those who were in urgent need; and this was agreed on. Mr. Saunderson then motored out to the factory at Fairview, found two of the employees in charge and instructed them to distribute roofing paper in five-roll lots to all who should apply for it. In this way, five thousand rolls were distributed in forty-eight hours. Another visitor, in the hurly-burly who also impressed himself upon the memory of this busy official, was Captain J. F. Cahan, an officer of the Canadian Engineers who was suffering from injury to the spine and could not move without assistance. He got himself a taxi and reported at Headquarters for orders. He was told to chase the people home and this he proceeded to do.

It was a long hard day. Every hour and every minute had its own particular difficulty or problem. By nine o'clock at night staff and H.Q. men were pretty well ex-

Search parties. "I cannot speak too highly of the services of my staff and the troops quartered in Halifax fortress. They worked day and night to do all that was possible to assist all concerned in this terrible disaster." Col. W. E. Thompson.

hausted. All the available troops had been working very hard, and, if they were to continue next day, they must have sleep and rest. The usual guards at various points had to be maintained, just as if nothing had happened. The total number of troops available had been diminished by a long list of killed or wounded. The whole city was "wide open," and night had come on. Colonel Thompson and his staff were "combing their brains" how to get the necessary guards, when there was a knock at the door of the office, and in came two American naval officers, Captain Stanford E. Moses, of the U.S.S. VON STEUBEN and Captain Howard Symington of the U.S.S. TACOMA. They asked, "Is there anything we can do?" The answer was, "Can you give me any men to patrol the streets?" "Any number?" "Can you give me two hundred and fifty?" The answer was, "Yes," and almost before the Headquarters staff could realize it, the efficient Americans had the required force of blue-jackets and marines on shore and had taken over the guardianship of the Halifax streets, thus affording the wearied Canadians the rest and sleep they needed so badly for the toil of the terrible next day, the day of the blizzard. This thoughful consideration on the part of the American officers is characteristic of the people they represented, and was manifested in a thousand ways by the

measures of relief which they put in operation later. The official report called the attention of Ottawa to "the whole-hearted, effective assistance" given by the officers and men of these two ships.

Colonel R. B. Simmonds of the 66th regiment was one of the first to report at Headquarters. He was in his house in town when the explosion occurred and thought that his house had been hit by the Germans. His post was York Redoubt and, after getting his family in a place of safety, he started for it. At Headquarters he was asked for a hundred men. He was able to telephone his orders and the needed men just caught the duty-boat before it left the wharf. They reached Halifax about eleven and went north. Their job of work was to clear the street, principally Campbell Road. The South Barracks were taken over for the headquarters of this regiment, which furnished guards, working parties, etc., as occasion required, and they never had men enough to meet the demands made upon them. Later, Colonel Simmonds was in charge of the working parties which searched the ruins of Richmond for the dead. The site of every house in the district was gone through and what was found identified as far as possible. Once the soldiers came upon a living dog which had fed upon a corpse; and once they found a strange mass of ice, which proved to contain the body of a woman.

One of the difficulties the soldiers had to contend with was the influx of men from the outside into the city, though this did not begin until the Saturday. The Armouries and Wellington Barracks had both been so damaged and overtaxed that they were not available and the huts occupied by the men on the Commons had been given up to the homeless women and children. There was no more accommodation, but relief parties continued to come in from the country, until they were asked to discontinue coming.

In his official report the General states: "I cannot speak too highly of the services of my staff and the troops quartered in the Halifax fortress. They worked day and night to do all that was possible to assist all concerned in this terrible disaster. Had it not been for their perseverance and the military hospitals I fear the conditions would have been much more dreadful."

The action of soldiers in such emergencies as that of December 6th is invariably taken for granted. The public assumes that they will work heroically, as a matter of course, and their official superiors are content to say that they performed their duties "cheerfully and energetically," stating parenthetically that they were "kept on duty day and night in some instances for several days without proper rest." "Working day and night" is no vague statement. Lieutenant W. E. Simpson, acting adjutant of the 1st Depot Battalion, N.S.R., remained on duty forty-eight hours without relief and showed "splendid ability in organizing the various details," according to the unemotional language of the official report.

Private soldiers as well as officers performed what is termed in official language as "noteworthy services." For instance, Private R. S. Hutchinson of the Pay Department was engaged all day Thursday in rescue work in the devastated area, all Friday he was employed on a motor-ambulance, all Saturday he worked on a motor-truck hauling relief material and he spent Sunday and Monday searching for bodies at Richmond. It is impossible to give all the names, or chronicle all the golden deeds of this great day, but the foregoing instances will suffice to show that the soldiers at Halifax did not fall below the high standard of the British Army, "at every turn where courage, skill and industry are wont to be employed."

Chapter 9

At The Armouries

All over Canada the old-fashioned wooden drill shed has given place to buildings of more modern type known as armouries. They are squat, solidly built structures of heavy stone with mediaeval-looking loop-holed round towers and battlements at various angles. Not only is there a large area roofed in for drill and military exercises, but space is given to permanent offices of adminis-

tration. Buildings of this type have been erected by the Government at important centres in the Dominion for the accommodation of the regular Militia regiments. In Halifax, the Armouries are situated on the edge of the Common at the corner of Cunard and North Park Sts. It is a very large building, too large, one would think, in time of peace, but during the war it has been used to the full. Across the street, long, low sheds have been run up, called "hutments" in Army phrase, and surrounded by a high wire fence.

All this accommodation was not too much for the bodies of troops assembling in Halifax preparatory to passing overseas. Here was the headquarters of the first Depot Battalion under the command of Col. H. Flowers, a Halifax man, who had always been a keen militia soldier, and who has seen two years' service in the 25th Battalion from Nova Scotia. In these quarters, there were also stationed two batteries of Canadian Field Artillery, the 74th and the 75th, which had been recruited in Ontario. There were also several hundred recruits for the British Expeditionary Force.

At the moment of the explosion, some of these troops were on parade on the Common outside, and some were in the Armouries. The shock of the explosion smashed glass and doors and injured the great span of the roof to an extent not realized at the time. The engineers were officially reported as having effected repairs and prevented it falling. But later, it was found necessary to remove and restore the whole roof. Many injuries were suffered by the men inside, chiefly B.E.F. recruits. Like the troops in the barrack square at Wellington, they were thrown to the earth. In their own phrase, "the ground flew up and hit them." There was very little confusion; discipline was immediately restored; and these various units were ordered to stand by and await orders. It did not take Col. Flowers long to learn that a great explosion had occurred in the north end of the city, although he was uncertain as to the exact scene of it and the extent of damage it had caused to life and property. He immediately detailed three parties from the battalion as rescue parties to proceed in three different directions, one to Pier 2, the important point of embarkation, one to Richmond, and one to the north end of the city by way of Agricola St. In organizing these details he was ably seconded by his adjutant, Lieut. W. B. Simpson, who is officially reported as having "displayed splendid ability" in so doing. It should be noted as an illustration of how men worked at this time that this young officer remained on duty for forty-eight hours without relief.

After the despatch of these rescue parties there remained a certain residue of the Depot Battalion. The Sergeant-Major was instructed to hold all available men in readiness for any emergency with water bottles filled, and the Battalion was reported to Col. Thompson at Headquarters as "Awaiting Orders." It may be said in passing that the readiness of Col. Flowers, the prompt-

10

ness and efficiency of the measures taken by him impressed Headquarters most favourably, and in the official report this officer is commended as "largely responsible for the very satisfactory manner in which he did his job." Two years' campaigning in France during the great war prepares a man for sudden and unforeseen crises. This was not Col. Flowers' first experience of explosions. Almost as soon as it got into the front line in France, his battalion had been blown up by a German mine. Relief of the injured at once claimed his attention. At the corner of the Armouries where three streets join, Cunard, Agricola, and North Park, he established picquets with orders to commandeer all passing vehicles and use them for the transportation of injured persons, because in a very few minutes people from the surrounding streets, men, women, children, bleeding and bruised, came flocking to the Armouries to obtain medical relief. It was at once plain to Col. Flowers that one of the great, immediate needs was all kinds of vehicles to convey those, who were not walking cases, to various hospitals.

A party was sent off post haste to the old Military Hospital which stands on its own grounds at the corner of Cogswell and Brunswick Sts., for all available medical supplies. On the prompt arrival of these, four dressing stations were established on the Common in charge of two officers of the First Depot Battalion, N.S.R., and two civilians who had had previous training in first aid. Four had been already established and each was besieged by throngs of patients needing immediate treatment. When Commander Howley with his wounds unstaunched reached this scene within half an hour of the explosion, he found such long queues of wounded awaiting treatment that he decided to go elsewhere. The medical supplies soon ran out and more had to be obtained from the inexhaustible reservoirs of the Ordnance, and a second time from the Military Hospital on Cogswell St. When bandages gave out the surgeons tore up their own clothing and worked naked to the waist. Capt. E. S. Ingraham, Quartermaster of the Battalion, is mentioned in the list of recommendations for his efficiency in bringing the necessary supplies to the spot. It was by using one of the commandeered cars that he was able to bring such speedy aid. That morning, injured persons bled to death on their way to hospitals and dressing stations. There was need of haste.

While this was going on, the hutments in front of the Armouries were being cleared out, the troops occupying them being assigned to various duties. The empty quarters were quickly filled with injured and shelterless women and children. They were supplied with bedding from the military stores, and hot broth was served to them through "the untiring efforts" of one of the officers stationed at the Armouries. Him, the official report does not particularize further, not even mentioning his name, although it supplies the welcome detail that it was "entirely due" to him that the refugees were made comfortable.

As has been stated several times, the deplorable rumour that a second explosion was imminent flew round the city soon after the first explosion occurred. It originated in the very real danger of the magazine at Wellington exploding. Its effects could only have been local, but only the fewest thought of that possibility at the time. The sight of men in uniform exhorting the crowds to go south, to the open spaces, to throw themselves on the ground, was sufficient to move the crowds and spread panic. The largest "open spaces" are the areas at the foot of the Citadel *glacis* known as the Common. The north end streets debouch into it, and soon it was crowded with people. The well and strong, infants, the old, the bed-ridden, some of whom had not left their rooms for years, found themselves in this mob expecting they knew not what that strange December day. The greatest hardship was endured by those who had found shelter, had their wounds dressed, and now had to be carried out of the different refuges and laid on the ground. In addition to their physical sufferings they had all the torment of nameless anxiety and suspense. The house of Dr. Mackintosh on Robie St. which skirts the western edge of the Common, had become a dressing station, like every doctor's office in Halifax and Dartmouth that day. Some twenty injured persons were carried out and laid on mattresses before the house, where they remained till noon.

The mob on the Common was composed chiefly of women and children. Some were very scantily clad and there was much suffering from cold. Here again the military came to the rescue. A party from the 1st Depot Battalion was detailed to carry blankets about and distribute them among the shivering crowd, in the words of the official report, "to lessen the suffering of the unfortunate people who were made as comfortable as it was humanly possible under the most adverse conditions." It is highly probable that few of these army blankets were ever collected and returned to store, or properly accounted for. They were found in various hospitals and shelters, then and later, the only protection of the helpless against the cruel cold. They were well "expended."

The hutments being normally filled with troops, and now occupied by the injured, the question of further accommodation arose. The solution was tents, a suggestion which the Deputy-Mayor had already made at Headquarters. By eight o'clock that evening no fewer than four hundred tents had been erected on the Common, as well as an emergency marquee hospital. They were furnished with floors, cots, blankets, light and heat. This canvas town sprang up not by magic, but by the most intense, untiring labour on the part of the Ordnance which supplied the material, the Army Service Corps which transported it, and the engineers who set it up and put all in order. After all this labour these tents remained empty and were never used. Apparently this accommodation designed to shelter the civilian population was not sufficiently well known, or else those in search of shelter preferred public buildings which were nearer at hand, such as the theatres, or even the very insufficient protection of their wrecked houses. Instead of returning to their huts, the troops remained on duty all night and it was, therefore, unnecessary to shift the injured persons into the less comfortable tents. These huts had been in fact organized there and then into a temporary hospital where the injured received every possible attention from the medical officer stationed at the Armouries. The official report notes that these men did exceptional work.

The figure of the demolished ant-hill applies well to Halifax that day; there was endless confusion, hurryings to and fro on errands of life and death, and aimless straying of the helpless. Some people undoubtedly lost their heads for the time being, but the vast majority kept steady, saw clearly the duty that lay nearest, and did it with wisdom and promptitude. One detail in the process of housing the injured citizens in the huts on the Common showed rare thoughtfulness. A complete record was kept of all those who passed through the hands of the medical officers and a list was posted on the door of each hut showing who were inmates there. Consequently, when distracted friends or relatives came inquiring for the missing, the military were able to answer all inquiries.

As has been stated, the recruits for the British Expeditionary Force were on parade in the drill-hall at the time of the explosion. This part of the building suffered most. The roof was so shattered and the girders were so broken and displaced. None of these men were killed, but many were injured more or less, or dazed for the time being. Captain J. R. Armitage, the officer in charge, was badly cut about the head, but within half an hour all had their wounds dressed, and he was able to lead a party of a hundred and fifty to Richmond to assist in putting out the fires. His exertions then and later were too much for Capt. Armitage and he suffered a long illness in consequence. Some of the men who remained on duty had been injured much more severely than appeared at first. For example, the Sergeant-Major worked all day with three broken ribs. In the bald language of the official report, ''This unit deserves every credit for the manner in which they conducted themselves especially when it is remembered that many of them have been in the service such a short time that they had not been uniformed.''

Chapter 10

At The Citadel

One reason for selecting the present site of Halifax was the ease with which it could be defended. There was bold water up to the shore and the hill behind was a natural fort. From the first, this hill has been fortified. Short's drawing of 1760 showed a square block-house on the summit, a flag-staff and a flag. In his prize essay, Akins states that the hill was eighty feet higher than when he wrote. About 1830, the obsolete eighteenth century works were done away and an elaborate starshaped fort took their place. This was constructed according to the best military science of the day; but long-range artillery has rendered it obsolete. It is now used as a signal station, a barracks, and a prison. From all points it commands beautiful views of the city, the harbour, the Basin, and the surrounding country.

During the war, the Citadel has been the headquarters of the 1st Regiment, Canadian Garrison Artillery. On the morning of December 6th, the quartermaster, A. M. Bauld, was on his way to the Citadel, coming up over the hill, and had just reached the signal station at the southeast angle when he was startled by a loud noise. It was immediately followed by an earthquake-like tremor which threw him to the ground. He looked north on recovering himself, and saw ''a magnificent sight in the sky,'' a sight he will never forget. A huge volume of dark cloud followed by a white cloud circling thousands of feet in the air, and in the centre, flames. His first thought was that the magazine at North Ordnance had blown up, but he did not realize the havoc made by the explosion. He at once went to the Citadel and found every office and barrack room completely destroyed. The sashes, windows, and doors were ''torn to pieces.'' His own office was, emphatically ''a sight,'' a medley of broken glass, demolished window sashes, and tumbled furniture. All was in confusion. He tried to bring some order out of this confusion and make repairs, and also gather together his papers. The men in the Citadel had not been seriously hurt although numbers had been cut by glass.

Major Bauld's work of restoring order was interrupted by a more pressing necessity. The slopes of the Citadel *glacis* were soon covered, like the Common at their feet, with hundreds of people who had been warned to leave their houses on account of the danger of a second explosion. Very many of these were wounded and in need of immediate medical attention. In Major Bauld's opinion, they were ''certainly panic-stricken.'' They flocked to the Citadel gate, the beehive-like entrance flanked by old French mortars taken at the siege of Louisburg. The usual rules were relaxed and on the demand of the wounded and bleeding for a doctor, they were admitted to the Citadel. Major Bauld and an orderly conducted them to the doctor's office, but there was no doctor. The regimental surgeon, Dr. A. McD. Morton, was besieged in his own house in Quinpool Road, by those who rushed in to have their wounds attended to. His sergeant had been taken off to Camp Hill Hospital to help there with the wounded and dying. It was perhaps an hour or more before they arrived at the Citadel. In the meantime, in Major Bauld's own modest words, "We had to do our best to give first aid." The wounded were coming in from Wellington Barracks, and even from Rockhead Hospital in the extreme north of the city. One of the barrack rooms happened to be empty and this was turned into a temporary shelter for the men, women, and children who swarmed in for aid. Hot tea, bread, and jam was served out to the patients, while they waited the arrival of the doctor. The more serious cases were sent off to hospital in a motor car driven by Lieut. L. L. Harrison. When Dr. Morton did succeed in reaching the Citadel, he did, in the words of the official report, "heroic work." It was five o'clock in the afternoon before he had finished and given at least temporary relief to all who needed it. But there was no rest for him. He immediately reported at Camp Hill Hospital, where he assisted the other doctors in their overwhelming task of caring for the injured who crowded that house of pain all that awful day. The men of the Garrison Artillery were brought in the next day, as many as could be spared from the out-forts, and assigned to various duties. Amongst others was the task of digging graves in the cemeteries. They worked faithfully and even in the most terrible storms which followed the calm of December 6th, there was not a complaint from any one of them. But all commanding officers of the various units report the same thing of their men at this time.

It is very seldom that a soldier tells what he has done. His tendency is to be silent or understate. But "Headquarters" ordered the officers commanding the various units to make inquiries as to special services. This came into being the official list of recommendations. For his work that morning, Major Bauld was included in the official list of recommendations because "in the absence of the M.O., who was detailed attending the wounded, he established a dressing station and assisted by a Medical Orderly, attended to the wounded who flocked to the Citadel."

While Major Bauld was walking up to the Signal Station, another officer of the R.G.A. was climbing the road to the entrance of the Citadel in his motor. This was Lieut. Leslie Harrison, the only son of Captain Harrison who salvaged the PICTON. He was just getting out of his car, when the explosion occurred. He was thrown violently to the ground. The noise and the shock suggested a bursting shell near him. He ran across the square to the south parapet, and looked seaward thinking, no doubt, like half Halifax, that the Germans were bom-barding the city. Thence he saw the portent of the flame-shot column of smoke towering above the North End, and he realized that a magazine of some kind had exploded. At once he saw gunners running out of all the buildings covered with blood from the cuts inflicted by the glass. He shouted, "Take cover," and blew his whistle. As soon as the danger from the flying fragments was over, Harrison ordered the fire call to be sounded; and the men who were suffering from cuts were sent to the care of the medical orderly.

About half-past nine, the Adjutant took command and Harrison left the Citadel in his car with the medical orderly, as many bandages as could be secured, and proceeded north to the scene of the disaster. He made two trips with wounded persons to the Victoria General Hospital, and then left the orderly at one of the dressing stations which had been formed before the Armouries. In his next trip, he took his load of wounded to the Halifax Infirmary in Barrington St. Thence he went to the extreme end of Gottingen Street and from this point, conveyed as many seriously hurt as could be found to Camp Hill Hospital. Among these was a child about eight years of age who died on the way, probably of shock, and a woman whose arm was blown off bled to death. Near Oxford Street, he picked up a woman who was prematurely confined on the way to the hospital. In the same street, he saw a baker's wagon filled with injured persons, the blood dripping from beneath. All that day, Harrison continued to transport injured persons or doctors and nurses from point to point as required. He was on duty continuously until his car was stalled in a drift at nine o'clock Friday night, when he left it and walked home.

The dry official summary of Lieut. Harrison's activities is instructive as showing how all flesh and blood details are omitted:

"This officer with the Adjutant's instructions left the Citadel shortly after the explosion in his car taking Med. Sgt. E. T. Morton with him and medical supplies. He proceeded to the North End giving emergency aid and conveying injured to the hospitals. He continued this work until 2:00 a.m. on the 7th, and then reported to Headquarters, and during the night took Major Willis to the various hospitals. At 5:00 a.m. he began conveying nurses and doctors from the terminals to the hospitals and continued till 9:00 p.m. driving officials and patients to and from wherever required being continually in his car for 36 hours."

Contrasting this severely condensed account with what precedes it, the reader may be able to fill in the outline of other paragraphs from the report, which summarizes the activities of other officers in the unit, in this fashion:

Lieut. O. A. MacC. Wilson:
This officer was detailed on the 6th for duty at Camp Hill Hospital where he remained for about ten days giving very valuable assistance.

Lieut. E. S. Thompson:
This officer spent 6th, with 23 men clearing away wood-work at entrance to North Ordnance magazine and searching the ruins for bodies, recovering about fifty. December 7th engaged in similar work.

Lieut. G. B. Isnor:
This officer spent the first 36 hours after the explosion driving his car, assiting in the search for places to house the homeless, conveying nurses and doctors from the Terminals to the Hospitals and helping with the distribution of emergency blankets, clothing, etc.

Lieut. L. G. Esther:
This officer on the 6th ordered to assist in putting up tents on the Common. Relieved at midnight and reported to Headquarters. 7th at Richmond recovering bodies.

Lieut. E. A. Bell:
This officer left Connaught Battery at 11:00 a.m. on the 6th in his car and spent the day conveying sick and wounded to the hospitals etc. and recovering bodies from the ruins. Returned to Connaught on the 7th.

Chapter 11

The Firemen

On December 6th some criticism might have been heard regarding the delay of the Fire Department in getting the engines to the scene of the disaster, but it was uttered in ignorance before the creditable facts were known. A little before nine o'clock the alarm was rung in Box 83. Edward Condon, Chief of the Fire Department, and W. P. Brunt, his deputy, set off at once in the official motor at top speed for Pier 6, near which the MONT BLANC was aground. A hose-wagon from the Isleville engine house and the fine new modern chemical engine ''Patricia,'' the pride of the department, hurried to the same spot. They were actually at the nearest available point for effective work when the explosion occurred. All but one reached it only to meet their death. The motor containing Condon and Brunt was flung up in the air and completely reversed. The two occupants were instantly killed.*

The first shock of the explosion damaged the ''Patricia'' but did not stop the work. The second

wrecked the engine completely and killed five of the crew. These were Michael Maltus, Frank Killen, William Broderick, John Duggan and Walter Hennessey. Heroism and self-sacrifice are all in a day's work of the fireman and risks of life and limb are taken as a matter of course. They pass, as a rule, unremarked by the public, but in this case a grateful city has testified its admiration for their steadfastness by laudatory resolutions and by providing for the families which have been deprived of their bread-winners. One of the crew had a miraculous escape. This was William Wells, engineer of the ''Patricia.'' The force of the explosion flung him across the street against a telegraph, or electric light pole. His own account is that he left the engine, or the engine left him, he did not know which, but anyhow they parted company. There he lay until the sea drove over the road, washing him up as far as the middle of Mulgrave Park. He was drenched and almost drowned and when picked up was not expected to live. He did, however, recover and regained his usual health.

After the explosion a second alarm called out the remaining engines and men of the Fire Department. They proceeded as quickly as possible to the north end of the City and worked under their own captains in different divisions west of Gottingen and north of Macara Street. The general superintendence of this force devolved upon Controller Hines. He did not know until late in the afternoon that the head of the Department had been killed, but imagined that Condon was fighting the fires on the eastern slope of the hill, so he concentrated his efforts upon the western section in the neighbourhood of the Cotton Factory. As already stated the fires rose from the ruins of separate houses. There was no sweeping general conflagration, on account of the calm weather, but in the event of the wind shifting and blowing from the north nothing could have saved the city from destruction. The loss of the Patricia with her crew, auxiliaries and apparatus was sorely felt. The plan on which the firemen worked was to control fires which seemed to menace the city and to let isolated buildings, like the Cotton Factory, burn. The grounds of Wellington Barracks are bounded on the north by Russell St. which marks the southward

* It is a noteworthy fact that heavy objects such as this motor were completely overturned. Numerous reports bear out the theory of whirlwinds being set up by the explosion. In the case of the tug Hilford, driven up on shore, the engine was found to be almost exactly in its proper position, but upside down, with the fire box in the air. A teamster driving a wagon northward along Water St. reported that after the explosion he found himself under his horses, which were facing the other way about. An invalid lady in a north end house was found by her daughter underneath her bed, which was then bottom upward. The head of the bedstead was resting on a trunk, which had stood at the foot of the bed, thus making the space between the bed and the floor. All the heavy furniture of the room was piled on top of the overset bed, and on the very top of all were the window curtains. The inmate escaped being crushed, because the head of the bed rested on the trunk.

limit of the devastated area. Just in front of the Barracks to the west runs Gottingen St. and just across the way from the barrack gate a grocer's shop took fire and was burnt to the ground. It was at this point that the firemen rendered perhaps their most efficient service in checking the spread of the flames, for all about were flimsy wooden houses, which would have burnt like tinder on the slightest encouragement. The hard work of the firemen at this point undoubtedly kept the fire from spreading south and averted a great danger.

When the unfortunate warning of the second explosion being imminent flew through the city, there were undoubtedly many who felt panic. Men were seen running south along Barrington St. with their eyes staring and along Robie St. as if German bayonets were behind them. Motors sped southward through the streets with refugees clinging to the footboards, and the screeching horns helping to spread alarm. Moreover, the orders to move south were communicated everywhere by men in uniform and were naturally supposed to proceed from some official source. But neither panic nor official command affected the firemen. Thousands of citizens made for the open spaces with all haste; but they stood fast. They would not leave their posts, thus saving, at the very least, the fire apparatus of the city from certain destruction. So they toiled all day, wet and cold, without food, without assistance, ignorant of their families' fate, until late at night, when they had the situation under control. Extinguishing fires was only part of their work. Rescuing women and children from burning houses, even giving first aid to the injured formed part of their duties. Late in the afternoon, willing and plentiful aid, men and machines, arrived from Truro, New Glasgow, Springhill and Amherst, but the essential work had been finished by the city's own employees, though diminished in numbers and material. The firemen of Halifax had done all that men could do before the eager helpers arrived. Then they obtained a much needed rest, and the firemen from New Glasgow and Truro patrolled the streets in case another fire should break out in the night.

Another who died in the performance of his duty was John Spruin, veteran fireman. He had had thirty years' service in the Department and was not liable for duty except in the event of a special call, but he saw the engine passing and the old habit reasserted itself. He sprang to the running-board to do his part with younger men. A sudden lurch of the machine flung him to the ground and he was instantly killed.

Chapter 12

The Second Alarm

A city is like an anthill. Destroy a portion of it with a careless foot and the busy population at first runs distractedly in all directions hither and yon, before it makes an effective rally and begins to repair the damage done. The effect of the explosion on the Richmond district was that of a paving stone dropped in a puddle, smiting, displacing and driving what it hits in all directions away from the centre. That day in Halifax the currents of population swirled and eddied to the various points of the compass, according to impulse which can be easily understood. There was the impulse, first, to reach a place of safety. The instinct of those injured was to reach some spot—hospital, doctor's office, drug shop—where they could find relief for their hurts. Those who were unhurt wanted to escape from danger, or to assist their helpless friends to get away. There was a movement of the population from the north to the south along the main arteries of traffic, Barrington, Gottingen, and Brunswick streets.

Against this wave of population surged a counter-current northward of men employed in the business portion of the city, intent on finding out what had become of their families. One observer in Brunswick St. noted their set, determined faces as they ran towards their homes. This northward setting current was swollen by masses of citizens who knew vaguely that something had happened in the North End, and wanted to find out just what the trouble was. In these, curiosity was quickly changed to distress, horror, and sympathy when they realized something of the awfulness of the calamity, and saw the bleeding helpless bodies carried in every kind of vehicle southward; for almost as soon as this swift destruction had fallen on the city, willing hands were hard at work in rescue and relief. Northward towards Fairview and Dutch Village, westward to the slopes of old Fort Needham and toward the Arm Bridge, the people streamed in search of relief, or simply to get away from the burning desolation of Richmond. Some went to Rockingham, to Bedford, to Herring Cove, even as far as Windsor Junction.

Barrington Street was perhaps most quickly filled with throngs of curious citizens. The upper end of the street near the Railway Station and Wellington Barracks was thick with people, when the unconsidered act of some individual in the crowd increased the confusion tenfold, and had even more serious consequences. When Lieutenant McLennan turned his extinguisher on the fire in the heater house, the natural consequence was a sudden cloud of mingled steam and smoke rising from the wrecked building. To the onlookers it must have looked as if it came from the magazine itself; the two were practically one building. The ruined houses in Russell Street just beyond Wellington Barracks were on fire. Nothing could be more natural than the supposition that the magazine was also on fire. It is said that some civilian in the crowd pointed with his cane to the cloud of smoke. He may also have shouted, or spoken his thought to his nearest neighbour. But the mere hint, the mere wind of the word would be enough. The crowd turned at once and surged back from the apparent danger, heading south and spreading alarm. Panic ran through the city. With incredible swiftness, the rumour went round, that there was great danger of a second explosion from a powder magazine, that all people were to leave their houses and take refuge in the parks and open spaces. There was nothing vague about the rumour. The definite statement was conveyed by soldiers throughout the streets. They were on foot, knocking at house-doors, or in vehicles such as motor-lorries telling the people to ''go south'' and even to throw themselves on the ground in the open spaces. Would-be helpers were turned back at North Street by police and soldiers and told why they should turn back. Naturally, they warned all they could reach, as the Harrisons did from their car.

And here is a mystery which had not been cleared up. The orders to leave the houses were carried over the city by men in uniform, chiefly private soldiers. The testimony of individuals in different quarters agrees in this point. It is hardly likely that these men should have done so without proper authorization, but it seems impossible to discover whether any orders were definitely given to this effect. If orders were given, the source from which they emanated is not known, or if known, the secret has been well-kept. A heavy responsibility rests with the officer who gave them.

Indeed, the danger about North Street Station and the East Gate of Wellington was real enough. Russell Street was ablaze from end to end. A shift of wind might have carried sparks and embers from nearby Russell Street to the magazine which McLennan and his working party were trying to make safe. Twenty-four hours later, on the night of the blizzard, the guard was kept busy putting out the live embers blown by the fierce gale from the still burning houses, through the openings in the magazine. Another source of danger was close at hand of which the public in general knew nothing. This was the North Ordnance, a magazine just across the street and railway inside the Dock Yard grounds. This was charged with high explosives and had been damaged by the concussion of the air-blast. The whole district of Richmond as well as the Sugar Refinery, the latter only a few hundred feet away, was blazing. Orders were given to empty the magazine of its dangerous contents and all that day, a strong working party of blue-jackets, under the direction of Lieutenant MacDonald, R.C.N.V.R., was engaged in carrying the boxes and cases down the hill and dumping them into the harbour. By the law of association, danger from fire suggests safety in water, and much

good ammunition was expended in the harbour, before the wastage was checked. This was a military magazine, and when the natural authorities found what was being done, they checked the dumping into the harbour, and instead, had the various cases piled up on the wharf edge, so that if the fire came too near, they could be pushed over into the water in the very shortest time. The work of removing this ammunition lasted from the morning till between four and five o'clock. Only a few yards away lay the PICTON with fifteen hundred tons of fused shell in her hold, and the litter from the damaged smoke-screen apparatus on fire. It was quite possible that one, or all, of these collections of explosives might have gone up at any moment. The destruction of life and property that would have been caused thereby would have been trifling compared with that wrought by the explosion of the MONT BLANC, but all the workers in the neighbourhood must have suffered severely. All that morning there was a stream of traffic passing along Barrington Street between the damaged magazine in Wellington on the one hand, and the emptying Ordnance store in the Dock Yard on the other. Removing the injured people from Richmond was like the evacuation of the wounded from the battlefield, only much worse because the modern military organization and appliances were lacking. It was carried on, as it were, through a pass guarded by three masked batteries, which might spring into deadly life at any moment.

The warning to abandon all houses and take to the open spaces passed through the city in all directions and was universally obeyed. The general movement was southward towards Point Pleasant Park. The Common, the great open space about the Citadel, as well as the slopes of the *glacis* itself were ''black with people.'' The population flowed into the grounds of the Halifax Golf Club, into ''Studley,'' the grounds of Dalhousie College, into the vacant fields west of Agricola Street, out the road which leads to Bedford, and that which leads to the head of the Arm and St. Margaret's Bay. An officer coming up from a shore battery to the city was struck by the sight of such ''hordes'' at this point. Another stated that their route could be traced by the trail of blood upon the road.

The hardship, suffering, and death caused by this panic can hardly be estimated. The sick, the aged, the bed-ridden were moved out of their houses. Those who had been injured were taken to the open and laid on the ground. Worst of all, in some cases, those engaged in rescuing injured persons from the ruins of burning houses of Richmond were forced away and left helpless ones to an agonizing death.

From North to South every dwelling, shop, institution, was emptied that morning and abandoned with open doors and windows, to whatever chance might befall. Windows were all gone and doors stood wide open. The police had other duties to perform besides protecting property. If there is a criminal class in Halifax, it missed its opportunity that morning, for there was no plundering or robbery. One small street urchin was seen carrying candy which he had looted from some store, but apparently he had no imitators. Later, wild tales ran about of ghouls plundering the dead, or thieves being shot by the military. They had no basis of fact. Desirable goods from shops were piled in the open, were left unguarded, and were not touched.

Though the population in general had taken to the open, the streets were full of traffic, for there was no cessation in the work of removing the injured to hospitals. On the Common, in the Golf Grounds, and at Studley, people stood in groups waiting without much excitement for what might happen. In some cases, fires were made to warm the scantily clad refugees. About noon word was passed round, again by men in uniform, that the danger was over, that the magazine had been flooded. People went back to their homes, or places of business and took up the duty nearest at hand.

The "second alarm," as it has been called, must be regarded as a second disaster. Its results were calamitous. Many lives were undoubtedly lost thereby; for the truth is that not a few engaged in the work of rescue thought first of themselves. The removal of the sick and injured and old and helpless from houses to the open spaces also caused much needless suffering. Besides, the shock to the nerves of the city as a whole was severe, and prepared the population to accept other rumours and feel other terrors.

Chapter 13

No. 10 Train

On the morning of the disaster, the night express from Saint John, known officially as No. 10, was nearing Halifax. It was made up of engine, postal car, baggage car, a second-class and a first-class coach, and two Pullman cars, in charge of Conductor J. C. Gillespie. At Bedford it was ten minutes late, and therefore, did not reach Halifax in time to share the destruction which overtook the North End. Indeed, this particular train never reached Halifax at all. It was approaching Rockingham when the shock of the explosion struck it. The cars were tilted violently over on the tracks as far as the safety chains would permit, and then clashed back into their usual position. The glass broke gently all along the train, coming inside but injuring none of the passengers. The engineer was thrown against the boilerhead and

badly hurt, but he stuck to his post as engineers do, and stopped the train. No one knew what had happened. A Canadian officer, lately returned from France, described his impression, "It was as if a torpedo had struck the train." After waiting about fifteen minutes, the train proceeded to Rockingham and then crept up to Willow Park Junction, to a point between the negro settlement called Africville and the wrecked district of Richmond, just before the streets of Halifax proper begin.

As soon as the train stopped, there was a rush of injured persons towards it—"hundreds," according to one eye witness. They were "as black as if they had been shovelling coal," and streaming with blood. Some were carrying helpless ones in blankets or sheets, and all were frantic with pain, or fright, and crying out for relief. But there was no medical man on board the train. One of the passengers volunteered to go for a doctor, but seeing the destruction of the city and the hopelessness of his errand, he turned back to give what help he could on the spot. The conductor of the train is like the captain of a ship. He is in command and he is responsible for lives and property. Conductor Gillespie was suddenly placed in a situation not provided for in the railway rules and regulations. The wires were all down, he could not get into communication with any one of his superiors or obtain instructions what to do. But he saw cold, barefoot, and torn people needing shelter and help. In his own words, he "went to work." The baggage and postal cars were emptied of their contents. Luggage and mail bags were thrown out beside the track to make room for the injured. Train crew and passengers were aided by willing helpers, soldiers, sailors, and civilians, who came upon the scene. On the men devolved the task of carrying the wounded persons and getting them into the cars. The women passengers set to work making bandages out of the bed and table linen found in the Pullman cars, and when that supply was exhausted they tore up their own underclothing. Water to bathe the wounds was obtained by running it off from the engine.

After labouring in this way for perhaps half an hour the workers became aware of something even more dreadful than the heart-rending sights before their eyes. Shrieks of agony rose from the ruins of the houses round about; and then they realized that the houses were on fire and in them were living, sentient, human beings in danger of the most horrible of deaths. The men left the women in charge of the wounded in the train, and organized themselves quickly into rescue parties. Working desperately, by the utmost exertions they saved life after life, but in some cases the heart-sick rescuers were unable to penetrate the barriers of flame, and those within perished with help only a few feet away. That was the chief horror of this day of horrors. The only tools available for attacking the burning piles were the axes and saws kept in cars in case of accident. Beams and planks were used as levers to prise the wreckage up and apart.

The only effective implement, said one of the rescuers, would have been a gigantic crane to lift up the heavy masses of woodwork off the people buried beneath. For the most part, the men had no tools, but their bare hands with which they tore the tangled planking asunder. After making some progress, they would be checked or thwarted by coming upon entire sections of roof or walls which could not be lifted or pushed aside. One party of six men was engaged in working at one house until one o'clock. In it were a man and his wife, another woman, and a small boy. When rescued at last, the man was quite unhurt, but his wife was severely cut about the face and blinded. On being brought out she kept her hand over the eye which had been destroyed so that her husband could not perceive her injury.

A worker in this party tells that the next house was on fire, and that there were four children in it. The parents "went on like maniacs," but it was not possible to get the children out.

Very soon after the train came to a standstill, men in uniform began to come upon the scene one at a time. Some had bandages on their heads, or arms, some were maimed, with one arm or one leg, a number were dressed "improperly," as the army phrase runs. These were undoubtedly hospital patients who had been dismissed from Rockhead that morning when the injured poured in for treatment. Others had come from the hospital at Pier 2. There were some fifty in all. On the train that morning was Col. E. C. Phinney who had been in command of the 85th Battalion, C.E.F. in France. He was in uniform and quickly organized these soldiers into working parties, and pursued the work of rescue as systematically as possible. They ascertained as well as they could if anyone was alive in a house. If there was no one, they let it burn and went on to the next. These men, collected by chance, worked remarkably well together, and showed the results of the discipline they had undergone and their familiarity with danger and death. The rumour of the second explosion reached these workers in the mysterious way that rumour is communicated, for they were not officially warned. Col. Phinney pointed out to them that there was no likelihood of avoiding danger by leaving their task. The best thing to do was to "stick it." Their response was, "Sure," and the informant added, "They went to it." That morning at least forty, possibly as many as sixty persons, were rescued there from the burning houses. They were chiefly babies, small children and old people.

Strange sights were to be seen about No. 10 train that morning. Col. Phinney recalls vividly the first case that came under his notice; it was a boy suffering from three wounds. A rivet had been driven into his right eye; the top of it was showing plainly. A piece of iron, apparently plating from the MONT BLANC had penetrated his chest, and another had gone into his right thigh. They were large pieces of plating and driven in deep, but there

was no effusion of blood. Col. Phinney examined the wound in the chest, and it seemed to him that the edges were seared. The wounded boy was quite calm, talked rationally, and said that nothing hurt him, but his injuries were so severe that they must have caused his death.

Another episode was the arrival at this point of several sailors, probably four or five, who had swum ashore from wrecked or disabled vessels in the harbour. One man was in his shirt and a pair of overalls. He had managed to save the ship's papers in a large packet. After talking sensibly for a little while, and saying that he thought the "old man" (his captain) was lost, he collapsed and was put on board the train with other injured persons.

About noon, Col. Phinney made his way to Headquarters and reported what had been done. He was given general instructions to return whence he had come and continue his work. He went back to Richmond with a brother officer through the wreckage and passed the many corpses. Some of these were "mangled." Others had no mark of injury on them at all, but were quite nude except that their boots remained on their feet. These had been killed by concussion. The same thing happens in modern warfare when large shells explode. Men may be stripped of their clothing and killed without any mark of violence appearing on them. There is a difference in the expression of those instantly killed compared to those in France. In France, the faces of dead soldiers wear a look of determination, teeth clenched, brows drawn. These wore a look of surprise, surprise not fear. The mouths were open and the eyes staring as if they were looking at they knew not what.

To return to Train 10, as yet none of the sufferers had received any attention beyond amateur first aid. The "rough bandaging" unavoidable in such conditions was noticed in the hospitals at Truro. But skilled help was on the way. That morning, Major C. E. A. DeWitt, a doctor and the son of a doctor, residing in Wolfville, had been ordered in from Aldershot to Halifax to attend a conference in the city. He had taken the early train and was approaching the city when the explosion occurred, but it was too far away to produce any special sound or disturbance noticeable by those on board. Not until the train reached Rockingham did Major DeWitt learn of the calamity to Halifax from Mr. Graham, the General Manager of the Dominion Atlantic Railway, who was waiting at the station. The D.A.R. train was sent back to Windsor Junction, while Major DeWitt was rushed into Richmond on an engine. His own account runs: "I arrived there about 11:00 a.m. No. 10 train was on the track with windows broken but no further damage. The condition of the track and surrounding was almost too horrible to describe. Men, women and children were lying round on the ground on boards, broken beds, doors, or anything they could get, and suffering untold agonies. Naturally, the work was difficult as I was the only medical officer in the district at the time. Fortunately, I had my hypodermic case, and morphine was a great blessing to many that morning.'' He had, he adds, one hundred and twelve surgical cases to attend to. Altogether there were two hundred and ten injured persons on the train.

De Witt's difficulties were many, but Conductor Gillespie had also his problem. He had "filled the train full;" it was the obvious thing to do, but it only increased his difficulties. "Then what to do with them?" Here was a trainload of broken, bleeding humanity standing on the track on the outskirts of a stricken, burning city, and it was impossible to obtain orders where to go or what disposal was to be made of the unexpected passengers. Gillespie had to decide the matter for himself. He sent the engine to the Roundhouse for a fresh supply of coal and water, and then ran the train back as far as Rockingham because, as he says, he did not know where else to go. Here he received the necessary authorization to return to Truro. The train left Rockingham at 1:27 p.m. and reached its destination at five minutes to four. Conductor Gillespie had proved equal to the responsibility so suddenly thrown upon him. Perhaps his chief satisfaction lay in the knowledge that he saved one woman's life by bandaging her wounds so as to stop the hemorrhage. The doctor told him so on examining the case. He also had the forethought to take down the names and addresses of all injured persons on board his train.

On the way to Truro, Major DeWitt was completely absorbed in his duties towards his trainload of patients. He did not know that at Windsor Junction another doctor and a trained nurse had got on the train, and begun to work at the other end of the train. Only at Truro did he discover that these were his father, Dr. DeWitt senior, and his sister. During the journey, three children died, and Dr. DeWitt performed two successful operations which deserve to be remembered for the difficulties overcome and one more proof that necessity is the mother of invention. He removed two eyes with no better instruments than a forceps and a pair of scissors. At Truro Station the people were waiting for the sufferers with open arms. An hour sufficed to transfer them all from the train to the three hospitals they had improvised that very afternoon. Unfortunately, all the local doctors had been gathered up in the special train and been taken to Halifax. It was impossible for the three DeWitts to leave their charges, and they "carried on." Doctors came from the country about Truro to assist, and Dr. Eaton, who had been left behind because he was too ill, got up from his sick bed to minister to the suffering. Major DeWitt's conduct came to the notice of Headquarters, and he was officially reported as having performed "noteworthy service." The report states curtly: "Major DeWitt worked then night and day for five days till he was finally relieved, arriving home a physical wreck, with an infected hand. He should have immedi-

ately gone sick, but he struggled on with his work, narrowly escaping the loss of his arm." The "work" referred to was his regular attentions to the soldiers in camp at Aldershot near Kentville.

Chapter 14

The Schools

The disaster of December 6th spared neither old nor young. A special horror was the slaughter of the innocents. It might have been thought that as the children were assembling at that time in the schools and as the schools suffered damage like all other buildings, that they were very dangerous places. The contrary is true. Far more children lost their lives outside the schools than in them. The escapes were little short of marvellous.

Naturally, the schools of the South End suffered less in every way than those nearer the north. When the crash came, the children of the Morris Street School rushed out of the building into the street, just as the Deputy-Mayor was passing on his way to the office. A good many were cut and frightened, a few were hysterical, but no one was seriously injured. Cuts about the head and face bleed freely and are alarming to look at, but they are not, as a rule, dangerous. This school served afterwards as one of the temporary hospitals.

In most schools the practice is to begin the day with prayers. The pupils of the Halifax Ladies' College, a large residential school for girls in Pleasant St. were assembled in the gymnasium for this purpose. It is a large room in the second storey at the back, its windows were protected to prevent possible breakage during ball games. Consequently, when the glass shattered, none of it reached the pupils. No one was hurt. The noise was alarming, but no confusion ensued. The pupils filed out the room and downstairs in an orderly manner. Below they found the Rev. Mr. Laing, the head of the college, and Mr. Harry Dean, the head of the Conservatory of Music, calm, collected and awaiting developments. No one knew what had happened or what might happen next. Presently, some of the younger children got brooms and dustpans, began to sweep up the broken glass and to tidy the room. The pupils remained in the building until they were ordered out during the second alarm, when they marched with their teachers to the golf links, and remained there quietly until word came about noon that all danger was past.

In Halifax the institutions of the Roman Catholic Church form several extensive groups. For example, about St. Mary's Cathedral in Spring Garden Road cluster the Glebe House for the clergy, St. Mary's Convent, Parish Hall and schools for boys and girls. These two schools are largely attended, and though the children were assembled in the corridors about to enter the different classrooms and although the broken glass from the windows rained about them, they escaped with a few slight cuts.

The County Academy is an obsolete brick building standing at the corner of Sackville and Brunswick Streets. It is at the foot of the citadel *glacis* and opposite to a barracks. There the pupils were also at prayers. They assembled in the large room at the top of the building and were actually singing the well-known hymn, "Peace, perfect peace," when the harmony was ended by the roar of the explosion and the crash of the shattering glass. Once more discipline prevailed, and the habit of mind acquired by fire drill asserted itself. The pupils passed out of the building without any sign of panic.

Much nearer to the scene of the explosion was the Bloomfield School, at the corner of Bloomfield and Agricola Streets. There are two buildings standing within the same yard. Owing to the growth of population in this district, the original building became inadequate and a second larger, more modern building was erected alongside. Both are needed, for the rolls show an attendance of eight hundred pupils. The force of the explosion wrecked both buildings, smashing roofs and windows, though not shaking either fabric to the ground. The old building suffered most. The roof collapsed and the desks were covered six feet deep with broken rafters, plaster, lath and planking. Fortunately, few pupils were inside the building. Some boys were caught, but they managed to crawl out from underneath the confusion with no injuries worth mentioning. The majority of the girls were lined up outside, and so escaped. There was naturally much excitement but nothing approaching a panic.

A notable instance of coolness and presence of mind occurred in the basement of the new building. There thirty-five small boys were in line and passing up the stairs on their way to the Assembly Hall. They were under the direction of a "guard," Roland Theakston, a boy of fourteen. At the unforeseen and most alarming sound of the explosion, he simply reversed his line, right about face, and passed them out safely into the yard.

The principal of the school, Dr. H. D. Brunt, was in his office getting some papers, when the window glass blew in on his face. His glasses were broken, but they saved his eyes. He turned instinctively towards the door, only to meet fragments of the heavy English plate glass from it in his hands and face. Like so many others, he thought first of boiler explosions in the basement and asked himself, "Where are the flames?" Next came the deafening crashing noise due to damage to building itself; and he thought of bombs from an airplane and tried to reach the basement. The exit to the southward is just next to the principal's office. Two swinging glass doors

open on a short flight of steps to the double doors which open directly into the school yard. Dr. Brunt found one of the glass doors had fallen down the steps, the transom light above the exit had been blown in and the double doors at the foot of the steps jammed inwards. He ran back up the steps to gather way and flung himself shoulder first against the door to smash it open. Before he was completely successful the pupils came streaming to the entrance, falling down the steps, sliding on the broken glass door and blocking the whole passage. The outcry and confusion may be imagined. Perhaps two hundred children were piled into this narrow space. It was impossible for Dr. Brunt to make himself heard, impossible to move himself, or to get the children out. And he expected fire. Then he remembered that he had his scout whistle hanging about his neck, and blew the "Rally." Some of the boys outside heard it, and came back into the school by a side entrance and reached the scene of confusion from the rear. They began to pull the children who were nearest to them away from the confusion and thus loosen the jam. Some of the older girls came and helped. In the meantime Dr. Brunt had succeeded in getting one door partly open and was passing the children between his legs one at a time into the yard. The spirit of comedy did not desert the city even on that tragic day. Some of the Bloomfield school pupils will not soon forget the incongruous sight of their principal, his face and hands streaming with blood and his attitude at the door. School boys have a ready sense of the ludicrous.

Other teachers in the school sustained cuts and bruises. A large room in the top storey was the home of the kindergarten under the charge of Miss Mary Armitage. She was badly cut by the broken glass and bled freely. The alarming sounds and sights terrified the little ones; they turned "balky" and could not be induced to leave the room. Their teacher had to carry them out and downstairs. In this work she was assisted by other teachers. H. J. Vickery the science master, had been struck by a transom which had been hurled from the old building into the new. He was hurt and dazed, but worked on, carrying the kindergarten children downstairs. Only about half an hour after the shock of the explosion did it occur to him to ask his Principal what had happened.

The schoolyard was for some time a scene of confusion. The mob of excited children was soon increased by dozens of eager parents uncertain as to the fate of their sons and daughters and fearing the worst. A party of twenty men under a subaltern officer came up at the run from Wellington Barracks to render assistance, but even before they arrived, all were safe outside. Dr. Brunt went through the building himself three times in ten minutes looking in every hole and corner to make sure that no child had been forgotten. After the parents and children had gone, the teaching staff remained behind salvaging the school property such as the manual training gear and domestic science material. They also saved the heating system of the school from ruin by running off the water. Otherwise in the windowless condition of the buildings, the radiators must have frozen and burst. It was four o'clock before the work of protecting the property of the taxpayer was done.

Another group of Roman Catholic institutions was to be found at the northern end of Gottingen St. near Wellington Barracks. Clustered about St. Joseph's Chapel, a small brick church, on a good Gothic model stood St. Joseph's Convent, Temperance Hall and school. Except the church, these were all frame buildings. The force of the explosion demolished the chapel, unroofing it and leaving only one wall standing. The ruin was complete. Father Gray, who had been celebrating mass, had a miraculous escape. He was at the door, and was hesitating to go out, when a mass of brick rubble was flung down just outside the door. There was literally but a step between him and death. It is a curious fact that while the solid structure of the church worked its downfall the light make of the wooden building saved them from greater injury. Houses in the North End that remained standing show unmistakable signs of having been shaken violently to and fro. Some persons in them so describe their sensations—as if the house had been gripped by giant hands, rocked swiftly in one direction and then the opposite. The dislocation of partitions, the collapse of floors and ceilings bear out this supposition. Some houses showed the outer sheathing standing out from the studding on the opposite sides. That means the house swayed away from its outer skin on one side, then righted and left the outer skin on the opposite side standing away from the main structure on the other.

St. Joseph's school was so shaken. It was a two-storey structure surmounted by a sort of cupola over the main entrance. The air blast removed in an instant the glass from every window, bashed in the roof, tearing off a part, and twisted the cupola about till it looked like a battered hat on the head of a drunken man. This school did double duty. In the morning it was devoted to the instruction of girls and in the afternoon, to boys, the school which accommodated the latter having been burnt down some time before. The attic roof caved in on the children of the eighth grade, pinning the principal, Sister Maria Cecilia, to her platform, which, with the whole floor, pupils and all slowly sank down into the storey immediately below. Although imprisoned between the ceiling and the floor, with the debris from the wrecked attic piled on top, she escaped all injury. She was unhurt but she could not get out, like Sterne's starling. Like the principal of the Bloomfield School, at the same moment, she expected fire to follow upon the collapse of the building and listened for the crackle of the flame. When they did not come, she was relieved of her anxiety concerning the furnace, which she had inspected that morning, and waited quietly for rescue. Like so many people

in Halifax that morning, she also thought of a German attack of some kind, and made up her mind that when she heard voices, she would not answer until she was sure what language they spoke. If they spoke German, she would "just keep still." Her theory of the accident was that the school had been struck by a bomb from an airship. Ultimately the voices she heard were English and belonged to a working party of soldiers who extricated her from her prison. All the children in the room with her also escaped unhurt.

One of the surprises of this event-crammed day was the cool and even heroic behaviour of mere children suddenly set face to face with the peril of death. One of the Grade Eight pupils was Cecilia McGrath, a remarkably well formed, intelligent and attractive girl of the Irish type with dark hair and grey eyes, about eleven years of age. That morning she was a little late and stood at the window of the cloak-room watching the tall pillar of smoke pierced with jets of red fire which rose in the still air from the burning MONT BLANC. It occurred to her that she ought to report the strange spectacle to her teacher and had just turned away from the window to do so when the explosion wrecked the school. But neither the dread crashing, rending noises, nor the strange sight confused her. She kept her head and deliberated coolly what she should do. Looking into the schoolroom she saw it slowly settling down into the lower storey, while the floor of the cloakroom on which she stood remained intact. After a little while she worked her way along the room on what remained of the floor supports until she came to a front window from which all the glass had been swept clean. Cecilia got over the sill and sat on the zinc pediment surmounting the window just below the one by which she had made her exit. After sitting here for some time, she let herself down carefully, hung by her hands to the lower edge of the pediment for a moment or two, and then dropped lightly to the ground—a storey and a half. She was not in the least hurt. Encouraged by her success, eight other little girls adopted the same tactics and escaped unjurt to the ground. This is how they were said to have "jumped out of the window." Doris Kenty can give no clear account of how she got out of the building. She did not want to drop from the window and so "waited for a while." She told the Principal that she must have come down the main stairway, though she does not remember doing so, and just "found herself outdoors." Apparently the central staircase was practicable for one of the Sisters met Doris on it, thus confirming her story. Cecilia McGrath got away from the school to see sights which are mercifully withheld from children's eyes—a woman with blood spouting from the severed jugular—her own mother in the flames of her own home. The horror haunted her and took her sleep from her; but time has restored her healthy normal state.

In the Assembly Room, the class was on the stage

under the instruction of Sister Ethelred. The large swinging doors were flung down violently crushing three little girls to death; but these were the only ones who lost their lives within the school building. Little Florence Fudge, aged thirteen, helped her teacher notably in getting her school mates out of the wreckage. On the ground floor, Sister Rita's eyes were blinded for a time by the blood flowing from her wounds. She called the children to her, so that she could determine by feeling if they were injured and to what extent. Margaret Zwicker led her blinded teacher to such children as could not come to her amidst the tumbled furniture and, working together, they two freed them all from the wreckage of the classroom.

In the basement the little girls of the primary department were preparing to go upstairs to the Assembly Room under the guidance of Sister Edwina. The shock of the explosion stunned her and made her blind for the time being. She told the little ones to take hold of one another's clothing and the foremost in the line to grasp her habit. Thus, with her living train following her, she groped her way in the dark to the staircase, up the steps, and out of doors. She knew when she had come into the open by the feel of the fresh air; but it was some time before she recovered the use of her eyes.

It would seem impossible that such an accident could happen to a building full of children with so little loss of life. While only three were killed in the school itself, fifteen girls were killed outside, and, of the boys who should have attended that afternoon no fewer than fifty-five were killed in or about their own homes. Many of the pupils were cut or bruised, and several of the sisters suffered from lacerations or fractures. The injured were laid on the ground in the schoolyard, and persons from the neighbourhood who were hurt were brought to the same spot. A priest gave conditional absolution. In the words of one reporter, the place was "an image of a battle ground after a deadly engagement." As at Bloomfield, the schoolyard was soon crowded with fathers and mothers, the prey of cruel anxieties. As a rule, the injuries to the children were slight, but the frightened blood-stained faces made those who saw them fear the worst. Ambulances and other vehicles came up to take the worse cases to the hospitals. The sisters cared for their fainting charges, securing wraps and covering for such as could not walk, before their own injuries were attended to.

Farthest north and only some seven hundred yards in a straight line from the point at which the MONT BLANC blew up was Richmond School, a two-storey wooden building. Normally three hundred children were in attendance, and should have been in it at the time, but on this very morning the hour for assembling had been changed for the winter, from nine to half past nine. The school was not open, but a few of the pupils had gathered in the yard or about the porches when the explosion wrecked the building. Only two were killed through

being in or about the school, but eighty-two who were not there were stricken in their homes or in the street. What would have happened if the three hundred children on the roll had actually been within the walls of the building when it collapsed is hard to say. The slaughter might have been terrific, or, on the other hand, they might have escaped in the miraculous fashion of the children of St. Joseph's. The fact remains that the great majority of the Halifax children who lost their lives on the fatal December 6th were not in school at the time. Apparently the schools were the safest places that day. In the two schools nearest to the accident, only five were killed out of the total number of one hundred and ninety-four school children who died that day.

On this day even children displayed heroism. One of the Richmond School pupils, Pearl Hartlen, age nine, was at home when the house collapsed. Her mother was knocked unconscious and half buried under the ruins, but the child pulled and dragged until she managed to get her mother clear, except for a part of her skirt which still held fast. Pearl has been described by her teacher as "dependable," the sort of child who can be trusted with younger brothers and sisters. Here she showed resource. She got down and bit and tore at the dress with her teeth until she got her mother free.

Unconscious fortitude was also manifested by Agnes Foran, aged twelve. She is very small and slight with fair hair and blue eyes; she would be described as frail in appearance, and as also of the "little mother" type. She and her mother were standing at the window of their house, No. 12 Merkel St., watching the fire when the explosion occurred. According to Agnes, "the sky opened." The windows were blown in, the furniture smashed, but the house did not collapse. Mother and daughter were thrown down on the floor. As soon as Agnes picked herself up, her first question was, "Where is the baby?" Mrs. Foran said that he was downstairs; Agnes ran down, found her three months old brother safe in his carriage and called up to her mother that he was all right. Her mother called her to come up and help her as she could not see. Agnes went upstairs and led her blinded mother down. Then she got cloths and water and bathed her eyes. When Mrs. Foran realized that she was blind, she had Agnes lead her into the street where she stood and called for help while Agnes went back into the house and got the baby out. She left the baby with her mother and hurried round the neighbourhood looking for someone to come to her mother's aid. She was unsuccessful, but about half past ten her father came, got a "man with an automobile" who took Agnes, Mrs. Foran, and the baby to the Victoria Hospital, where they received immediate attention. Just about the time her father arrived at their house, Agnes became sleepy. A chair was got for her to sit on. Her father examined her and found her clothing saturated with blood, and bad cuts on the body. It was not until late in the afternoon

47

The Orphanage.

that Dr. MacDougall operated on her. He found a piece of glass about half the size of a woman's hand driven into the child's stomach. Only a pin-head of it was showing. It had to be cut out, and twenty-nine stitches were necessary to close her wounds. The doctor was much impressed by the steadiness of this little heroine who has now completely recovered.

One case more. Norman Roberts, aged eight, is the son of a first officer in a cable ship who lived at 26½ East Young St. Norman is a stout, strong, little boy, with very dark eyes and hair and a swarthy complexion. On the morning of the disaster, he and his mother and little sister, aged two, were in the kitchen of their flat. The force of the explosion threw Mrs. Roberts on the floor and piled the door and the furniture on top of her. She was partially stunned but can remember Norman asking, "Where are you mother?" before she lost consciousness. When she came to herself, she found herself in Agricola St. several blocks away, and her belief is that her little son dragged her there. Mrs. Roberts was badly burned from contact with the stove, but neither of the children was hurt. At first Norman threw burning things out of the window thinking that he could keep the house

from burning by doing so. He led out his little sister Mabel, aged two, because she was frightened and wouldn't go alone. Neighbours saw the boy at the door of his house tugging at his mother. After they were all out, the house took fire, and burned to the ground. This boy evidently has the protective instinct well developed. Six months afterwards, when they were all living in the tenements at the Exhibition Grounds, there was an alarm of fire and Norman's first concern was to get his mother and sister to a place of safety.

Presence of mind and resource were shown by Doris Myra, aged thirteen, daughter of Edward Myra, labourer, 52 Union St. Her mother was so severely hurt by the collapse of the house that she afterwards died in the hospital. Doris did her best to drag her dying mother out of the burning wreckage. Not succeeding at first, she managed to get a rope, fastened it around her body, and so with great efforts hauled her out into the street, and safety.

The janitor of Richmond School was killed in the schoolyard, but two teachers inside the building were not injured. In the basement a carpenter, G. H. Libby, was at work. He was just thinking how comfortably he was situated for the winter with a good indoors job, when the force of the explosion struck the school. It drove in the window and flung the glass, the mullion, and even the

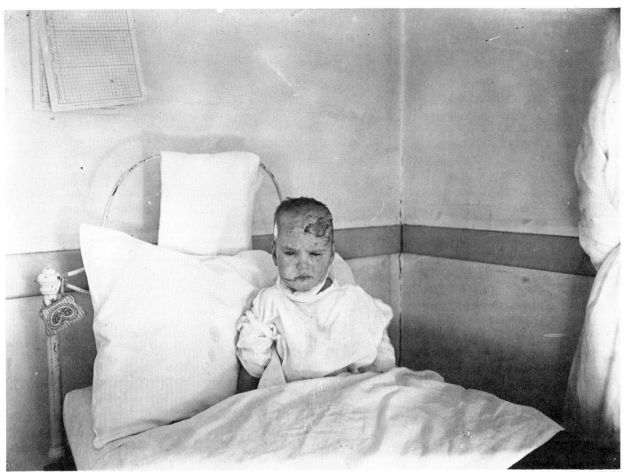

A young victim of the explosion.

lead weights from the sash across his bench. He himself was thrown violently against the brick wall and his head was gashed by the flying glass. He caught his head with both hands, and so remained for what seemed to him "five minutes," not daring to move for fear of the falling debris. Then he felt water falling over him. Then the smoke cleared away and he saw daylight through the window, through which he managed to crawl, but could not see very well, for one eye was injured. After getting through the window, he fell down a steep embankment. Badly shaken as he was, he made his way down Rufus St. to Creighton's Corner and then up Roome St. to his own house, No. 111, to find it a flaming ruin. His first thought was that all his family were in it and he began to tear away the debris to get at them. He heard a woman calling to him, and turned to look at her but did not recognize her. Again he began to tear at the rubbish with his bare hands. The woman called again: "Jack, you can't do anything there. They're all dead." Then he realized that it was his wife. She was black and almost naked. She said: "You're bleeding to death. Let's get to a hospital."

The two started for the road along which the car ran; this was Gottingen Street, but there was no street to be found. Together they walked as far as North Street without assistance, whence an ambulance took them to the Military Hospital in Cogswell Street. Their missing children were brought to the same place. They had been flung into the gutter and buried in rubbish, but someone dug them out and carried them over to the adjacent open space called Mulgrave Park. On their way to assistance, they saw strange sights. As she walked, Mrs. Libby struck her foot against something, looked down. It was a child's head without any body. They saw a woman cut in two at the waist, opening and shutting her eyes, and gasping her last. Another woman, big and fat, was walking along quite naked, holding up with her hand her left breast which was hanging by a shred of flesh. She had her eyes turned up to the sky and was streaming with blood.

7

Chapter 15

At The City Hall

A city is not merely a large number of houses, containing so many inhabitants. It is an entity, a government, an organization. How the organized government of Halifax met the crisis of December 6th deserves to be placed on record.

When Halifax was founded, city planning was still governed by mediaeval ideas. The aim was to make a city a compact, defensible, strong place, sheltering the greatest number of people within the narrowest limits. It included a central square in which citizens might be mustered or assembled for warlike or pacific purposes. In the plan of Halifax this square is known as the Grand Parade, and for a century and more it was the centre of the city's life. There the earliest laws were proclaimed and there the troops of the garrison were drilled. At the southern end stands the old parish church of St. Paul's with its hatchements and its mural tablets, an epitome of Halifax history. At the northern end was the first Dalhousie College, which, after a chequered career of fifty years, made way for the present city building, the centre of the city administration. It was wrecked by the explosion; that is, glass was broken in all the windows and the rooms were in confusion. The hands of the clock in the tower overlooking the Parade stopped at five minutes past nine. This city building was the second main ganglion of activity on the day of the disaster and the trying time which followed. It was the centre of the civilian organization as Headquarters was the centre of the military organization to meet the emergency. Here the city took control and functioned as a government.

On December 6th, the Mayor of the city was absent from it and his duties devolved upon the Deputy Mayor, Henry S. Colwell, the head of the firm of Colwell Bros. That morning he was on his way from his house to his office walking along Morris Street with a couple of friends when they felt the unearthly rumble and roar of the explosion. "The ground came up to meet them" and they "doubled up." One man dashed across the road exclaiming, "D....d German shell" and at the same moment came the crash of breaking glass in all the houses. The frightened children came rushing out of the school nearby and the people from their houses. In two or three minutes everyone seemed to be in the street. All seemed to have sustained injuries more or less severe; and there was a cry for first aid. Mr. Colwell looked north and saw the huge cloud of smoke, "like a water spout," as he described it, a mushroom-shaped, black portent in the sky above Richmond.

Almost at once the rumour ran round that the magazine in Campbell Road had blown up, a close guess not unlikely, for Halifax had experienced the effect of ex-

ploding magazines sixty years before. To the Deputy Mayor it was plain that a great calamity had occurred. As was natural his first thought was of his son, a young lieutenant on duty that morning at Wellington. The latter had indeed a miraculous escape from death. At that moment he was in the attic of the Officers' Quarters, the nearest point to the MONT BLANC, when the roof smashed in. But he got off with a few bruises. Mr. Colwell's next thought in view of the damage everywhere about him was what might have happened to his own home. Posting back to his residence on South Park Street, he found all well and then he remembered his official capacity. In his own words, "I realized I held the most important position in Halifax."

Any action taken by the City as a government must originate with himself. He went with all speed to the City Hall, where he remained on duty continuously for four days and four nights, with something like two hours' sleep out of the twenty-four.

It was about half-past nine when the Deputy Mayor reached the City Hall. The material damage found its counterpart in the disorganization of the personnel. The city officials and clerks were looking after their own houses and families as were the members of the police force. Here he first learned of the loss of the "Patricia" and her crew. The situation he had to face was that of a whole community suddenly smitten as by an evil spell. The machinery for preserving order and protection against fire had broken down; and there was no ready made machinery to bring about larger measures of relief. It appeared that half the city was on fire, and no one could say how far the conflagration would spread. To check the fire was evidently the first concern. The Deputy Mayor turned at once to the organization that had plenty of men and full control of them—the military.

Taking with him the Chief of Police and the City Clerk, the only two officials in the building, he walked up the street to headquarters and found Colonel Thompson in his office. He explained the situation as he saw it, how the City was in need of assistance of all kinds. Among other measures of relief he suggested to Colonel Thompson putting up tents on the Common to shelter the people who would be destitute and homeless. For he was impressed thus early with the magnitude of the calamity which had befallen the city. Colonel Thompson responded at once, and in the most forceful way, issuing orders and despatching mounted men in all directions.

At the close of this hurried interview, a stranger handed Mr. Colwell his card and asked if he could be of any assistance. This was Mr. W. A. Duff, Assistant Chief Engineer of the Canadian Government Railways. He had already been very busy that morning. He had his experience of the explosion at the Queen Hotel and, for ten or fifteen minutes, had helped giving first aid to wounded people in Blackie's Drug Store. Taking a motor belonging to the Cook Construction Co. he went to the North Street Station, found it badly wrecked, and saw that it would be impossible to get trains out or in. He then tried to get to Rockingham via Richmond, his idea being to get into telegraphic communication with the railway headquarters at Moncton. He did not reach Rockingham in the first attempt. There was more urgent necessity than that of sending news. He put as many wounded people as could be carried in the motor and took them to the Victoria General Hospital. He then left immediately for Rockingham a second time and reached about ten o'clock. At this point he sent a message to General Manager Hayes stating what had occurred in Halifax, the approximate damage done to property, an estimate of the killed and wounded, and asking him to have all the doctors, nurses, and relief supplies possible sent to Halifax with the greatest despatch. Duff told Colwell what he had done. Colwell asked him, ''for God's sake'' to send out additional messages to the different towns of Nova Scotia and New Brunswick asking for further relief, such despatches being signed by the Mayor of Halifax. How fruitful these messages proved to be was seen in the instantaneous rally of the whole province to the aid of the stricken city. Mr. Duff's action put in motion the most powerful machinery for the aid of Halifax at the earliest moment, nothing short of the whole activity of the Canadian Government Railway system under the personal direction of the General Manager.

Before the interview was over, a soldier rushed upstairs and ordered everyone out of the building, announcing that a second explosion might happen at any minute and that the results would be far worse than those of the first. Such a warning could not be disregarded. Colwell and the Chief of Police went out of the building and saw ''great hordes'' of people fleeing along Pleasant Street to the urgent cry, ''Go south.'' There was scarcely anyone in the crowd who was not bleeding. It was a stampede and the acting Mayor and Chief of Police were swept along with it. They had not gone far along Pleasant Street, perhaps the length of a block, before they decided to take their chance, and retraced their steps in the direction of the City Hall. There the only room which could be used at all was the City Collector's office which occupies the southeast corner of the building and looks upon the Parade. A long desk or counter runs right across it. In the narrow space outside, citizens come to pay their dues. The inside is taken up with desks and smaller offices. The room was unsuitable for any but the purpose for which it was designed, but it was the only one available. It was the scene of the meetings whence proceeded the action of Halifax as a corporation.

On his way to the City Hall, Mr. Colwell met Lieutenant Governor Grant and Mr. R. T. MacIlreith, at one time Mayor of the city, and invited them to come with him for the purpose of holding some meeting or consultation on what should be done. Minutes exist of the meeting which ensued, but it is to be regarded as a coun-cil-of-war. The forms were complied with. At half past eleven, the Deputy Mayor had convened five members of the Corporation and told them he had instructed the City Clerk to call a meeting of the City Council for three o'clock that afternoon, ''it being absolutely impossible to notify the members of the Council earlier owing to the existing conditions.'' Still, something could be done at once for the need was very great. ''He felt the present attendance of so many members of the Council afforded an opportunity for the immediate, though, of course, informal, consideration of the situation and any steps which should be taken at once.'' Rescue and relief were the two great matters to be considered. Obviously, this was a task for the best brains and strongest energy available in the city. It was also a task for many, not few. In the words of the minutes, ''It was necessary that an executive committee and various sub-committees should be organized forthwith to carry on the work.'' This proposition the Deputy Mayor laid before the members of the Corporation present and then proposed that the Council meeting should forthwith become a citizen's meeting by the inclusion of the citizen present. The Lieutenant Governor of the Province, McCallum Grant, was moved to take the chair and the Deputy Mayor was appointed secretary of the joint meeting.

The business of this meeting was the organization of committees. An executive committee of seven was appointed with five sub-committees, one to take charge of transportation, that is, the organization of means to convey the injured to hospitals, doctors and nurses to points where they would be needed, and all kinds of supplies for all kinds of purposes. Perhaps this was the most urgent need at the moment. There was a committee to obtain and distribute food, another to provide shelter for the homeless, another to dispose of the dead in a mortuary, and still another to deal with the all-important matter of finance. These six committees were struck there and then and given power to add to their numbers. The included some of the very best businessmen in Halifax, as was proved by the results they so soon obtained. This meeting, perhaps the most important in the history of Halifax, was over in three-quarters of an hour.

A second attempt was made to hold a regular meeting of the Council at 3 o'clock the same afternoon. Like the meeting of the morning, it resolved itself into a joint meeting of the citizens and Council. The Lieutenant Governor was again chairman. Among the citizens present were Gen. Benson and a representative of the naval authorities. This meeting simply ratified and confirmed the action of the morning meeting, and the appointment of the various committees, which were by this time all hard at work. The chairman of the Finance Committee was able to announce that a credit had been opened at the Bank of Nova Scotia, and that the chairmen of the various committees were authorized to draw upon that fund to any reasonable amount in any cases where cash should

This page and opposite: Halifax Relief Offices.

be immediately required. The chairmen of the various sub-committees present "reported progress," and the meeting adjourned, having lasted an hour and a quarter.

Later, changes and modifications were made in the committees, perhaps the most important being the enlisting of women in the general relief work. The work branched out in all directions and extended far beyond any possibilities considered on December 6th. Out of the Halifax Relief Committee grew the Halifax Relief Commission, appointed by the Government of Canada, endowed with city building powers and handling millions in money. But all the later development grew naturally out of the action of the Haligonians, who on December 6th envisaged the situation so clearly and took such prompt measures to meet it. Confusion was inevitable, mistakes were inevitable, but there was no panic, or idle wringing of hands, or tame submission to fate. Before any help could come from outside, Halifax, as an organized government, had begun to help herself with feverish energy. The record stands for all to read in the minutes of the City Council.

When the afternoon meeting was over, the Deputy Mayor moved into the City Auditor's room, where he was "nailed down to a table." For four days and four nights he did not leave the building. Indeed during this time of stress and strain, day and night seemed to run into each other. All sorts of applications were made to him as representative of the city's authority. The office was besieged and the building was thronged by all kinds of people on all kinds of errands. Written orders were wanted for such articles as rubber boots, for food, for clothing. There were telegrams to reply to, inquiries—"What can we send you?"—which had to be answered at once. Most of the people who came were eager to help, but what they needed was direction, and they looked to the acting head of the city government for it. The aid of Mr. MacIlreith in all consultation was highly valued. Gradually the work divided, Mr. MacIlreith giving most attention to the organization of relief, and Mr. Colwell to what may be called the normal work of the city.

"Bob" MacIlreith is a college-bred man, a lawyer by profession, and a sportsman, interested in yachting. He was well acquainted with the city affairs and management, having served as alderman and also as mayor. His home is across the Arm, whence he made his way soon after the explosion into the city. He met crowds going away from the centre, but none were going in his direction. He received many warnings of a second explosion being imminent, but he held on his course. His meeting with the Deputy Mayor had most fortunate consequence for, from that time on, his experience, sound judgment, and executive ability were apparent in the whole relief organization during the first trying days.

Mr. MacIlreith was struck with the way "fellows seemed to fit in." He was looking about for a secretary of the executive committee when Mr. Ralph P. Bell met him in the corridor and offered his services. The offer was gladly accepted; Mr. MacIlreith went on about his particular errand; when he returned half an hour later, Mr. Bell was installed with stationery and stenographer ready for the transaction of business. Mr. Bell was a most energetic and efficient organizer, and his good work made him the inevitable secretary for the Halifax Relief Commission when that body was formed. In the same way, when Mr. MacIlreith was looking about for someone to invent a system of medical relief, he encountered Col. Paul Weatherbe who had come to see what he could do. The two had known each other from boyhood, they soon came to an understanding, and one more department was competently organized.

During Mr. MacIlreith's term of office as Mayor, the TITANIC disaster occurred; and hundreds of the drowned were brought to Halifax for identification and burial. It was his duty at the time to see that this work was properly carried out; and his experience then gained was of much practical value now. He instructed those in charge of collecting the dead bodies to ticket them carefully, giving names and addresses, place where found, and such particulars as would lead to identification later on. Together with Mr. Johnson, the City Engineer, he motored out to the various North End Schools to select a mortuary. After inspecting three, they decided that the basement of the Chebucto School was the most suitable place for the purpose. It became the stage for many scenes of distress as the vain search for the missing ended among the long rows of sheeted dead. The trip only lasted half an hour or so, and the two were back at the City Hall.

The City Hall must be understood as the centre of all relief work during the first few most trying and difficult days. Food was given out to all applicants. "Hundreds upon hundreds came there with their baskets and were served food." Clothing and blankets were collected here and handed out over the counter. Medical relief was first organized here under the able direction of Col. Paul Weatherbe, R.C.E. This officer went to the City Hall on the eventful morning of the 6th, met Mr. MacIlreith and asked what he could do. He was given the task of finding a system in dealing with the injured. By one o'clock he had a staff organized for district medical

Snapshot showing an early movie camera taken by a friend of William Fowlie. Mr. Fowlie enters this book rather briefly in Helen Gucker's reminiscences. However more of his story is told in Michael Bird's chronicle of the explosion *The Town that Died*.

relief. Provision was made for the registration of cases as they came in, and also of doctors and nurses. There was a medical supply department with telephonists, stenographers, dressers, and messengers. In addition, this officer organized eight special dressing stations throughout the city. He was ably assisted by Capt. T. I. Byrne and Lieut. J. G. Ryecroft. They worked day and night, snatching a little sleep on mattresses in the City Engineer's office, until they were worn out, and the original committee was merged into another of wider scope under military authority. Saturday the 8th was a ''most hectic day;'' the situation was getting beyond the control of the sorely overtasked workers, when the arrival of the Massachusetts State Relief train with sixteen doctors and some twenty nurses, as well as hospital supplies, brought most welcome and timely reinforcements.*

* See page 136, ''Report of the Massachusetts Halifax Relief Expedition.''

The organization of transportation on the very day of the explosion was one of the marvels of that time. Some system was running two hours after the MONT BLANC blew up and it was running smoothly by eight o'clock that night. The city authorities were less peremptory in their method than the military. From the Lieutenant Governor they obtained some sort of order-in-council to commandeer motor cars. Its legality might not have stood much testing, but it was sufficient at a time when red tape was dispensed with. Cars were commandeered in the morning on this authority by the police and sent from the street to the City Hall whence they were despatched on various errands. Alderman F. A. Gillis was not present at the morning meeting of the City Council when the committees were struck. He was engaged in taking wounded to the hospitals and did not know of his appointment as Chairman of the Transportation Committee until the afternoon. Then he went about the city with Mr. W. A. Black, a member of the committee, asking owners of private cars to lend them for public use. By evening they had control of between two hundred and fifty and three hundred cars. This was in addition to those which had been taken over by the military. The

Transportation Committee was informed that there were seven thousand persons to be moved from the North End, and they set about their gigantic task.

Not only were there thousands of sick, maimed, and wounded to be moved to the hospitals, thousands of homeless ones to various shelters, and hundreds of dead to the mortuary, but building material, glass for temporary repairs, as well as food, clothing, and fuel had to be transported to various supply depots and thence to shelters or homes of the sufferers. In addition, there were whole cargoes of supplies to be shifted from the wharves to the distributing warehouses, and hundreds of carloads of freight from the freight shed to warehouses. The work was done during exceptionally trying weather. Snowstorms, rainstorms, and bitter cold followed hard on the explosion and made transport in Halifax well nigh impossible. An extract from the official report of this committee gives some slight idea of its activity: ''Our records show that we handled on an average of two thousand five hundred requests for teams and motor trucks per day for the first two weeks following the explosion, and over three thousand requests per day for motor cars, necessitating the use of eight phones to handle the calls alone.'' Many vehicles, men horses, and motor trucks were loaned by nearly every town throughout the Maritime Provinces. It was found necessary to build what was practically a new garage and turn a vacant building into a hotel for the chauffeurs.

By eight o'clock on the 6th, a canteen was started in the Treasurer's Office, to supply meals for the teamsters and chauffeurs engaged in the work of transportation, as well as for the over-driven helpers and officials in permanent session. The supplies came from the Food Committee and a food shop, Colwell's Delicatesse.

In all the activities of the City Hall, women had a large and important part. They showed initiative, organization and endurance. Three were specially prominent in the work of relief at this centre, Mrs. Clara MacIntosh, head of the St. John's Ambulance, Mrs. Barbara Freeman and Miss Jane Wisdom, a trained Social Service worker. They are not women who would be described as physically robust, but on the contrary, rather delicate; nonetheless, they ''carried on'' with sympathy and efficiency to the utmost limit of their strength and beyond it. To Mrs. MacIntosh was due the excellent suggestion of a careful inspection of the Richmond district to discover the exact condition of the population remaining in that quarter. It was not enough to give relief on the spot to those who were able to come and apply in person; there should be an effort to reach those who were too ignorant, or too proud, or who were simply unable to come to the City Hall for help. The meeting was hardly over before this lady began organizing volunteer visitors and sending them out with coal, food, clothing, first aid.

The situation in the City Hall has been described by an eye witness who went to help on December 8th: ''I entered the Mayor's office, where Mrs. MacIntosh was installed and asked for work and was told to wait . . . At the desk taking orders were Mrs. Frank Bell, Mrs. Norwood Duffus, Miss Young, Miss Hunter, Mrs. George Hensley, Miss M. Brown, and Miss Wisdom. These ladies took down on a pad, names, addresses, size of family, and what was required, whether coal, food, oil, or blankets. (Tar paper was also distributed but we gave no orders for it.) These pads were handed to Mrs. Freeman at the desk, who wrote the names and addresses on small typewritten orders, which she signed, 'Relief Executive, City Hall, J. B. Wisdom per B.F.' The coal orders were given upon the Dominion Coal Co. and Cunard's, the food upon John Tobin and Co., the oil upon the Imperial Oil Co. . . . The blankets were distributed in the City Hall by Captain Isnor, who found a very able assistant in Miss Young. The blankets ran out frequently, but were always quickly restocked as relief shipments arrived from outside points.

''I saw that if I wanted a job, I should have to get it myself, so I grabbed a pad and began taking orders at the desk, running errands for Mrs. Freeman and answering the telephone which rang incessantly with all kinds of messages . . . Controller Murphy . . . remained cool and efficient in spite of the tremendous demands that were made upon him.

''A continuous string of people came to my desk, many seeking the registration and transportation departments which were further down the hall, as was the emergency medical bureau under Colonel Weatherbe. Most of those who sought food, etc., were from the less striken areas. We gave to all without question, though some were patently undeserving. Our only orders were from Controller Murphy to 'give everything to everybody.'

''Mrs. MacIntosh attended to sending out the V.A.D.'s and allotting districts to be visited, but although she worked heroically, it was really too large an undertaking for her. She received some assistance from Miss Hunter and a Salvation Army colonel (a woman). It was noticeable of the workers during the first days that they were eager to do anything, even the most insignificant errand. Housemaids and shopgirls worked shoulder to shoulder with women who had probably never raised a finger to help anyone before.

''About eleven o'clock the coal people refused to deliver any more coal, as they had not the transportation facilities, and the food department on the second floor of the City Hall was opened. Henceforth, relief was only to be delivered to the most urgent cases, and that by special messenger, boy scout, cadet, or some other voluntary helper. With the inauguration of the food depot, we stopped issuing food orders, all names and addresses being taken upstairs; however, we now began giving out tickets of admission to the Green Lantern. In the afternoon, the Salvation Army was given charge of the coal,

16

and this relieved us of coal orders, but as practically everyone came to our office first and had to be referred elsewhere, our work was not diminished. At 11:30 I went to lunch, returning at 12:30 to relieve Mrs. Freeman. Henceforth, I was authorized by Miss Wisdom to initial orders. The afternoon was much the same as the morning. We were helped by two splendid Salvation Army men who had come from Truro. Telephone messages kept pouring in, usually for some other department of the City Hall. The cadets and boy scouts were mobilized into an excellent messenger service. Miss Cunningham of the Provincial Secretary's staff typed out lists of those to whom relief had been administered . . . Many people who had taken in refugees asked for relief for them. We also received scores of offers to accommodate nurses or sufferers, usually from people of the poorer classes.

"About six o'clock doctors and nurses began to arrive in lots of from ten to one hundred. They arrived at the South Terminals, and demanded transportation which it was almost impossible to supply as all the horses were absolutely exhausted. The evening continued busy until eleven o'clock. As Mrs. MacIntosh & Co. had worked until two the preceding morning, I volunteered to spend the night in the office for them. It was far from pleasant. There were no windows in the room, and the rain poured in. The heavy wind kept all the doors slamming and creaking. The only heat was furnished by a diminutive oil stove. Mr. McIlreith and Assistant City Engineer Johnson spent the night in the latter's office; as did several cadets. Dr. Ryan and several orderlies remained in the Medical office. The telephone rang steadily with various messages until 2:00 a.m., most of which had to be transmitted to the Medical Department. From 2:00 to 3:30, I typed out lists of those who had received relief. At about 4:00 a.m., an emergency call was received to send nurses to the hospital ship OLD COLONY, on which one nurse had collapsed. The Superintendent of the Victoria General offered to send two, but we were unable to obtain transportation, as the storm made motoring impossible, and horses were out of the question. The transportation and information bureaus had closed about twelve. All night long until 4:30, there were occasional callers, mainly policemen who wanted company. There was one call for food for the refugees at the Strand Theatre, and a French sailor, Octave Ducasse off the H.M.C.S. LADY EVELYN, brought in two dollars for the Relief Fund. At five, I had half an hour's sleep, but at six things began to happen again, albeit spasmodically on account of the storm. The condition of the streets delayed Mrs. McIntosh and Miss Wisdom so that I was in charge of the office until 10 o'clock. The weather prevented the rush of Saturday, but there was nevertheless a steady stream of people. We had many calls from voluntary helpers for rubber boots and oilskins, so we gave orders on various shops which were always signed by a controller. I was able to leave the office at about 11:30 and did not return until Monday morning at nine.

"On Monday, our office was practically a clearing house and an information bureau. We did little but refer people to the various departments, write tickets of admission to the Green Lantern, give orders for rubber boots, and attend to such urgent cases as were brought to our attention. Mrs. McIntosh, devoting all her attention to the Medical side, had withdrawn to the Council Chamber. Miss Wisdom was conferring with the officials of the American Red Cross. So that the office was practically in the hands of Mrs. Freeman, myself, and the two Salvation Army Ensigns, with an occasional voluntary helper. We still answered countless telephones for the city fathers. Worthy of notice is the unflagging courtesy and patience of the telephone operators. Food depots had been opened at the Armouries and St. Joseph's Hall. Discrimination was being inaugurated with rather questionable success, as, according to our experience, the Green Lantern turned away many deserving cases. However, grafters were unpleasantly evident, particularly self-styled 'soldier's wives.' On Monday, the Relief Executive at the City Club was fairly well organized. Miss Wisdom had taken her place on the Rehabilitation Committee. We remained in the office until 11:00 p.m.; but business was slack in the evening.

"On Tuesday, Mrs. Freeman and I were in full charge of the office. We gave out information and tickets of admission to the Green Lantern. The transportation office had been moved to Bedford Row. (N.B. This office also gave orders to people who wished to leave Halifax, of whom there were many.) The information bureau had been transferred from the City Clerk's office to St. Mary's Parish Hall. The reconstruction bureau was established at the Halifax Hotel, moved from the Engineer's office which still attended to plumbing.

"All this may have been politic, but, as no advance information was given out, the people still came to the City Hall, and had to be referred on, and as the various offices were widely separated, and there were no trams, it meant a great deal of additional and tiresome walking for those who were seeking relief. Mrs. Freeman and I remained in the office until 9:30 when we relinquished it to the city officials, and the remnants of the original relief committee passed out of existence.''

16

17

5

Chapter 16

The Rescue

The roar of the explosion had hardly died away, the "black rain" of the MONT BLANC's explosives had not ceased to fall from the sky, with flakes "as big as half a dollar" before the work of rescue began. All over the Richmond district, the survivors began at once to help those who needed help and were nearest to them. A house would collapse burying the family beneath the ruins. A father or mother would struggle to extricate their children from the ruins, or it might be, the children would try to drag out or lead out their injured, unconscious, or blinded parents. Individual effort of this kind was instinctive and universal.

A few incidents may be cited from hundreds by way of illustration. George Oak of 28 Russell Street is a man about fifty years of age. He lost a leg three years ago and wears a stump. This was blown away in the explosion, when his house fell, and he himself was badly injured. Crippled as he was, he was seen dragging himself over the ruins of his poor house and tearing with his hands at the pile of bricks from the fallen chimney which covered the body of his little daughter. He was unable to rescue her, and the child was burned to death.

Mrs. Henry Bayers is a grandmother. Physically she is a giantess, the stature of a tall man. Her home was her pride, for she represents the thrifty, saving, working class type of the North End. She and her husband owned their own house, making additions and improvements as the family increased and their savings mounted. They had just installed electric light and had their first bill for it rendered, when disaster overwhelmed them. In the same house lived her married daughter who had a young baby, another daughter who was a professional pianist and a crippled son who was also musical and played with his sister at dances and concerts. That morning Mrs. Bayers was bathing her two grandchildren by the stove when the house collapsed. She put the two babies in a place of safety "on a board" and then lifted the stove off her daughter, burning her hands severely in doing so. The floor gave way and she went down into the cellar. The ruins caught fire, and the flames had begun to lick her clothing, when by a desperate effort she succeeded in freeing herself without assistance. Throughout she triumphantly retained her spectacles. Although she had lost her house and all her belongings which represented the thrift of a lifetime, she was found in hospital with her arms bandaged to the elbow, cheerful and content in the thought that it was no worse, that her husband had escaped the fate of other men on the waterfront, and that her son was the sole survivor from Hillis' Foundry.

The story of "Kid" O'Neil, ex-pugilist, is stranger still. He lived in a house directly opposite the point at which the MONT BLANC blew up. His wife, Annie, was watching the spectacle of the burning ship, and called him from bed to witness it also. He got up and dressed; with his wife, her mother and her aunt, they mounted to the fourth storey in order to obtain a better view. After the explosion, "Kid" found himself pinned down by the kitchen stove across his chest and two dead women at his feet. He and his wife were the only survivors out of the eighteen persons who lived in the house. His wife had fallen close beside him. When she recovered her senses, she put out her hand and touched his sweater. When she understood his helpless condition, Annie O'Neil ran out and begged a man, "a big hulk" to come and help. She was rudely refused. What happened next is best told in "The Kid's" own expressive language. "She comes back and battles and battles with that big stove. The fire is comin' near, an' my clothes begin to burn. My wife pulls an' drags at me until all the clothes is pulled off me; an' my God, I don't know how she does it, but that little woman has lifted the stove off'n me. An' she weighs but a hundred and five pounds." Even then the rescue was only half completed. O'Neil was in a fainting condition; the dead woman, his wife's mother, lay across his feet; he could not help himself and he begged his wife to save herself. Her answer was, "I'll never leave you, Bernie. If I can't save you, I'll die with you."

She put her arms around his neck and his courage revived. Somehow he managed to free his feet, but he was unable to walk. His wife picked him up on her back and carried him along until he fainted. And once more he urged her to save herself. Once again she looked for help and could find none. She put the "Kid's" legs over her shoulders and dragged him face downward the road, "like a wheel-barrow." Somehow she managed to get him down to the harbor where she bathed his wounds with the salt water. His chest had been torn open and a huge mass of flesh and muscle gouged out by the flying glass; he was bleeding freely. The cold water revived him and he was able to walk with his wife's assistance. Except for one shoe, he was naked; she took off her skirt and put it on him. At last they met with a policeman who put them in a motor and sent them to the Infirmary. Kid's tribute to the heroine who showed such determination was, "she ought to have been a prize-fighter herself."

Rev. C. J. Crowdis is the pastor of the Grove Presbyterian Church, a large and thriving congregation. The night before the disaster, it had celebrated the occasion of having paid off the last of its debt. Mr. Crowdis was running along Kenny Street, which leads to the water, in order to see the fire, and had reached a point just above the MONT BLANC when she blew up. He was flung down on his back by the ground shock, bruising his head, but immediately he recovered his footing. It seemed to him that the air was filled with everything flying and falling. This is how Mr. Robinson described his impressions looking from the bathroom window of the Naval College at the same moment. All the houses in the quarter collapsed like houses made of cards. ''Not more than a minute after I fell, the houses were as level with the ground as they were an hour later.'' They looked as if they had been pressed down. This testimony to the instantaneous collapse of all the houses in Richmond is very striking, though in some cases the collapse must have been more gradual than this statement would indicate. A sergeant on the Citadel Hill saw, as it seemed to him, all the houses of Richmond sway away from the blast of the explosion, recover themselves, and then topple down.

Mr. Crowdis immediately ran back to his own house on Gottingen Street, No. 565. He found the manse flat, his wife and her two sisters buried in the ruins, but his two children, Jean aged six and Donald aged four, were standing in the middle of the street unhurt. Their escape borders on the miraculous, because at the time of the disaster the sister of Mrs. Crowdis, Mary Kennedy, was helping the two children to dress in their bedroom. She was pinned down under a beam of the house and had to go to hospital for several days. The children were not at all hurt. The little girl's own account of her escape was, ''I jumped through the window and Donny jumped after me.'' When found by their father, these tots had already gone to a neighbour, Mrs. Milligan, to get her to come and help their mother and aunts. The other sister, Marjorie Kennedy, was standing with Mrs. Crowdis at a back window in the hall upstairs watching the fire when the house collapsed. She was very badly hurt, suffering dreadful lacerations of the face, neck, and chest. It did not seem possible when rescued, that she could live, but she ultimately recovered. But Mrs. Crowdis was most frightfully injured. One eye was so filled with glass that later it had to be removed; her forehead seem to be crushed in, a cut in her neck laid bare the jugular vein, one bone of her right forearm was split lengthwise and a piece of glass was driven in behind the left knee cap. On her body she had no fewer than thirty severe lacerations besides bad cuts on the limbs. Unaided, Mr. Crowdis dug his wife and her sisters out of the ruins and laid them on mattresses which he also succeeded in dragging out of his house. Other houses near by were on fire, but the ruins of the manse did not burn at all.

Mr. Crowdis got his wheelbarrow out of what was left of the barn, and put his wife in it. She was bathed in her own blood and must have seemed to her husband to be in a dying condition. He put little Donald in the rude conveyance beside her, and bidding Jean walk along beside him, he started to the nearest hospital, that for convalescent soldiers at Rockhead, nearly a mile away. When he reached it, he found this building a ruin, and very little could be done for injured persons there. About one o'clock a good friend of the family came to the hospital and removed Mrs. Crowdis and the children to his own home at Fairview. Here her injuries were attended to as well as possible in the circumstances, and the same night upon her arrival, she was placed upon the operating table, and received the skilled treatment so sorely needed. She lost an eye, but, in other respects made a complete recovery.

These stories are only typical of hundreds which might be told of the prompt, instinctive efforts to aid those who were nearest and dearest. In too many cases, however, the would-be rescuers came on the scene only to find that they were too late or that their best efforts were unavailing. A young officer, lately invalided home from France, hurried to the devastated area, to render what aid he could. Among his experiences was this: ''Approaching the ruins of a house, I first heard the loud sobs of, and then saw, a sailor walking up and down in a dazed and distracted way. His sobs were so heart-rending that I could not help asking him if I could help him in any way and what the trouble was. 'This is my trouble, sir', he said between great sobs, and taking me around to the other side of the tumble-down house, he knelt down beside three prone and lifeless bodies. They were those of his mother, wife, and daughter.''

There were many, many cases like this, but such a death, to be instantaneously struck out of life, was merciful compared with what hundreds suffered that day, for many were pinned down under wreckage or imprisoned in places where they could not escape and suffered death by fire. The second alarm, as it was commonly called, forced rescuers away and conscious human beings were abandoned to an agonizing death.

In addition to the countless efforts of individuals, a rude organization for the recovery and transportation of wounded sprang up almost at once. The injured and the dead were carried to the nearest open spaces away from the ruins and burning houses, and the injured were removed as soon as possible in vehicles of all sorts. The lines of old Fort Needham can still be plainly traced on the hill above Richmond. It forms an open space in the very heart of this district. Into it were carried the wounded and the dead from the blazing streets on every side. The ground about the old fort which had never seen an attack was littered like a battlefield with the dying, the dead, the wounded and those who were striving to aid them.

The motors of Halifax were in great demand that day. Owners drove their own cars or turned them over to the City or the Military. Motors were ''commandeered'' at various points such as the Armouries, and sent flying wherever needed in response for urgent calls for help. The City Hall was the central point or nodus of this activity. Thither motors came for orders and were sent as required. In many cases, cars fell into the hands of very unskilled amateur chauffeurs and they were soon disabled or ruined in consequence. The cars at one garage in the South End are reported to have been damaged in this

The dead were laid out to be identified.

one day's driving to the extent of $27,000, but saving life was more important than saving machines. Every kind of vehicle was used, express wagons, coal carts, flat wagons, even the hand trucks for luggage from North Street station; in fact, everything that had wheels was pressed into service that day. Mr. A. O. Saunderson saw a low cart near Kempt Road dragging along on three wheels; the fourth was broken. On the cart were four men and three children, he could not say whether they were boys or girls, all swathed in bloody bandages, and being driven to the Armouries. It had stopped to take on a woman who was being carried on the door out of a house nearby. Mr. Saunderson thought that she would have been "shaken to death" by the jolting of this crippled conveyance. He saw the woman placed in a coal cart on the empty sacks and driven off to the Armouries.

It is only just to say that wherever there were soldiers there was organization. A barber, driven out of his shop by the second alarm, went south from George Street, as far as Spring Garden Road where he rallied and convinced himself of the futility of flight. Here he met a friend driving a wagon of the Dominion Express Company who asked him to bear a hand. Together they worked moving injured persons from the district about North Street Station. They found whenever they returned from a trip to the hospital that there was always someone to tell them where to go for the wounded who had been collected and lend help in lifting them into the wagon. These two worked on undeterred by the possibilities of a second explosion. Indeed the teamster fought off panic-stricken people trying to get into his wagon with oaths and stronger arguments.

Halifax that day was one vast turmoil. The main streets were soon encumbered with crossing currents of humanity on foot, and along the main arteries of traffic proceeded ceaseless streams of vehicles of all kinds, at all rates of speed from tearing motors to crawling carts, each bearing its melancholy load of torn, bleeding, human beings. One eyewitness saw a man's leg drop from a cart that was crossing the Common. These streams of vehicles moved between the collecting points in the devastated district such as Fort Needham and Hungry Hill, and the various hospitals in the city. The resemblance to a battlefield struck many beholders. The dead were collected and laid together in groups. One observer that afternoon, an officer returned from France, saw the whole hillside flecked with patches of white. These were the cloths laid over the corpses which had been collected.

To tell in detail the story of the rescue would require not a chapter but volumes, for hundreds of willing helpers were engaged in it, and each one had his own experience. When questioned, the general response is to the effect that nothing was done worth mentioning, or, that only the obvious thing was done which everybody was doing. Where all did so well, soldiers, civilians, sailors, it is hard to discriminate, indeed impossible. But perhaps the highest praise that day must be awarded to the returned soldiers, who in the hospitals and elsewhere labored with severe physical disabilities for those who were suffering greater need. They gave up their beds in the hospitals and served as nurses and stretcher bearers. Men who were not fit to work at all "carried on" until they literally dropped. A typical case is that of Mr. Ralph

4

Survivors from Africville walking along Gottingen Street.

Proctor. He is a young man not yet twenty-one years of age who served in the 85th Battalion and had been severely wounded at Vimy. Two vertebrae have been destroyed, he has sustained permanent injury to his right leg, and a bad wound in his lung. The doctors have forbidden him to lift any weight for at least a year.

On the morning of the disaster he was at Smith & Proctor's place of business, 582 Barrington St., in the office on the second floor. Here, as everywhere else, glass was broken, doors were forced, partitions were broken down, and yet in spite of it all, only one man was hurt, and he not badly. Proctor assisted in bandaging him up and then saw people passing in the street cut and bleeding. He realized then that the damage was not confined to the premises, but something far more serious. He set out for his own house, 306 Gottingen, above North Street, which he reached about half past nine. It was a wreck. In his own words, "Things were in an awful mess." This man who was forbidden to lift any weight had to dig his car out of the ruins of his garage, using a crow bar to move the heavy timbers. When he got it out, he found that a chimney had fallen across the street which he would have to move before he could get the car out of the yard. With the help of some soldiers who were passing, he succeeded in removing this obstacle, and then proceeded in his car along Gottingen to Richmond. Most of his work was done in Macara and Russell Streets, which run at right angles to Gottingen on the edge of the devastated area.

The first passenger he picked up was a man whose left arm was hanging by a shred of flesh. He was walking along the street holding his injured arm. Proctor opened the door of his car and the man got in beside him. He filled up his car with others badly hurt but not so seriously as the first man, and drove to Camp Hill Hospital. There the man got out of the car without assistance and began to walk up the steps with his arm around Proctor's neck who supported him. After a step or two, the man fainted from loss of blood and Proctor carried him into the building.

Proctor stuck to the route he had first taken and plied between the devastated area and Camp Hill Hospital. Many of the cases he carried were very serious. One man had the jugular severed but they managed to stop the bleeding in time. He saw a man with a piece of wood, part of a window sash, driven through his neck from left to right like a skewer. In Russell Street, he found a girl with every stitch of clothing gone, simply bathed in blood. She seemed to be terribly injured but later it was found that she had only surface cuts. However, there was hardly an inch of her body that was not cut or scratched. One woman had her breast completely cut off. A man with his side crushed in died in the car on the way to the hospital. The most pitiful case was a little child of five with a broken spine.

"It affected me far worse than anything I saw in France. Over there you don't see women and children all broken in pieces."

Proctor drove his car over fences and collapsed houses without any regard for its feelings. He had punctures and blow-outs and detached tires, and travelled part

60

of the day on the flat tires. It took $350 to pay the damages it sustained.

In Macara Street every second house was on fire. Once, when he had three injured persons in his car, he was passing a burning building at the very instant of its collapse. Two beams, one of which was burning, fell across the car smashing a mudguard, the cowl, and the windshield. Previously to this, the wound in his lung had opened and he had a hemorrhage, as he drove. "With this and the knowledge that I had swallowed glass I was pretty scared." However, he "carried on" after the fashion of the Canadian soldier. In his own words, "there was nothing else to do." He "carried on" until eleven o'clock that night.

His activities on Friday, the day of the blizzard, and Saturday, the day of the bitter cold, deserve to go on record. In spite of his exertions on Thursday, he was at work the following morning at half-past eight. His car had been commandeered, but he drove it himself. His work was picking up homeless people and taking them to various shelters, namely, the Academy of Music and St. Mary's Hall. In the morning he made six trips to Richmond in his disabled car through the blinding snowstorm. He found people huddled together without any shelter whatever, some just crouching against walls which happened to be standing. Some were at the reservoir. This form of rescue was the work of the people with motor cars on the Friday. In the afternoon, he was taken over by the Military, for he was still in uniform, and drove under orders until nine o'clock. Then he went to his brother's house at Armdale for the night. On Saturday morning he had to get a horse to drag his car out of

the drift, and he drove it in from Armdale to the city through the snow. Still acting under military orders, he carried food to the various hospitals, met the doctors at the various incoming trains, and took them to their destinations. This was late on Saturday evening. Proctor "was feeling all in then, and pretty grumpy—didn't talk to them at all." Sunday was the day of the fierce rain storm which washed the streets bare, for on Saturday night the temperature arose, the snow melted, and the rain fell in torrents. Rarely has Halifax known such violent extremes of weather as those which followed the explosion. Proctor worked his car in the tropical downpour from the City Hall to the Academy, thence to the Armouries, and then the long-suffering machine began to "go bad." Still he managed to humour it round as far as Smith & Proctor's shop. After a brief rest inside, he tried to start the car again, when the rear axle broke. He was trying to repair it when he suddenly fainted on the sidewalk. In his own words, "We both went at once."

That is the record of a returned soldier of the Canadian Expeditionary Force. Beside it may be put the record of a returned officer.

Capt. J. F. Cahan, C.E.F., represents the best type of Canadian manhood. He is a college-bred man and an engineer by profession. He "joined up" early in the war, leaving wife, young family and profession at the call of duty. He was severely wounded at Courcelette, receiving injuries to the spine which paralyzed him from the waist down and which caused intense and almost uninterrupted

10

Identification of personal items saved from the destruction.

pain. The best treatment procurable has been unable to cure or mitigate his sufferings. He never knows a natural sleep. For a year and more he had been living at Belmont, a beautiful old retreat on the shore of the North West Arm, fighting down his sufferings with heroic determination.

When he learned on December 6th what had happened, he sent his man-servant and constant attendant, for he cannot move without assistance, into the city to obtain a taxi-cab. He got himself into what remained of his uniform, for most of it had been left in France, his idea being that an officer in uniform would be able to pass cordons of soldiers and be more generally useful than he would be in mufti, and proceeded with his servant to Headquarters where he reported himself to Colonel Thompson. His general orders ''to chase the people to their homes'' were exceeded. Under his direction his servant raided a drug store, securing bandages, peroxide, etc., needed for first aid. Thus the two spent the day bandaging wounded persons in the street and conveying others to the various hospitals. Capt. Cahan did twenty dressings with his own hands. It was eight o'clock in the evening before he had finished his good work and returned to Belmont, exhausted but ''happy'' to think that he had been of some service. It was three weeks before he recovered from the effects of his exertions on that day.

On December 6th, there was no lack of eager rescuers who worked without a thought of self. Many were injured themselves, or arose from sick beds in hospitals to help. Many worked to the point of absolute exhaustion. The rescuers worked with a will, without a thought of self, returning again and again to the district where they were officially informed another deadly explosion might occur at any moment. They take no credit for what they did; they say, ''I did nothing worth speaking about;'' or ''I wish I could have done more;'' or ''What else could I have done?''

Chapter 17

The Hospitals

The hospitals of any city are designed to meet what may be called the normal flow of patients in ordinary times; they are not designed to cope with a sudden, unforeseen influx of hundreds upon hundreds of wounded, as if from a nearby battlefield. The main hospital is the Victoria General; and, second in importance to it, the Military Hospital in Cogswell Street. The conditions of the war had compelled an increase of accommodation. To meet the needs of convalescent soldiers, the Presbyterian divinity school at the Arm known as ''Pine Hill'' had been taken over by the government. But this was not enough. A large temporary lath-and-plaster hospital had been run up on rising ground at the back of the Citadel. The whole district is known as Camp Hill from the fact that troops lacking barracks used to live there under canvas. The city cemetery is situated here and is called Camp Hill Cemetery; and the new emergency hospital is called Camp Hill Hospital.

The Victoria General Hospital is a two-storey brick building standing in its own grounds in the south end, near the School for the Blind, All Saints' Cathedral, and old Dalhousie College. On a little rise of ground beside the drive was erected the gallows on which the four pirates of the SALADIN were executed in 1844, a notable event in local history.

On the morning of December 6th, Dr. G. H. Murphy was in the operating room getting ready for a ''case,'' which was being put under anaesthetics. A grating, rumbling sound, different from anything he had ever heard, startled Dr. Murphy into going to the window to discover if he could what had caused it. He came directly under the glass skylight when it crashed down, cutting his head and stunning him. His impression was that the building was coming down and the thing to do was to get out of it as soon as possible. He found himself in the open air with his head and hands covered with blood, and he saw the ''dense, grayish smoke rising like a dark pillar over the north end of the city.'' Dr. Murphy was the only person injured in the hospital and neither the patients in the wards nor the attendants suffered anything beyond the slightest cuts. Most came off unscathed.

After having his wounds dressed and visiting his house which was close by Carlton St. to see what damage had been done there, Dr. Murphy hurried back to his duty at the hospital. He writes, ''I wish I could describe the scene at the hospital adequately. The ground in front was jammed with autos, wagons, and every conveyance capable of carrying a sufferer. The hallways and offices and every bit of floor space in the hospital were littered with human beings suffering with all degrees and manners of wounds and injuries. The wards already well filled with the regular patients seemed to take on almost magical expansion to make room for broken and dying men, women and children.

''Dr. Puttner who was acting superintendent turned no one away. He pressed every available nook in the big building into service, and his big-heartedness and good judgment never stood him in better stead than during the trying hours of that fatal Thursday. Besides those brought on stretchers was an army of walking victims seeking some kind of first aid. Many of them turned away on seeing the human wreckage around them unwilling to take the time and services of doctors and nurses from those whose needs were greater than their own. Notwithstanding the crowding together of the wounded they gave little evidence of the suffering they endured. There was little groaning or complaining, and, apart from the occasional crying of the wounded babies and little children, an almost uncanny quiet pervaded the wards and available spaces of the hospital. Nor among the friends and relatives of the stricken ones who searched hither and thither among the human bundles was there any evidence of anguish or hysteria such as might be popularly supposed to obtain under such conditions. There were pale faces enough but their eyes were dry. There were no tears. 'Tears were not yet brewed'.* The suddenness and horror of the disaster were too great to find expression in that way; the shock to the nerve centres induced a form of anaesthesia, a certain callousness which I believe to be a common enough condition when a human organism is acted upon by the grimmest of all the stern realities of life. It is when the stunning effect has passed off that reflection reaches 'the fountains of grief''.

It was impossible to get all the patients inside the hospital at once and many were simply laid on the ground outside the building, while the rescuers hurried off for others. Into the Victoria General, as into the others in the city, soon poured a throng of amateur helpers, chiefly women, and from the neighbourhood of the hospital. One lady avers that she did everything but amputate. The patients lying on the ground waiting to be taken into the hospital suffered from cold. Their clothing soaked in their own congealed blood chilled them. There was an urgent need for hot water bottles, which were collected in the neighbourhood and brought to the uncomplaining sufferers. One of the voluntary helpers, a young girl who worked here all day, described the condition of the hospital in the morning as ''chaos.'' By evening, however, order had been brought out of the chaos and the local staff had the situation thoroughly in hand. One reason for the improved condition was that numbers of patients with slighter injuries had been sent to their homes, or to improvised hospitals and shelters. Another reason was that the Victoria General was self-contained. It has no fewer than three operating rooms with complete modern equipment. These were taxed to the full, day and night, with the regular surgical staff of the hospital at work in them, almost without a moment's rest. The many difficulties of treating such an influx of patients were greatly increased by the crowd of distracted visitors seeking for missing relatives or friends. There was also a plentiful supply of splints, dressings, instruments, etc. Additional mattresses were obtained from the Ordnance and the American hospital ship, OLD COLONY.

* Macbeth Act II, Scene IV: ''What should be spoken here, where our fate hid in an augerhole may rush and seize us? Let us away our tears are not yet brewed.'' Spoken by Donelbain after the murder of his father King Duncan.

The hospital staff felt the loss that day of Dr. Murdock Chisholm, the senior surgeon. He was severely cut in the neck and at first reported dead. Not only was the staff deprived of his assistance but of his valuable advice. The loss of such a skilled operator in this crisis was very serious.

The Victoria General was the scene of a triumph in surgery. Dr. D. L. MacDougall reached the building in his car about half an hour after the explosion and did not quit it until the following Sunday. For thirty-six hours he stood beside the operating table dealing with the most serious cases. There was a continual stream of major operations. Surgeons in the wards prepared and diagnosed the cases, getting them ready for the table, and others attended to them after the operation was complete. The work was not hastily done. Each case was thoroughly treated and did not need to be done over again. The last major operation was performed before the first of the American surgeons arrived in the city. Just across the street from Victoria General Hospital is the School for the Blind. It was used almost at once as a shelter and emergency hospital. The building consists of two main members joined together by a covered-in passage. The pupils and staff escaped very lightly, although the glass was broken in all the windows. One teacher was severely cut in the neck, but her injury was promptly attended to and she recovered. During the second alarm the children were turned out into the yard, where they remained for two hours. About noon, a woman student of Dalhousie College, who resided in the house of a teacher in the School for the Blind received an urgent call to put on warm clothing and come and help. She found the sitting room at the entrance of the School crowded with injured persons, and thirteen children were in the nursery. People were busy preparing beds and turning three classrooms into a temporary hospital. Later in the day, she was sent over to the Victoria General Hospital with the message that fifty patients could be accommodated at the School for the Blind. When she reached the V.G.H. she was asked, ''Can you wash cuts? Go in and get to work.'' She went in to the room on the left hand side. The inmates were mostly children with slight cuts on the head and were simply covered with blood and dirt. Here she spent two hours dressing wounds, and becoming faint for lack of food, went back to the School for the Blind about dark. On her return, she was again employed in washing children, dressing their injuries, and putting them to bed. About 10 o'clock, the soldiers who had been helping had to be fed. One man did the cooking. The gas had been turned off for fear of fires and explosions from leaky mains and they had ''to run round by candlelight,'' serving food.

The glass from the broken windows was not gathered up. More pressing work took precedence. At the entrance to the School this Dalhousie girl saw a working man with his clothing partially torn off and bare footed.

He was hesitating about walking in over the broken glass. She took off her coat and laid it down for him to walk on, and was much surprised to hear him remark, "Not exactly Sir Walter Raleigh."

Some of the injured at the School for the Blind had not received any treatment. One woman was badly cut in the face, body, and arms, as well as being badly bruised, but only her eyes were bandaged. She looked as if she had been dragged through the dirt. Another injured woman in a similar condition said she had crawled through the cinders for a city block. The Dalhousie girl was struck by the patience of the injured children she tended. One girl of eight with a bandaged face sat without saying a word. When the bandage was removed next day, it was found that her face had been cut open to the bone from the middle of the forehead almost to the end of the nose. There was also a boy with both arms and legs broken as well as being badly cut. This observer did not think that they were "dazed," for, being questioned, they answered sensibly. This helper did not reach her lodgings until six o'clock next morning. By daylight she was back again at the School for the Blind working as on the day before. This experience is typical.

Camp Hill Hospital is a large, low, two-storey affair of light construction, designed to accommodate solely convalescent soldiers returning invalided from service overseas, for many reach Halifax in no condition to endure the fatigue of the long railway journey home. It had only just been put in commission and contained about one hundred convalescent soldiers. Some time before, one of the staff, discussing its defects, complained that the wards had only one hundred and forty cubic feet air space instead of the orthodox one hundred and sixty. That allowance must have been seriously lessened on December 6th when probably fourteen hundred victims of the explosion were crowded into space designed for 240. The situation of Camp Hill Hospital at one end of the Common made it the natural receiving station for all injured in the neighbourhood. It soon became congested. The entrance was blocked with ambulances, motor cars, lorries, carts, flat wagons, vehicles of all descriptions, discharging their loads of wounded. The convalescent soldiers were turned out of their beds which were speedily filled with more urgent cases. Sometimes there would be two in a bed, or even more in the case of children. When the beds were filled the patients were laid between the beds and under the beds. Every room, every office, every nook and corner was filled with the injured. Mattresses were laid down along the corridors in a double row, and filled with patients. It was almost impossible to walk along without treading on some sufferer. The building was, of course, windowless, and all suffered from

Christmas in unidentified temporary hospital.

12

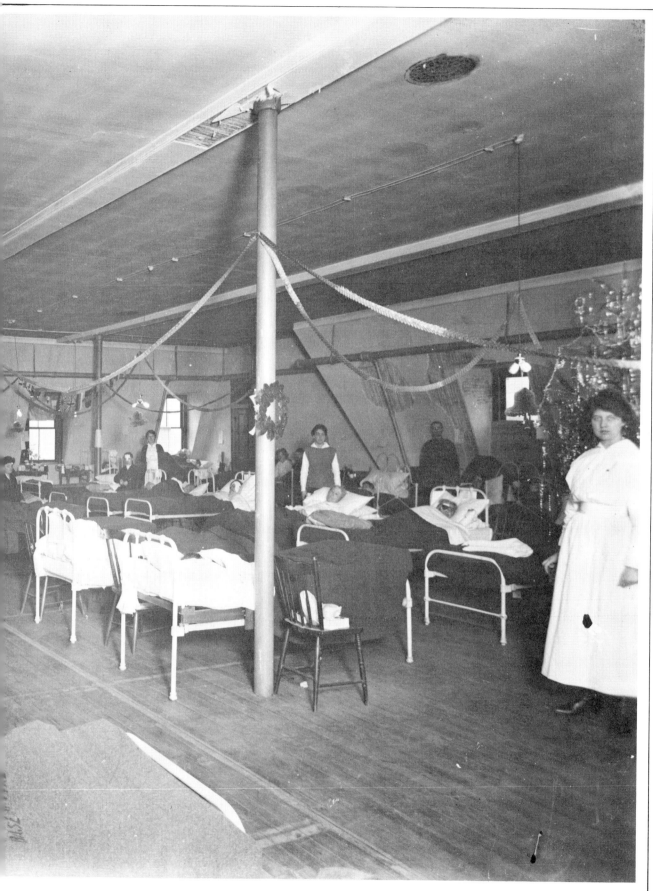

65

the bitter cold. The medical staff was entirely too small to cope with such a flood of suffering. The operating rooms were insufficient to meet even the most urgent cases, and had to be supplemented by the kitchen tables. Cooking and surgical operations went on there together. Here as elsewhere, a host of willing workers flocked in to give assistance, but even so the situation was beyond them.

A woman medical student of the fourth year, who lives in Robie St., started for the Victoria General within half an hour of the explosion but, seeing injured people being carried past, stopped at Camp Hill Hospital to give what help she could. She saw stretcher bearers carrying the injured persons from the various ambulances, wagons, etc. into the hospital. The hundred convalescent soldiers were working "like slaves," although some were hardly able to crawl. What struck this competent observer was "the organization without any organization." Without anyone in command to order and direct, everyone was working intelligently and without clashing. For instance, the stretcher bearers never ceased carrying people in. Voluntary helpers went to the kitchen, or to the wards, wherever they could be of use. They quite lost any thought of themselves in what they had to do, and she was surprised at the way girls behaved, who had absolutely no experience of such work. Inside there was no one directing or in control. She went into the first ward on the right hand, saw a doctor whom she knew at work, and began to assist him. A military nurse gave her a hypodermic outfit and told her to continue to give it until the morphine was exhausted. A morphia tube holds twenty-five tablets but there were not more than fifteen in this. When the supply was exhausted, an orderly was sent for more but could not get it anywhere in town. This medical student administered the morphia to those who were making the most outcry. She asked some of the wounded if they wanted the anodyne and got the answer, "Give it to someone who needs it more."

At first the hospital was not full or crowded, but the volunteer stretcher bearers soon filled up the beds. There were unlimited supplies of bedding and mattresses but nothing else that was needed. The operating room was unfurnished and there were only one or two pans to a ward. She had to go to a kitchen for kitchen utensils to be used in the operating room. The doctors brought what they had themselves but this was not enough. The stretcher bearers kept carrying in the injured as fast as they could. There were four rows of mattresses in the ward besides the beds. In the dining-room, mattresses were laid on the floor touching one another and covered with "the living and the dead together." As already mentioned, the various offices, closets, etc., were filled with people lying on the floor on mattresses. In one was found a woman and her baby, a girl about a year and a half old, soaking wet. They had been left without attention all day; the child was unconscious and died from ex-

posure. Other lives were lost simply and solely because there were not sufficient doctors and nurses and appliances. In the wards, conditions gradually improved. The windows were stopped in some way or other and there was plenty of light. In the corridors it was different. There it was dark, and the swinging doors at each end were constantly opening and shutting, letting in the icy wind. The patients were shivering with the cold. There were no hot water bottles, but heated bricks were used instead. It was in the corridor that Lieut. Balcom lay for four days with a compound fracture of his thigh, refusing to be treated because others needed attention until it was too late. When the doctors examined him they found that the leg had to be amputated and he did not long survive the operation. Here too lay a couple of cadets from the Naval College suffering from severe cuts about the face. One of them lost an eye and the other was terribly scarred.

Camp Hill will almost be a synonym for horror. All who were there say one thing, "The sights were terrible." One visitor called it a "shambles." "You couldn't tell the living from the dead sometimes." The patients were "bathed in blood." "The black rain" made them like negroes, soaking their clothes and dyeing the skin underneath. In addition, the dust and dirt and falling plaster covered the persons and filled the wounds of those who had been taken out of the wrecked buildings. The injuries were of all kinds,—broken bones, scalds, burns due to the contact with stoves or boilers, contusions, maimings, internal injuries—but undoubtedly the most ghastly wounds were those inflicted by the flying glass. Heads and faces, bodies limbs, were rent and gashed in all conceivable ways. Huge pieces of flesh were gouged out by glass. In other cases, incredibly large fragments of glass were imbedded in the flesh. Two cases, both women, at Camp Hill had their faces literally cut off. One was described as "lying on the left side like a trap door." The face had been cut across the forehead, round to the cheek, and through the corner of the mouth. The frontal and nasal bones were sliced away and the base of the brain was exposed. The wound was clotted with dirt and hair. This patient died. The other woman injured in the same way, almost as terribly, recovered. Faint with loss of blood, she was crying in an inarticulate way for water when she was noticed by this medical student. The difficulty was to find a place to put the water.

It is impossible to relate in detail what happened in all the hospitals that day. It was the same story everywhere of the injured swamping the accommodation and being tended by heroic doctors, nurses, and voluntary helpers who labored day and night in their unceasing ministry of mercy. One episode, however, must not go unrecorded.

The hospital farthest north in Halifax was at Rockhead. It stands on a high bluff overlooking the Basin, and on the morning of December 6th was occupied by some eighty convalescent soldiers. It is built of reinforced concrete, which stood the shock of the explosion very well. The windows were all broken, the roof was gone, the plaster came down, and the furnace pipes were broken. Little damage was done to the patients beyond some superficial cuts due to the broken glass. About ten o'clock, it was visited by the surgeon in charge, Dr. W. Bruce Almon, who motored up from his house in Hollis St. alarmed for the safety of his patients, who, he feared, might have shared the fate of so many that morning in Richmond; but the reinforced concrete had resisted the strain of the air shock. After satisfying himself that little harm had been done, Dr. Almon was about to leave the hospital, when wounded refugees began to pour in from the surrounding district. In all, there must have been between eighty and ninety, and Dr. Almon and his assistant were busily engaged in tending to their wants until six o'clock in the evening. The convalescents, none of whom was in a very serious condition, were allowed to leave the hospital for the city, and their beds were occupied by the wounded civilians.

In the afternoon, the two doctors were reinforced by a party of four women who had come out to Rockhead almost by accident. Two were students of Dalhousie College who had sallied out to do what they could wherever they found opportunity. One of them had gone to her lodgings and torn up her own clothes in order to make bandages, and with these they had filled their pockets and their muffs. At a druggist's in Robie St. they got some iodine. They then met a middle-aged man staggering along, hardly able to walk. He had been cut about the head and his wound had been dressed at the Victoria General Hospital. He was suffering mental distress, as well as physical, for his little boy had been burned to death that morning. One on each side, the girls supported him to his brother's house in Gottingen St. near Cunard, where they left him, and continued their journey northward. On their way they met two other women, strangers to them, but also Dalhousians, and joined forces. They raided the drugstore at 162½ Agricola St. but got only one roll of adhesive tape and a small bottle of antiseptic. The floor was inches deep in glass and plaster. At a grocer's shop, they bought a small bag of sweet biscuits, which served as their only solid food until next day at noon. About 2 o'clock they reached Rockhead. It was so dilapidated with the windows broken, doors smashed in, and the roof down, that they thought it was not inhabited. On going in, they found broken glass lying everywhere, which they never had any time to clean up completely. The water pipes had burst and the floors were flooded. All the beds from the upper floors had been crowded into the first floor ward, so close that in many places they had to draw up in order to pass between them. Some convalescent soldiers were acting as nurses under the direction of two military doctors. The four amateurs applied to them and were given permission to do what they could. One instructed them to leave the bad wounds alone, as they were better with the blood congealed.

The doctors had their hands full and these four novices set themselves to the special work of women, putting things in order, cleaning wounds, feeding the patients, and making them comfortable as far as possible. On the floor in the office, they found some twelve or thirteen children covered with blood. The first thing was to bathe the wounds, which were chiefly minor cuts in the arms and hands, and then to make the women and children as comfortable as they could under the circumstances. They kept on their hats and coats for the weather was cold, and they had to walk on their heels through the standing water on the floor. In the basement, they found the kitchen in the charge of a woman cook. This was not damaged. There was a huge caldron of tea on the stove, and this they kept taking to the patients as required. There was nothing to eat except the biscuits they had brought themselves, but late in the afternoon, rations arrived in sufficient quantities, consisting of bread and butter, ham and eggs, and cake. To the workers, "there were no incidents particularly outstanding. It was the same thing over and over." But they carried on until noon the next day. Towards morning, when all the patients had been attended to, they lay down in their clothes and tried to sleep, but they could not on account of fatigue and excitement.

The telephone wire connecting Rockhead Hospital with the rest of the system had been broken, and it was not until late in the afternoon that transport could be obtained to convey the patients to the other hospitals, for Rockhead was uninhabitable. Not realizing the seriousness of the situation, some of the boys driving the various conveyances to the hospitals wanted to stop work at the end of the day. It was only by dint of much coaxing, cajoling, and the use of moral suasion, that one of these helpers noted for her force of character kept them at it until the hospital was completely evacuated. During the night, three of the little girls died from the effects of the burns they had received. At twelve o'clock on Friday, in the midst of the fierce storm these four women came away in the ambulance along with three corpses. They wanted to walk in but the orderlies would not allow them.

One of the injured in Rockhead Hospital was Private Thomas Pringle of the Composite Battalion. On the morning of the 6th he was on guard at Pier 8. He had brought a shovelful of dirt out of the guardhouse when he saw a flash and was flung forward on his face. A "great wind" was roaring and sweeping everything with it. He rose to his feet, only to be thrown down on his face a second time. The wind stopped abruptly and then "everything seemed to be going straight up in the air." A minute after the shed fell upon him, and the wave raised by the explosion almost drowned him. In his extremity he prayed. The water receded as far as his chin. He crawled out from under the wreckage with one arm disabled, three vertebrae broken, bleeding from his cuts and soaked to the skin. He was not conscious of the injuries to his spine which were afterwards discovered. He thought that the explosion was local, and started for Wellington Barracks to report it. Bleeding and weak, he was still able to walk. He crawled under a freight car on the track, because he had not sufficient strength to climb over the couplings. He made his way as far as Gottingen St. where he was told that the Barracks had been abandoned, and he was advised to make his way to Rockhead which he eventually reached, his strength giving out just as he reached the steps.

About midnight Pringle was discovered by one of these volunteer nurses, wet, cold and suffering. Somehow or other he had been overlooked and had received no attention whatever for fourteen hours. She got him a cup of hot bovril but he refused it, and was asked why, "Don't you want it?" He answered, "Yes, but the woman beside me has not had anything either." So, the comforting cup was passed to the one who needed it more, but eventually Pringle got his bovril. He was made as comfortable as possible in the sorry circumstances, and between four and five o'clock in the morning he was transferred in an ambulance to the Military Hospital at Cogswell St. Like so many others, he was black as a negro from the "black rain." When his skin was finally cleansed, he was found to be a fair man of the extreme blond type. It was many months before he could walk and make a complete recovery. He will never forget the kindness of his amateur nurses in that night of suffering.

The episode of Rockhead illustrates in little what was done by the women of Halifax in the hospitals that day—the readiness of their help, their initiative, and their constancy to the duty immediately before them. The story was repeated a hundred times that day, but for the most part it must remain untold and unchronicled.

Chapter 18

The Shelters

How to relieve the suffering of the hundreds of injured was not the sole, though it was the most urgent, problem for the administration of Halifax to solve on December 6th. There was also the problem of the thousands who had suddenly found themselves without house or home, in need of clothing, of food and of shelter. A large number of houses had been destroyed utterly; many more had been rendered untenantable. The streets and open spaces were encumbered with crowds of people who did not know where to lay their head that coming winter's night.

This particular difficulty was recognized early in the day by numerous citizens and, at the same time, they perceived the way to meet it. The solution was in the use of the less damaged public buildings, such as the theatres. Almost at once, the managers of the various places of amusement, the Academy of Music, and the Strand, hurried to the City Hall to offer their buildings to be used for any purpose the administration might decide upon. Among the buildings used as shelters were St. Paul's Parish Hall, St. Mary's Parish Hall, the Academy of Music, the Salvation Army Citadel, the Dispensary, the quarters of the Knights of Columbus, the City Home, the Monastery of the Good Shepherd. The list is not complete. In addition, countless private citizens offered to house the shelterless in their own homes, specifying the number of families or of individuals they could take in. One could accommodate two men; another, a man and wife; a third so many children, and so on. A record was kept of these offers in the City Hall. Indeed, one of the difficulties of the administration that day was dealing with the numbers of those who were importunate to help.

At half-past ten on the morning of the 6th, the chairman of the House Committee of the Knights of Columbus called upon the Deputy Mayor and put the fine quarters of this influential organization at the disposal of the City. The offer was gladly accepted. This building is a fine stone mansion in Hollis St., once the home of a wealthy Haligonian and now serving as a comfortable and modern club. In the afternoon it began to be filled with refugees.

To this shelter were designated two nurses who came in on the relief train from Kentville. These were Miss Jessie Parker of Wolfville and Miss Miner of Walbrook. On their arrival, they found some fifty persons; their injuries were for the most part slight, but there were some bad burns. This was a refuge for families. Even on the 6th, there were few missing from the different little circles, but they were destitute; they had lost all their possessions. The various groups formed, as it were, one big family of which these two women took charge.

The first thing to do was to relieve suffering. They sent for a doctor and got the wounds and burns "fixed up." Then they made up beds with the cots provided by H.M.C.S. NIOBE and blankets from the Ordnance stores. There was no stove in the building, which is used as a recreation club and does not furnish meals, so they obtained a three-burner oil stove, on which they did all the cooking that was done. They heated water for bathing the children in washtubs in the good old fashioned way. Later, regular bathrooms with modern appliances were installed and hot water was obtainable by a less laborious process. On the first night all shook down together, men and women indiscriminately on the floor of the huge ballroom in the top storey; and this arrangement lasted for ten nights. Then the ballroom and the other rooms of the club were divided up by partitions of beaverboard. At first the women inmates were too frightened and dazed to render any help; later, they lent a hand in the heavy work involved in housekeeping for such a large family; but the burden of the first few stenuous days fell on these two women who did everything— cooking, washing dishes, etc., as well as regular nurse's work in dressing wounds. When they felt that it was no longer a charity they asked for a cook and two assistants—a very modest requirement. They were up at six every morning and never in bed until midnight, sleeping on the floor until cots were obtained for them. Between fatigue and the harrowing tales she heard, Miss Parker could not sleep. The worst case in the shelter was a woman whose eye was injured. Part of the brow and the upper eyelid hung down on her cheek. There was no anaesthetic obtainable. The doctor cleansed the wound of dirt and gravel and put in nine stitches. The patient was "wonderfully brave. She did not make a single moan." Members of the Knights of Columbus assisted most energetically in making this shelter one of the very best in the city by obtaining what was needed to transform a club into a temporary hotel. Later this shelter housed one hundred persons, of whom fifty were children. For these schooling was provided with one teacher for the Catholics and one for the Protestants. It was closed on March 31, 1918. Miss Parker remained till the end. On Christmas Eve, the Knights of Columbus presented both nurses with gold wrist watches in recognition of their efficient self-sacrificing labours.

The Y.M.C.A. in Halifax is a new building of the familiar modern type, half club, half hotel with reading room, gymnasium and auditorium attached. It stands on the very site of the old Masonic Hall, once a scene of Howe's oratorical triumphs. Near it in Salter Street was the old Main Guard in the eighteenth century, "within the pickets," when Halifax had to defend herself against the French and Indians. Here all the window glass was shattered by the force of the explosion. The magnitude of the calamity and the probable need of dressing stations was soon realized by those in charge. Capable and willing hands began to put the place in order. The front lobby and the reception room on the second floor were cleared out. The assistant secretary, Mr. J. G. Reid, the engineer, and a couple of dormitory men had been working at this for an hour, when the first patients began to arrive at ten o'clock. At the same time, the secretary of the local Y.W.C.A. came in with a welcome reinforcement of young women from that institution. They were set to work cleaning, dressing wounds and making up the dormitory beds. Willing volunteers, both men and women,

flocked in offering their services. By night the floors were wholly cleared of broken glass and the windows were covered with tar paper; the engineer kept steam up well, so the building was never cold.

By half-past eleven, a soup kitchen was opened. This "kitchen" is a diminutive affair in the second storey, furnished with two small ranges, one for gas and one for coal. The gas being cut off, only the coal stove could be used. How the ladies of Halifax managed with such meagre appliances to feed the hundreds of patients, refugees, helpers, staff, is one of the many marvels of the time. They worked day and night. Mrs. W. A. Henry was in charge for the first twenty-four hours without rest and continued to cook for a fortnight. Among others who aided was Mrs. McCallum Grant, the wife of the Lieutenant Governor. The first meal served was dinner to the Y.W.C.A. workers. Canned soup, especially tomato soup, was the great standby; bread and butter and cheese were also served the first day. With soup this should form a satisfactory emergency ration. In the afternoon, the "Green Lantern" restaurant sent over a barrel of soup, a most welcome addition to the commissariat. That little Y.M.C.A. kitchen deserves to be celebrated; its capacity to produce what was required seemed to be without limit. From it, many a cold, wet, tired worker received the comforting sustenance which enabled him to carry on when it was needed most. "Admirable piece of work" is the testimony of one eye witness of what was done here by the ladies of Halifax. By six o'clock, according to the log of the physical director, three hundred cases had received their first dressings. That night there were fifty patients in the beds upstairs, the regular occupants finding quarters elsewhere; and at least a hundred other homeless persons sheltered within the building. Food was supplied without question to all who asked for it all that night. At midnight mattresses were brought from the City Hall; there were not enough, and many of the refugees sat up in the room adjoining the kitchen all night.

On the morning of the 6th, Mrs. J. G. MacDougall went with Miss Scott to offer their services at the Halifax Infirmary. It had soon become congested with injured people and new cases were taken to the Y.M.C.A. just across the street. The two ladies saw the injured being carried in, crossed over and walked in over glass and furniture and began to lend a hand. Miss Scott attended to the dressings and Mrs. MacDougall became matron of the improvised hospital. The latter lady had been a trained nurse of wide experience, which proved most valuable in this emergency. "Everyone went to her for direction." She has testified to the way the work of relief was carried on in this particular shelter. Her praise of all concerned is warm. As a nurse, she was struck with the way the untrained voluntary helpers worked. "They could do anything." They could "special" patients, i.e., in the absence of trained nurses, they could be depended on to observe critical cases and make accurate reports. None of these girls knew what "hours" meant; they would come on at eight o'clock in the morning and work on till midnight. The soldiers and sailors acting as stretcher bearers were not under orders, but working on their own initiative. They were "magnificent"—"so tender in moving the patients." They were eager to be of service. "Wherever you went, there were half a dozen boys with hands out to help you." Lieut. Reid, who had a room in the building, was tireless, working day and night without rest. He was efficient, faithful, helpful, always on hand when wanted. When Dr. Codman reorganized the hospital on his own lines, Reid was made adjutant.

Like so many other qualified observers, Mrs. MacDougall bears testimony to the incredible fortitude of the sufferers. The patients were in a dreadful condition. Some were without clothing; many were so blackened that they were mistaken for negroes. One girl had her hair standing out with plaster. During the three weeks that she acted as matron, she never heard a complaint from a patient of being neglected or of a helper of being tired. Here too the spirit of self-abnegation reigned. "There are some worse off than me. Take someone else."

There were two deaths the first night, a child whose lungs had been filled with water, and a returned soldier, who was so bruised and battered as to be unrecognizable. He was brought in unconscious with both legs broken. One patient, a woman, went violently insane.

The story of these two shelters represents in general what went on in all the others. In all, there was the same instantaneous grappling with the unforeseen difficulties. The organization made itself; because where there's a will, there's a way.

In Dartmouth, the four bunk houses of the workmen employed by the Imperial Oil Company were filled by the homeless people, the regular occupants being sent elsewhere. Here the refugees were well treated as they were everywhere. "I don't know what we should have done without them," said one Dartmouth pastor. The company simply adopted these people, saw to their provisioning, etc. in a most generous manner. In the Monastery of the Good Shepherd, the delinquent girls gave up their beds to the homeless ones and slept on the floor.

Halifax is rich in charitable institutions. There is a school for the blind, for the deaf, for delinquent boys, refuges for the old, etc. The Old Ladies' Home was badly shattered by the explosion, but some of the fifty-eight inmates refused to be excited by it; they would not dress hastily or even get up out of bed when called upon to leave the building. They went out in the "grass islands" in Robie Street and sat on chairs borrowed from the surrounding houses. Some wandered off and found shelter in the Armouries or at Camp Hill. At last the matron shepherded her flock back to the dismantled build-

ing where for two days the old ladies sat on chairs in the kitchen, the only habitable portion of the building. It is not surprising that two of the old ladies died and three lost their reason from shock and fright. Eventually a remnant found refuge in the basement of Fort Massey Church, where nineteen beds were crowded in among the furnaces. It was a case of any port in a storm. In addition to those who found shelter in these public buildings, many were taken into private houses. There were few homes in Halifax on the night of December 6th which did not hold more than their regular number of occupants. Complications sometimes ensued. A large hearted family at Fairview with a house to match took no fewer than fifty persons. They were made comfortable in the various bedrooms or on straw shake-downs in the kitchen. Others sat about all night on chairs. One daughter drove the worst injured in to the city hospitals, while the father and a friend stopped the windows and effected repairs.

In the same neighbourhood, a milkman found room for no fewer than eighteen persons in his small house and fed them, refusing to apply to the Relief Committee for provisions for his guests. His answer was, "Can't a man do something?"

Rockingham is a picturesque hamlet on the shore of Bedford Basin, four miles from the city. A large convent school, Mount St. Vincent, in its own grounds is the chief building, and Halifax people have summer cottages there. One of the residents, Mr. R. A. Brenton, saw the refugees streaming out of the stricken city on foot or in every kind of conveyance as if before an invading army, and he dealt promptly with the situation caused thereby. He "commandeered" the village store to secure food supplies; and had the various summer cottages thrown open as shelters, as well as the mansions known as "Sherwood" and the "Wayside Inn." Within this area were at least one hundred and fifty persons, scattered as far as Carney's Lake. They were supplied with food, fuel and clothing. Efficient first aid was given by Mr. Bruce MacDonald. Mr. Brenton sent his own family "up the line" and took into his house six Maltese sailors of the S.S. COLONNE. He gave away clothing and his supply of coal. On his representations, the village grocer supplied every applicant for food with what he needed, keeping a rough account, though without any expectation of ever being paid. The people of Rockingham did their utmost for fellow beings in distress. Everywhere a wonderful spirit of helpfulness was abroad. What happened in this village is simply one more instance of organized relief springing into life wherever needed. In the circumstances, it is difficult to see what more could have been done, or to say that it could have been done better. The measures taken were prompt, generous and rational.

And yet, in spite of every effort, there were hundreds of injured people who in Halifax received no attention and hundreds of others who had no sufficient shelter for days and nights of storm and Arctic cold. They clung to their houses even when they were unfit for habitation. It might have been thought that all would be eager to get away from the devastated area for fear of a repetition of the horrors. But many did not know what relief had been provided for them; others were too proud to apply for charity, or even to let their wants be known; and again, others were dazed with their sudden bereavement and refused to leave what remained of their homes. Mothers are pictured sitting with their children about the unlighted stove, waiting for the husband and father who would never return. Only by snatching up the children and carrying them off could these desolate ones be induced to leave the ruins of their pathetic tenement. These frequent refusals to move greatly complicated the work of relief.

The experience of a lawyer, Mr. C. J. Burchell, K.C., is illuminating. On the day of the explosion he was busy moving wounded to hospitals in his car or transporting doctors and nurses from point to point. He did not reach home until one o'clock in the morning. At half past seven he was called up by telephone and directed to meet doctors and nurses at the South Terminals and take them to Camp Hill. He breakfasted and then went back for more doctors and nurses. At nine or a little after, he reported at the City Hall and was assigned two streets, Kane and Livingstone, from which to remove injured and homeless. He worked at this task all day, until his car stuck in an impassable drift at eight in the evening.

Most of the houses he worked on were "destroyed," but still harboured human beings suffering from more or less serious injuries. In a backyard in Kane Street he found a shack which looked as if it might have been at one time a henhouse. It was a tiny place; but it was the home of John Latter, an old fisherman, and his wife. The woman was badly cut about the head; the blood had matted her hair; but when found, she had not had time to dress her wound or tidy up. This couple had gathered into their poor two room cabin no fewer than eleven persons in greater need than themselves. These included a mother with her four-day old baby as well as two or three small children, and a girl so badly scalded about the legs by water upset from a stove that she could hardly walk. Besides there were others hurt more or less. How they managed to crowd in such narrow quarters seems impossible, but there they were when rescued. Poor as the building was, it was better than exposure to the blizzard that was raging. Perhaps in all Halifax that day there was no more misery packed within such narrow limits. The pluck of the woman with the young baby excited the rescuers' admiration. She was able to walk up the steps of Pine Hill.

The last trip Mr. Burchell made was to Hungry Hill just before dark. His objective was a house which proved to have the whole side blown in and "things . . . so badly tumbled together" that he had to get down on his hands and knees and crawl into the wreckage. He hailed the people supposed to be inside several times before getting any response. At last his hail was answered and he crawled down to where a sergeant and four women were huddled about an oil stove. He took the women away, but the soldier remained as he had to go on duty.

In a house at the corner of West Young and Agricola he found a woman with her three children living in the kitchen of their house. There was no door but a bit of curtain had been stretched over the opening. Mr. Burchell tried three times to induce her to leave the place, but in vain; she was afraid her furniture would be stolen. And it was blizzard weather.

Such cases could be multiplied from the experience of all the rescuers. They present a very feeble and partial image of the total suffering, misery and privation endured by the people of Halifax in the first dreadful days. They show also the system and the thoroughness with which the work of relief was carried out.

Chapter 19

The Rally of the Province

The interests of Halifax the capital and Nova Scotia the province have often been divergent, and at times even antagonistic. Howe's struggle to win responsible government was in a way a quarrel between the city and the country; but if any feeling of old differences yet lingers anywhere, there was no sign or symptom of it in the day of the city's calamity. The rush to help was as prompt, as instinctive, as generous throughout the province as it was in the stricken city itself.

The telegram sent to General Manager Hayes by Mr. W. A. Duff set the powerful machinery of the Canadian Government Railway system operating. On December 6th, no fewer than four separate trains were despatched from Moncton for Halifax. The first of eight cars carried the General Manager, railway officials, doctors, nurses and hospital supplies. The second of nine cars brought the Moncton Fire Brigade. The third brought food supplies and more doctors and nurses. The fourth brought gangs of workmen and gear for clearing away the wreckage on the railway tracks. A train of ten cars from College Bridge brought the Amherst Fire Brigade; and still another train brought doctors and nurses from Sydney and New Glasgow. All these special trains were speeding through the province on the very day of the disaster, each provided with means of help and succour. The best intelligence and energy available were working at high pressure that day in one great task of meeting an emergency.

The prompt action of another railroad man brought help to Halifax from another quarter at the earliest possible moment. As already stated, Mr. George Graham, Manager of the Dominion Atlantic Railway, was breakfasting with his wife and daughter in his private car at North Street Station when the roof crashed down. They all escaped without injury and made their way out of the ruined building into Lockman Street whence they could form some conception of the calamity which had smitten the city, from the sight of the shattered buildings and of so many injured persons. Leaving his wife and daughter on their way to the centre of the city, Mr. Graham started for Rockingham on foot, walking and running. By the shortest route it is at least three miles. He reached it about ten o'clock and sent the following message to Kentville, the divisional point:

"Organize a relief train and send word to Wolfville and Windsor to round up all doctors, nurses and Red Cross supplies possible to obtain. No time to explain details but list of casualties is enormous."

In response to this message, a train was made up which left Kentville shortly before noon with doctors and nurses. One nurse, on being notified, left a smoothing-iron on her best blouse and ran to the station. More doctors and nurses were taken on at Wolfville and still more at Windsor. The only other stop was at Windsor Junction where Dr. DeWitt senior and Miss Nellie DeWitt were transferred to No. 10 train bearing its wounded to Truro. About three o'clock this special from Kentville got to Richmond where some delay occurred. About four, Col. Bell and Col. Phinney came to the train and directed the eager helpers to make their way to the City Hall. They had to walk about half a mile along Campbell Road through the debris and the smoking ruins. They saw unforgettable sights. "In one place the dead were piled up like cordwood." At North Street, motors were waiting to take them to the City Hall. At this point they were distributed among the various hospitals. One of the Kentville doctors testifies: "I was surprised to find a better organization for application of relief for sufferers than I anticipated and the attempt to establish order out of chaos seemed fairly successful. We were distributed by an efficient auto service to the various hospitals where our services were most required."

The urgent telegrams sent out broadcast by Mr. W. A. Duff through the request of the Deputy Mayor had also most important results in prompting various communities to corporate action and in bringing medical help to the city. Two doctors motored all the way from Lunenburg, reaching the city in the afternoon of the 6th and immediately getting to work. The services rendered by these practitioners from the outside was most valuable and very much appreciated. They worked tirelessly day and night, desiring no publicity and getting none. A typical case would be the improvised hospital in the Y.M.C.A. Dr. E. A. Codman came from Boston and organized it according to his own original and admirable system, but the work of attending to the patients was done by Dr. Duncan and Dr. P. R. Ford of Liverpool, N.S., who remained at his post for two weeks. "We could have gone down on our knees and blessed him," said one enthusiastic co-worker. Writing to a Halifax friend under the date January 2nd, 1918, Dr. Codman says: "I received a very nice letter from Mr. Moriarty giving me the resolutions adopted by the Board of Directors. I have never received so much undeserved credit as I have from my Halifax trip, for all the real work was done by you people in the transformation of the Y.M.C.A. building into a hospital."

To give in detail all that was done by the different communities would be impossible within the space allotted. Everywhere was a swift outpouring of generous sympathy which took the practical form of unstinted giving of time, labour, money or money's worth. Windsor made provision to receive a trainload of hospital patients which could not be despatched on account of the weather of Friday. The Red Cross of Wolfville worked three days in gathering clothing and making surgical bandages. It took in and sheltered a number of the refugees, and Acadia University offered the hospitality of its buildings to the School for the Deaf.

Truro is the nearest to Halifax of the larger Nova Scotia towns. It is a beautiful and prosperous place, an important railway and educational centre. It is the seat of the County Academy, the Provincial Normal School, and the Provincial Agricultural College. The news of the disaster reached Truro early and the shock was distinctly felt at nine minutes past nine. Glass was broken in the windows of the hotel and the doors slammed in the Academy. The great exploit of Truro was the astonishingly rapid transformation of three of its public buildings into hospitals on the very day of the disaster, and having them ready for the patients when No. 10 train arrived. Immediately upon the news of the explosion an emergency meeting of the citizens was called by sounding the fire alarm denoting help needed out of town. In the absence of the Mayor, Col. John Stanfield presided. It was decided to turn the Court House, the Academy, and the Firemen's Hall into hospitals or shelters and no time was lost in getting to work. Mr. D. G. Davis, Principal of the Academy, naturally took charge of this part of the work. The boys were sent out to gather cooked food with which a car was soon loaded for Halifax. Beds and bedding were obtained from shops and private houses. The Assembly Room was turned into a ward, and the Cloak Room into a kitchenette. By dusk everything was in readiness and some fifty patients found accommodation here. Not a few were taken into private houses, for kind-hearted people "picked them off the door step" and carried them to their own homes. The Academy cadets rendered most efficient aid. During the two weeks and three days that this hospital remained open, there was only one death. At the end of that time the remaining patients were transferred to the military hospital. The Court House was also swiftly tranformed into a hospital through the energy of Mrs. Eaton and Mrs. John Stanfield. They were notified of their appointment to this task at a quarter past one and, by half past three, they had everything in order. The courtroom itself was used as a woman's ward. There were also a men's ward, a children's ward, a kitchen and an operating room. Here some sixty patients were accommodated. The Court House Hospital did "not cost the town a cent except for drugs."

The Firemen's Hall was used chiefly as a shelter, in the charge of Miss Francis as trained nurse. On account of its nearness to Halifax, Truro received a large number of refugees. On December 7th there were at least 400 destitute persons to care for and a Shelter Committee was formed to deal with the situation.

Nearly all the food used in the emergency hospitals was contributed by citizens or local restaurants. The country people sent in butter, eggs, vegetables, poultry, etc. as free gifts. It was noticed "the poorer people also worked hard and made many sacrifices." Over $8,000 worth was received in voluntary contribution and more than 200 people were fitted out with new clothing. The laundry bill for three weeks was $400. There were ten deaths in the Truro hospitals and patients were discharged as they improved and were able to leave. Just before Christmas the remaining patients were removed to the Willow Street School, which had been converted into a hospital. It was a church-like building not the most suitable for the accommodation of the sick, but it was made habitable and kept spotlessly clean. At first it accommodated between 80 and 90 patients. The other buildings had to be taken over for their usual work.

An American doctor who visited these hospitals writes: "The Town of Truro in my opinion comes in for a good share of credit for the excellent organization of medical care which I found on my visit to the town. Cleanliness of the wounds and freedom from sepsis contrasted strongly with those we left in Halifax. The doctors as well as the townsfolk showed the greatest enthusiasm and interest in their work and the results obtained bespoke the attention that the injured had received."

The towns of Nova Scotia have not all been run in one mould. Each has its individuality, but perhaps no one has more character, more strongly marked than New Glasgow and that character is emphatically Scottish. In the days of lumbering and wooden ship building the town thrived and when wooden ship building failed, it turned its attention to steel industries which have grown and thrived. The town has prospered exceedingly during the war on munitions contracts.

The distress expressed here for the stricken city was very genuine and sympathy manifested itself promptly in the most practical ways. The special train bearing doctors, nurses and firemen with provisions for two days was ready to start at eleven o'clock, one hour after the call for help had been received. It reached Richmond about four, and at 5:40 the party reported at the City Hall and the doctors and nurses were distributed among the various hospitals in Halifax and Dartmouth. More doctors and nurses were gathered up by the special train from Sydney which passed through New Glasgow later in the night. One doctor and one nurse were detached to give help in the hospitals of Truro. On the way down, there had been a conference on board the first emergency train as to the most practical measure of relief which could be undertaken for the benefit of Halifax. It was decided that the best thing would be an emergency hospital in New Glasgow and Col. Cantley was asked to take the matter up with the authorities of both places. Much time was consumed in necessary consultations with the city fathers at the City Hall, with the General Officer Commanding No. 6 District, with the Principal Medical Officer, with the General Manager of the Canadian Government Railways; but in the end Colonel Cantley had his plans complete. He motored out to Rockingham at eleven o'clock that Thursday night, and telegraphed to the Mayor of New Glasgow that the best way to assist Halifax was to turn the West Side School into a hospital of a hundred beds. A special train of five cars would start on Friday with the patients to fill it.

No time was lost in New Glasgow. Colonel Cantley's message was received shortly after eleven o'clock. By two o'clock the plans had been made, and by seven o'clock the next morning, Friday, carpenters began taking the desks out of the new school which had been selected as a hospital. By nine o'clock a gang of cleaners, mainly volunteers, and including pupils of the High School, began scrubbing the walls and floors. Plumbers had come in with the carpenters to make the necessary installations. Placards asking for cots were placed upon the trams, and transportation was arranged for these from the City Hall. By 6 o'clock that evening, a hospital of a hundred beds was in absolute readiness and a kitchen was in operation. Friday will be long remembered as the "day of the blizzard," but the blizzard was not allowed to hinder the good work. On Saturday, the cot capacity of the hospital was increased to a hundred and sixty and the plumbing was complete. Everything was in readiness even to the temperature charts for patients who had not yet arrived, and their night clothes laid out on the beds.

The West Side School is a large brick structure standing on an eminence about half a mile "across the river." It is spacious, airy, with high ceilings admitting plenty of sunlight, altogether an ideal place for a hospital. Over three thousand dollars were spent in fitting it up. Three first class bathrooms were installed and a room was built for the use of the Superintendent. Many electrical appliances were donated by the Pictou Electric Light Co. which supplied all current free. The kitchen was in the charge of a trained dietitian and the various churches took day about in looking after the kitchen, cooking the meals, sweeping the wards and corridors. As a hospital of a hundred beds, it was ready on Friday evening. But the patients did not come, nor any word of them. Great was the disappointment when Colonel Cantley stepped off the train on Saturday with only two patients to show. The reasons why were simple. The special train of five cars was ready at the South Terminals at noon, provisioned and waiting for its passengers. An effort was made to fill it, but only two or three ambulances could be mustered to transfer the injured from the hospitals. It was a day of storm, snow fell heavily, the fierce wind piled it into unpassable drifts. Transportation broke down. The ambulance available actually made three or four trips with patients to the train, but the weather was so severe that they had to be taken back whence they came. Colonel Cantley telegraphed the facts to New Glasgow, but the telegram was not received until Sunday evening. No one who saw the conditions in the Halifax telegraph offices will be surprised at the delay.

Being Scotch, New Glasgow is not easily turned aside from any determined course of action; now it was not to be balked in its good intentions. On Sunday afternoon an informal meeting of the leading citizens was held at which it was decided to make a second effort to give the help that was so sorely needed. A special car was attached to a working train which started at one o'clock with bales of clothing to the value of $2,500, which had been purchased in response to a request from Halifax that very day. The train reached Halifax the next morning. Colonel Cantley and R. M. MacGregor, M.P.P., set out in search of authorization. After hunting from pillar to post they found the Principal Medical Officer at the Nova Scotia Technical College, the distributing point for Red Cross supplies to the various hospitals.

The plan agreed upon was to begin with the patients in the OLD COLONY American Hospital ship lying at the Dock Yard then to take them from Camp Hill and the Victoria General Hospital. A troop ship was expected about this time from overseas and the train which is always in waiting to transfer the wounded soldiers was available. It consisted of three military hospital cars, two colonist cars, one day coach as well as the private car from New Glasgow—ample accommodation for a hundred and fifty patients. As at least one meal had to be served on the train, the commissariat was stocked up with bread, soups, etc.

The train was ready at eight o'clock on Monday night. When the first patients began to arrive, Mr. Don

Fraser and Mr. MacGregor were alone at North Street Station which by this time had been cleared of all the wreckage. The various improvised ambulances drove up to the station grill and these gentlemen dragged the sleighs to the doors of the carriages and lifted the patients on board. In the background they had noticed men with tripods. They were the inevitable "movie" photographers making pictures of the "first patients taken out of Halifax to Toronto." The thoughtful Americans on board the OLD COLONY refused to allow their patients to leave without sufficient warm clothing. This, Mr. MacGregor obtained from the depot at the Masonic Hall. It was necessary to obtain the consent of the patients to be taken away and some refused to leave at the last moment. Altogether eighty were taken on board. The train left Halifax at 3:00 p.m. and reached New Glasgow at half past ten; with it returned the indispensable local doctors who had worked so hard in Halifax. As on the previous Saturday, the station was roped off and comfortable vehicles were ready to transfer the patients. Within an hour the work was done and they were all comfortably housed in the West Side School. Nowhere did the victims of the disaster receive better medical attention or kinder treatment.

The work was done with characteristic thoroughness. Within twenty-four hours an emergency hospital had been created. In addition to the cots with their necessary linen, etc., there was an operating room made ready with four tables; there was a dispensary with a full stock of dressings and drugs; there was a diet kitchen with two ranges and "jacket" heaters, ensuring an ample supply of hot water; and there was a lavatory accommodation with bathrooms both on the main and upper floors. The whole building was wired and electric connections made both for heat and light.

There were many donations of money, clothing, etc. The country folk sent in gifts of butter, cream, eggs and poultry. On being discharged from the hospital, every patient was completely equipped with clothing. Even spectacles were bought for such as needed them from a private relief fund in the hands of the Superintendent. There were six wards accommodating eighty-six patients. On December 31st there were only forty remaining, but these were all serious septic cases. At Christmas there was a tree for the patients, furnished with the proceeds of a dollar subscription which amounted to $325. That Christmas will be long remembered by every patient who was fortunate enough to be the guest of New Glasgow that day. One eye witness reported that the hospital looked like a "grocer's shop and a fruit shop," and one of the beneficiaries testified, "They couldn't have done more for us if we had been paying the highest price of board."

The return of the New Glasgow doctors on the Tuesday was imperative. They had been working day and night with few intervals of rest; they were needed not only at home but on the train itself to look after the patients. The experience of Dr. G. H. Cox, oculist of New Glasgow, who came on the first relief train, is typical and illuminating. He was just leaving his own house to go and perform an operation at Stellarton when he learned of the explosion. He returned from his work at Stellarton to find a special train made up, carrying the fire engine, 3,000 feet of hose, forty firemen as well as doctors and nurses. He rushed home, filled his bag with dressings, chloroform, etc., and caught the train just as it was moving out at 11:30. Doctors and firemen were picked up at Stellarton and Westville. At Milford they passed No. 10 train carrying wounded to Truro. They reached Africville about five o'clock, got out and walked along the track and then found the road, making their way through slush, mud, and wreckage and over mutilated corpses. The thick smoke was streaked here and there with jets of flame from the ruins of cellars. Now and then the wind lifted the pass of smoke a little and showed heaps of bodies, which soldiers were putting into carts. It was like ''going from one corner of hell to another,'' like Pliny's description of the flight from Pompeii. Richmond suggested Dante's Inferno to another well-read physician from Kentville.* At North Street, motors took the party to the City Hall where they were assigned to various posts. Dr. Cox was assigned to Camp Hill. He began operating at half past six and stopped at half past seven next morning for a rest of only three hours. He operated at first in the kitchen, where the buffet was running.

Three New Glasgow firemen, Daley, Douglas and Silliker, practical men, who came to Camp Hill to do what they could, ran a coffee canteen in the diningroom during the entire night. The patience and fortitude of the ''cases,'' their tenderness for one another were wonderful. They did not mind having their eyes taken out, and were willing to walk to and from the operating table, but this Dr. Cox would not permit. Everyone had chloroform, except where cocaine alone was necessary. He went all over the building, along the rows of mattresses and cots, passing those eyes that looked ''bright'' and attending only to the most serious cases and those that were nearest at hand. Some faces were torn to tatters, ''as if clawed by a tiger.'' The wounds were stuffed with plaster and dirt. Some eyes were literally ''bags of glass.'' Sometimes an eye would be forced up into the middle of the forehead. Eyelids were torn to shreds and had to be patched. There were cases of facial paralysis owing to the nerves being severed. There were seriously mutilated noses and throats to be treated. One woman with her face blown away had been found by her husband in the ruins of their home nursing a dead baby. During the first night it was impossible to keep a record of the cases. There were more pressing needs. Dr. Cox found ''plenty of good assistance,'' and he admired how quickly Camp Hill was ''licked into shape.'' By Friday morning he had gone all over the cases on the lower floor of the hospital and took three hours' rest which he sorely needed, as he is a man of slight physique and not robust. By the afternoon he was able to have the use of a regular operating room, with trained nurses and proper appliances. He worked until the following Tuesday when he returned to New Glasgow.

* See the Personal Testimony of Dr. W. B. Moore, p. 106.

75

The Documents

COPY OF TELEGRAM TO PROVINCIAL PREMIERS

& Dartmouth

The Capital City of this Province has been overtaken
with an appalling disaster. You will see the Public
Appeal for help in the Press. The Province of Nova Scotia,
while doing its full duty in the emergency, nevertheless
invites, and will welcome, the most generous aid from the
sister Provinces.

Prem Prov

Premier of P. E. I.,   Charlottetown
W. E. Barrett

Hon. W. E. Foster
St. John

Sir Lomer Gouin
Quebec

Hon. W. H. Hearst
Toronto

Hon. T. C. Norris
Winnipeg

Hon. W. M. Martin
Regina

Hon. Premier Charles Stewart,
Edmonton,
Alta.

Hon. H. C. Brewster
Victoria, B. C.

Form 2903 D

WESTERN UNION CABLEGRAM

NEWCOMB CARLTON, PRESIDENT

GEORGE W. E. ATKINS, VICE-PRESIDENT   BELVIDERE BROOKS, VICE-PRESIDENT

CLASS OF SERVICE DESIRED	
	Full Rate
	Half Rate Deferred
x	Cable Letter
	Week End Letter

Patrons should mark an X opposite the class of service desired; OTHERWISE THE CABLEGRAM WILL BE TRANSMITTED AT FULL RATES.

Number
Time Filed
Number of Words

Send the following Cablegram, subject to the terms on back hereof, which are hereby agreed to

_____ 191___

To   Blomidon,

London.

Estimated fifteen hundred people killed and many thousands injured. Fifteen thousand homeless. City north of North Street comprising area of two square miles practically destroyed. All buildings in City and Dartmouth badly wrecked. Relief trains arriving from United States and Canada with surgeons and nurses. Situation well in hand.

Murray.

Charge P. S. O.

CANADIAN PACIFIC R'Y. CO.'S TELEGRAPH
TELEGRAM

FORM T. D. 1

CABLE CONNECTIONS TO ALL PARTS OF THE WORLD

J. McMILLAN, Manager Telegraphs, Montreal.

FRA 53 A 653 exa

CP Toronto Ont Dec 7-17

Hon G H Murray

Halifax NS

Government of Ontario on behalf of people of ontario sending tonight to corporation of Halifax two carloads assorted glass with putty and man to superintend. One car beaverboard with nails one car tar sheeting with nails six thousand sheets and three thousand six hundred pillow slips provincial health officer colonel McCullough and Provincial sanitary engineer dallyn leaving tonight to give their assistance

3.32p   430p   R A Pyne   Acting Prime Minister

CANADIAN PACIFIC R'Y. CO.'S TELEGRAPH
TELEGRAM

FORM T. D. 1

CABLE CONNECTIONS TO ALL PARTS OF THE WORLD

J. McMILLAN, Manager Telegraphs, Montreal.

B112RAP-37--3ex

ReginaSask--decr7th

723

Hon.Geo.A.Murray   Halifaxns

On   behalf of the government and the people of the province of Saskatchewan I extend sincere sympaty to the sufferers in the Halifax disaster please suggest how this province can best be of assistance

W M Martin

Premier of Saskatchewan

733pm   Not ans'd

Still photograph from newsreel of explosion, probably shot mid-December. There are several 16mm copies of this early newsreel showing the devastation and relief work, including some sadly deteriorated footage of the Hydrostone neighbourhood rebuilding project. 16mm copies are in the collections of the Public Archives of Nova Scotia and the Nova Scotia Museum. The CBC have a copy of the Nova Scotia Museum copy. A 35mm 1954 copy of the original negative is in the collection of the Public Archives of Nova Scotia.

COPY OF TELEGRAM FROM HIS MAJESTY KING GEORGE V.

TO THE GOVERNOR GENERAL.

Buckingham Palace.

6th December 1917.

Most deeply regret to hear of serious explosion at
Halifax resulting in great loss of life and property.
Please convey to people of Halifax where I have spent so
many happy times my true sympathy in this grievous calamity.

(Sd.). GEORGE R. I.

Still photograph from newsreel made after the explosion.

CANADIAN PACIFIC R'Y. CO.'S TELEGRAPH
TELEGRAM
FORM T. D. 1

CABLE CONNECTIONS TO ALL PARTS OF THE WORLD
J. McMILLAN, Manager Telegraphs, Montreal.

136 RAO GOVT 42 GOVT

LONDON DEC 8/17

PREMIER MURRAY

    HALIFAX

IN THE UNPARRALLED DISASTER WHICH HAS OVERTAKEN HALIFAX YOU HAVE

MY DEPPEST SYMPATHY HALIFAX AND NEWFOUNDLAND HAVE

CLOSE TIES KNIT IN THE CENTURIES WE WILL ALL BE WITH YOU IN

ASSISTING IN YOUR COMMON NATION AFFLICTION

E P MORRIS

CANADIAN PACIFIC R'Y. CO.'S TELEGRAPH
TELEGRAM
FORM T. D. 1

All Messages are received by this Company for transmission, subject to the terms and conditions printed on their Blank Form No. 2, which
terms and conditions have been agreed to by the sender of the following message. This is an unrepeated message, and is delivered by request
of the sender under these conditions.

J. McMILLAN, Manager Telegraphs, Montreal.

Ra G118   O 49   **IF YOU CAN'T ENLIST—INVEST!**

   Edmonton Alta Dec 11 - 1917

HON G.H. Murray

   Premier Nova Scotia, Halifax N.S.

People of Alberta sympathize deeply with sister Province of Novascotia

in fearful calamity to your capital city have taken immediate steps

towards organization of province for aid to the sufferers expect

hearty response from public in addition to government aid within next

few days. When funds will be forwarded.

147am.   Charles Stewart

HERALD

HONEST ADVERTISING.

Nova S
Win-th
Newsp

EMBER 10, 1917

VOLUME XLIII,

MOMEN

Practically All the Germans in Halifax Are To Be Arrest

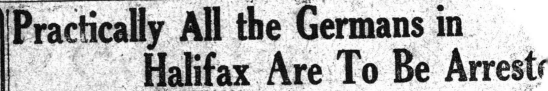

ONE MILLION DOLLARS FROM DOMINION GOVERNMENT

Sir Robert Borden, who was in Halifax yesterday and leaves this morning to spend Monday in Kings County, announced that, pending full consideration of the needs of those who have suffered by the appalling calamity which has befallen Halifax, and, to a lesser degree, the neighboring town of Dartmouth, the Canadian Government has appropriated one million dollars for immediate relief. The amount thus provided will be immediately at the disposal of the Citizens' Finance Committee, or such other constituted authority as may be entrusted with the duty of administering the relief fund.

Sir Robert expects to arrive in Montreal on Wednesday and to be in Ottawa on Thursday.

THE MANAGING EXECUTIVE WITH FULL POWER

The citizens meeting on Saturday night appointed a permanent committee of twenty-two and these named an executive to be the cabinet and directing force. This executive consists of R. T. MacIlreith, G. S. Campbell, Hon. R. G. Beazley, D. MacGillivary, A. E. Jones, H. R.
Dennis, W. Black, on, G. F.

Sixteen of
Taken Into C
Night and

The Deash Roll
to Grow and Now
Believed the Numb
Will Pass 2,000.

Sir Robert Borden
nounces $1,000,000
Dominion Governm
For Immediate Rel

HALIFAX, Decemb
ng upon in
tions   ilitary a
ties,   olic
han
sale
dent in
been a nu
Germ

d the old
and the
use and
peared in
t yet fully
ge to ship-
of a very
ors every-
in many
ses were
which at
ce of the
class and
, and fire
the explos-
een hundred
thus been

SURVIVORS — MONT BLANC

MONT BLANC survivors. Mrs. Aggie Marsh was standing outside her home, her three-week old baby in her arms, it was such a bright sunny day. She could see smoke from a ship in the harbour. As she stood enjoying the sunshine, a row boat beached close by and its occupants ran towards her. She did not recognize them but noted the great hurry and anxiety, even fright, in their movements. They were shouting at her, gesticulating wildly and pointing to the woods. Were they crazy? Suddenly the nearest grabbed her baby from her arms and ran towards the trees; his colleagues following on his heels. Furiously Aggie screamed and ran, chasing after them, determined to rescue her child from these lunatics. The straggle of runners reached the woods in time to be saved from the blast and debris.

WEST HOUSE MUSEUM OF PHOTOGRAPHY. AGGIE MARSH INCIDENT RELATED IN INTERVIEW WITH BERYL RIVOALLAN

OPPOSITE: HALIFAX HERALD LIMITED

NO: **19190**
25984/17

King House Jamaica.

27

December 1917.

Sir,

I have the honour to confirm the telegram which was sent to you on the 19th Instant as follows :-

CODE:-

Landbaron of Jamaica passed the following resolution begins subserial Council at its first sitting adiantando dreadful calamity records its deepest sympathy trackways citizens of Halifax immingled appalling largish and heavy diacassia property cargoblock the recent diasatrous explosion and hereby votes the smellmuch pigeontoed adrogated the sufferers ends the amount is being tacsonia cabalgador.

TRANSLATION :-

Legislative Council of Jamaica passed the following resolution. Begins. That the Council at its first sitting after the dreadful calamity records its deepest sympathy with the citizens of Halifax in the appalling loss of life and heavy destruction of property caused by the recent disastrous explosion and hereby votes the sum of £1,000 in aid of the sufferers. Ends. The amount is being transmitted by cable.

I have the honour to be,

Sir,

Your most obedient, humble servant,

Governor.

His Excellency,

The Lieutenant-Governor,

Nova Scotia.

International communications were often coded because of the war. This is a coded telegram from the Governor of Jamaica and its translation.

HALIFAX DISASTER RECORD OFFICE

ARCHIBALD MACMECHAN, B. A., (TOR.,) PH. D. (J. H. U.,) F. R. S. C.

DIRECTOR

CIRCULAR No. 1

This Office has been established by the Executive Committee of the Halifax Relief Committee in order to collect material for a comprehensive report or history of the recent disaster. Its object is to ascertain the facts.

The importance of this undertaking must be evident to all. Even more apparent is its difficulty, indeed, impossibility without the hearty co-operation of the entire community. Information is urgently desired as to:

1. Phenomena of the explosion; sound; impressions; testimony of eye-witnesses; effects of glass; freaks; etc, in Halifax and within the Province.

2. Personal narratives of escapes.

3. Rescue and relief work on the 6th, 7th, 8th, 9th, of December, particularly narratives of doctors, nurses, soldiers and sailors.

4. Names and addresses of all those who assisted in relief, or gave voluntary aid in the hospitals, or sheltered homeless people.

5. Damage done to various institutions and establishments, with particulars of injuries to *personnel*, and of material damage; measures taken to make good damage done, date at which normal business was resumed, etc.

Suggestions

1. All communications should be written or typed on one side of paper only.

2. Heads of institutions and business firms are desired to dictate their statements to their stenographers, or typists.

3. For purposes of record, notes, memoranda, etc., are almost as useful as statements written out in full.

NOTE: Confidential statements may be made. Unwelcome publicity will be avoided.

Representatives of this office can call for statements, if desired.

Appointments may be made with the Director at Room 24, Chronicle Building.

HALIFAX DISASTER RECORD OFFICE

P. O. BOX 25

HALIFAX, N. S.

The Halifax Disaster Record Office was opened on December 17th. This circular was its first publication and was widely distributed.

4/3 [signature] 1917

LIST OF PATIENTS IN VARIOUS HOSPITALS, DEC. 10TH.

Camp Hill	277
Victoria General	135
Knights of Columbus	12
Halifax Infirmary	50
Children's Hospital	12
Pine Hill	70
St. Mary's College	114
Station Hospital	30
Bellevue	152
Hurley Crest	2
Dr. Mader's	2
Y.M.C.A.	66
Halifax Ladies College	86
Total	**1008**

Executive Information Committee.

[signature] ....Chairman.

Fotocopy

After the blizzard. A still photograph from a newsreel.

Weather Reports

Thursday, December 6th
　　9 a.m. Fair. Frozen ground. Light N.W. wind. No precipitation. Temperature: max. 39.2, min. 16.8.

Friday, December 7th
　　9 a.m. N.E. wind, velocity 19. Snow falling. At noon N.W. gale. Afternoon, blizzard conditions. 9 p.m. N.W. wind, velocity 34. Precipitation 16.0 in. snow. Temperature: max. 32.2, min. 24.8

Saturday, December 8th
　　9 a.m. N.W. wind, velocity 20. Intermittent sunshine. 9 p.m. N.W. wind, velocity 11. Precipitation 1.2 snow (in a.m.). Temperature: max. 29.8, min. 15.

Sunday, December 9th
　　9 a.m. S.E. gale, velocity 39. Streets icy and almost impassable. 9 p.m. S.W. wind, velocity 27. Precipitation .99 rainfall (1.40 a.m. till noon). Temperature: max. 50.41, min. 14.6.

Monday, December 10th
　　9 a.m. S.W. wind, velocity 11. Afternoon, blizzard (worst in years). Kneedeep drifts. 9 p.m. W. wind, velocity 20. Precipitation 5.6 snowfall (2 p.m. till 5.40 p.m.). Temperature: max. 34.2, min. 16.8.

Tuesday, December 11th
　　9 a.m. Clear. W. wind, velocity 18. 9 p.m. W. wind, velocity 11. No precipitation. Temperature: max. 18.2, min. 6.6.

Wednesday, December 12th
　　9 a.m. N.W. wind, velocity, 15. 9 p.m. N.E. wind, velocity 3. No precipitation. Temperature: max. 17, min. 2.

From information kindly supplied by D. L. Hutchinson, director of the Saint John (N.B.) observatory, and F. B. Ronnan, Halifax Station. All temperatures in degrees fahrenheit.

"Social Leadership"

"It is the events of the first few hours which are of special interest to the sociologist. The word most descriptive of the first observable phenomenon was leadership. The soldiers were foremost in the work of rescue, of warning, of protection, of transportation and of food distribution. But the earliest leadership that could be called social, arising from the public itself, was that on the part of those who had no family ties, much of the earliest work being done by visitors in the city. The others as a rule ran first to their homes to discover if their own families were in danger. From this body in a short while however many came forward to join in the activities of relief.

　　As already said those with no social, family or property ties were among the first to begin relief work. But many of these started early simply because they were present where need arose. Many indeed of the uninjured folk at a distance seemed unable to realize the terribleness of the immediate need in the stricken area. In fact, owing to the collapse of communication they did not for an appreciable time discover that there was an area more stricken than their own, and devoted themselves to cleaning up glass and the like. But within a quarter of an hour a hospital ship had sent ashore two landing parties with surgeons and emergency kits. With almost equal dispatch the passengers of an incoming train—the railroad terminal at the time being in the north end of the city—were on hand, and were among the earliest first-aid workers. One, a Montreal man, was known individually to have rendered first aid to at least a half hundred of the wounded."

Both excerpts are from *Catastrophe and Social Change: A Sociological Survey of the Halifax Explosion* **by Dr. Samuel Prince.**

... colour Walnut age 2 8'

Jimmy Conrod
slightly burned leg. age 3½

New Crowdis
slightly bad cuts on body
eyes injured, it is hoped not
permanently. Badly cut about
face and throat, one wound
exposing the jugular vein.
serial wound.

Donald Crowdis
Walnut age 4

James Crowdis
Walnut age 6

Mrs. Mr. Crowdis
Walnut

Gordon Hollis
slightly cut and bruised
about face. also suffering from shock. age 11

... badly cut about face and
throat.

Baby Bottanio
burnt about face and arms
and also with a bad cut on
both lips and chin.

three grown up Bottanio girls
Walnut.

small Bottanio boy
Walnut

Mrs Davey
minor cuts about face
and throat.

Dorothy Davey, aged about 6
Walnut.

Mrs S? ...
his wife.

Baby Green, aged 3 or 4 mos
slight cuts, and fractured
Walnut

J. MacEldoney (2)

Personal Testimony

Jessie MacEldoney

Com? to me in H.D. R.O. Dec. 20. 1917

Wm Gunn (& Mrs. Gunn) retired J.C.R. conductor — lives next door to Macaloney — brought up (no children) Mrs. Wm Cameron living in Richmond — Ida Gunn (adopted in infancy) — also brought up W. G. nephew Fred Gunn & Charles Colbett — Mrs. Will Cameron killed in ruins of house — husband & area then & Dorothy killed

B. (about 11 yrs old) also Father & — & & — hurt: son Gordon the son (yrs 35 hospital: — Fred Gunn at Fairview business employ — of J.C.R.) — in bed, came home from late run — conscious of girls — went to Richmond to Ida — unaided — very fond of bodies out took the two bodies found to comfort bodies

lay side of roadway — unable to get conveyance — trying to Fairview — Mrs Cameron & daughter killed meanwhile — Mrs. C. by splinter of (axe) in right light of neck &, cut beside — Dorothy's head badly cut — forehead broken — no slack of suffering on other face of — f. had walked back these faces — asked neighbor to Fairview — horse & for loan of to bring to Fairview (3 little girls: 7th Day Adventist wife) I was refused "His horse was slippery — was the reason alleg? the horse refused was of home to convey Mrs. (onward) to hospital. Refused on the same ground "Horse was slippery" (Kathleen M. saw this! Gunn finally obtained fish — wagon in Richmond & brought bodies to Fairview some two in

**Notes by Jessie MacAloney of interviews with survivors
for the Halifax Disaster Record Office.**

Memoranda

1.

Con'd by Mrs. Best P.O. Dep.
at lunch Dec. 18.

wife Thomas Graham Pts.
(Press Cards Dept) went all
over town, as far as Arm
Bridge giving aid — wounds
were carried as far as A.B.
on alarm of ?second explosion — true 1?.a.m (?)
N.B. interviewed.

Charles P. Sullivan Railway
mail Clerk res. Maynard St.
In Yarmouth on Dec. 6. (like
about 40 others) eager to
get to Hx — "would have
bought a Train" — did obtain
a special.

C.P.S. did get home — found
his wife well & helped
into rescue work helped
to straight through until
Sunday — turned up on Monday at Best's office asking
for "orders" — B. "Never mind
orders". man broken, hysterical

Memoranda 2   Dec.19

crying — dirty — eyes sunken
in his head — the
cheek and jaw bones show-
ing— It is B's belief that
he had not had a square
meal since the previous
Wednesday. B. took him
with many protests to Maders'
great difficulty to get him to
Café (tried Hotel). It steadies him
the Hotel) and coffee.
with food
Sullivan helped to fill
a truck with 60 dead
bodies.

Best will send him to me.

Halifax Relief Committee

HEADQUARTERS: CITY CLUB BUILDING

PRIVATE PHONE EXCHANGE
CONNECTING DEPARTMENTS

HALIFAX, Dec. 15/17 191

NOVA SCOTIA

Fred. Mathers, Esq.,

Halifax, N.S.

Dear Sir:

With further reference to your cable of the 10th
inst. we have been able to locate the following people:

Dowling--75 Maynard St. O.K.

Jenkins 62.Maynard St. O.K.

Elliott family--57 Gottingen St O.K.

Ellard family--28 London St. O.K.

Cameron--182 North St. O.K.

Donovan--92 Bloomfield St. O.K. gone to Sydney

Elford-- 41 Bloomfield St. O.K.

Hennessey family--29 Macara St O.K. reported gone
to Truro.

Dellapinna--2 Kent St. O.K.

Hockley--412 Robie St. O.K.

Hayes--141 Argyle St. O.K.

Clarke--4 Bland St. O.K.

Lee family--11 Maynard St. O.K.

Edmonds--90 West Young St. Mrs Edmonds at
Acadian Hotel. Mr Edmonds in Hospital

Ryan, Mr & Mrs at Acadian Hotel and Mrs. Ryan,
Jr. at Acadian Hotel. Elizabeth, daughter of
Harry Ryan dead. Rest O.K.

Fennerty--214 Agricola St. George Fennerty age 16
dead. Thos F. injured, not serious. Rest O.K.

Melvin--255 Maynard St. Ethel killed. Rest O.K.

Stelling family--94 Seymour St. O.K.

Folkins--180 Robie St. O.K.

Ash family--203 Brunswick St. O.K.

Boreham O.K.

Coulstring--879 Barrington St. Alex injured, not
serious. Rest O.K.

Buxstead, 207 North St. Ted seriously injured.
Others O. K.

Carr--205 Lockman (1023 Barrington) O.K.

265 North Rd
Dec 23rd Ashton gate
Bristol
England

Dear Sir
Could you give me
any news about my
Son & his family.
I have called to them
Dec 8th as soon as I
read of the Disaster
but cannot get any
answer. I am over here
from Toronto. My

2

Husband is in France
& my other Boy in
St Thomas Hospital
with his right foot
off & other wounds.
I am nearly ill
worrying over them
in Halifax not know-
ing if they are dead
or alive. A reply
would be grateful
to a anxious Mother
Yours truly
Florence S. Holm

One of the many letters received by the Halifax Relief Committee. Every effort was made to answer all such requests.

The Chairman,
Adjourned meeting of December 21st.

Sir:

      The undersigned Committee, appointed at a meeting held

in the Executive Council Chamber on December 21st, to consider

and report upon the form of Commission proposed to take over

and carry on all work instituted and to be undertaken in con-

nection with the rebuilding of Halifax and vicinity and the re-

habilitation of citizens following the destruction of life and

property by the disaster of December 6th, beg leave to report

as follows:

    1. Your Committee's first act was to call in the Mayors of
       Halifax and Dartmouth, who thereafter attended all the
       meetings of the Committee.

    2. Your Committee recommends that the Federal Government be
       requested to immediately institute a full and exhaustive
       inquiry by competent authority into all the causes that
       led up to the explosion of December 6th, 1917. And fur-
       ther that the responsibility for the circumstances which
       permitted the collision between the S. S. "Imo" and the
       S. S. "Mont Blanc" in the Narrows of Halifax Harbor on
       that date be fixed.

    3. That a commission of not less than three or more than
       five members be appointed by the Federal Government,
       to hold office until its work is completed.

    4. Your Committee did not as a Committee secure an inter-
       view with the visiting federal Cabinet ministers, but
       different members of your Committee, in conversation with
       these ministers, found that they believed a Commission
       should be appointed with wide scope and powers to deal with
       the questions which have arisen and will arise in connection
       with the matter.

    5. Your Committee concur in this opinion that the powers of
       the Commission should be wide. They should be authorized
       to take over and carry on under their direction the work
       now being done by the Halifax Relief Committee, including:
         (a) The work of furnishing temporary relief.
         (b) The support of those incapacitated.

(c) The maintenance of those dependent on people who lost their lives.

(d) Compensation for injury to property and person, and loss of life.

(e) Reconstruction of devasted area, including any change of location deemed necessary.

(f) Rehabilitation of citizens who have so suffered in health or property as to render assistance of this nature necessary.

6. That to such extent as may be necessary in the opinion of the Commission, so far as it relates to the devasted areas, the Commission be vested with all powers possessed by the Mayors, Wardens, Councils and other public bodies including public officials appointed by or under the provision of existing City Charter, muncipal and civic bodies, Board of Health, etc., with any necessary supplementary powers.

7. That in addition to the above, without intention to restrict the generalities of paragraph 5, the Commission should have power:

(a) To enter upon and clean up all properties, in order that public health may be conserved.

(b) To condemn and raze all buildings not in their opinion worth repairing.

(c) To make temporary repairs.

(d) To provide temporary housing.

(e) To appraise and estimate damage.

(f) To act as public administrators.

(g) To expropriate.

(h) To receive, appropriate and expend all contributions public or otherwise.

All of which is respectfully submitted.

Approved.

The Rotary Club of Charlottetown

"HE PROFITS MOST WHO SERVES BEST"

W. H. TIDMARSH, PRES'T.
H. M. VANBUSKIRK, VICE PRES'T.
WALTER S. GRANT, SECRETARY
W. A. STEWART, TREASURER

DIRECTORS
J. R. BURNETT
J. O. HYNDMAN
A. A. POMEROY

SERGT. AT ARMS
J. E. MCLARTY

CHARLOTTETOWN, P. E. ISLAND
CANADA

January 24th, 1918.

WHEREAS a state of war exists between the British Empire, France et als, against Germany and her allies, and

WHEREAS the Dominion of Canada as an integral portion of the Empire is in a state of war, and

WHEREAS owing to this state of war, the City of Halifax, in the Province of Nova Scotia suffered on December 6th, 1917, tremendous loss of life and property, due to the explosion of a transport laden with munition of war, and

WHEREAS at the time of the disaster the navigable waters of Halifax Harbour were under the direct Control of Officials of the Dominion Government, and

WHEREAS the Port of Halifax is a National Port, and is being employed for National uses and purposes, and it's benefits being enjoyed by every Province in Canada all the Provinces are entitled to bear in the loss, and

WHEREAS the only equitable way to distribute the loss is through the Dominion Treasury, BE IT THEREFORE

RESOLVED that in the opinion of the Rotary Club of Charlottetown the Dominion Government should bear the entire cost of and make full and ample monetary provisions for the rehabilitation of the City of Halifax, and BE IT FURTHER

RESOLVED that a copy of this resolution be forwarded to Sir Robert Borden, Prime Minister of Canada, to the Premiers of the Provinces of Canada, requesting them to use their influence to further the object of this resolution.

The Governor General of Canada and his wife, the Duke and Duchess of Devonshire, visited Halifax in mid-December. In the above photograph taken on December 21st, the Duke can be seen (centre) surrounded by officials and members of the V.A.D. and the Halifax Relief Committee. The meeting was held at the premises of F. B. McCurdy, stockbrokers. Photograph by W. G. MacLaughton, a Halifax photographer best known for his panorama photographs of the devastation.

JOHN E. WOOLLEY, Chairman
JAY N. WHIPPLE, Business Manager
PHILIP BARRY, Assignment Editor
WILLIAM J. CARR, Managing Editor
WALTER E. DONALDSON, Managing Editor
JAMES M. PETICOLAS, Managing Editor

TELEPHONE 7100
YALE STATION
NEW HAVEN, CONN.

February 3, 1918.

Mr. Ralph P. Bell, Chairman,

    Relief Committee,

        Halifax,

            Nova Scotia,

                Canada.

Dear Sir:

    Would you be so kind as to write a few words for pub-
lication in the YALE DAILY NEWS on the relief work in Halifax
after the terrible disaster. The NEWS conducted a campaign, for
clothes to aid the sufferers in your city, among the University
men. The collection was forwarded through the kindness of the
New Haven Red Cross.

    Consequently we know the men here will be interested
in the work which they feel they have in a very small way aided.

    Thanking you very much for anything you may write on
this subject, and wishing you success in your fine work, I am

        Yours very truly,

        Hervey P. Clark

RECEIVED 1918 FEB 8

102

February 11, 1918

Harvey P. Clark, Esq.,
Care Yale News,
New Haven, Conn.

Dear Sir:

In acknowledging yours of February 3rd, I wish to express to you and through you to all those associated with you in the splendid contribution of Clothing for the aid of the sufferers here, our very sincere thanks for their thoughtful and tangible expression of sympathy. I am afraid that I am hardly competent to write a news item for your publication which would be suitable, and which would adequately describe conditions existing in Halifax immediately following the catastrophe of December 6, but the following paragraphs, however, will I trust, be of some personal interest.

Thursday, December 6th, was a beautiful clear fall day, scarcely a cloud in the sky, no wind, and just that tang in the atmosphere such as one likes to feel in football weather. At 9 o'clock labourers and mechanics were at work in various parts of the city; clerical help and employees in the various business places were either already at their posts or hurrying to get there, and the business and professional men were in some cases still at the breakfast table, reading the morning paper or leisurely strolling down to their offices, when just like the snap of a whip, there came a rumbling—a pause—then a terrific roar which shook the entire city from one end to the other, and what had been a peaceful well ordered community was changed in the twinkling of an eye into a mass of wreckage and shattered humanity.

No words can begin to describe the scene that followed. With 2,000 people killed outright, another 5,000 or 6,000 seriously injured, many of whom were blind as a result of flying glass, and an additional third of the population more or less badly cut, the memory of that eventful day is not a pleasant one to look back upon.

Almost immediately the whole Northern district of the city was in flames and with the report that another explosion was likely to occur the population of that most badly devastated district who could still run or walk, streamed south and west in an attempt to reach some open place, where they felt they would be safe. Hysterical mothers and fathers looking for their children who had been killed as they sat at their desks in school, practically everyone with blood streaming from terrible gashes in the face and head, rushed hither and thither in a vain attempt to save some of their belongings or rescue some of their family or friends.

The day passed so rapidly that almost before one realized dusk began to creep over the city and the awful first night commenced, and with the night came snow and the first real touch of winter. The agony had suffering of the next 48 hours cannot be described in any way. Hospitals so overcrowded that one could scarcely walk without treading on some poor unfortunate human wreck. Houses so badly shattered that it was impossible to keep out the weather, and the storm increasing to a blizzard brought about a crisis that tried the nerve of the strongest man.

Within an hour after the explosion occurred an emergency relief had been established at the City Hall with Robert T. MacIlreith, ex-mayor and Chairman of the Public Utility Board, as Chairman. Associated with him was a small band of public spirited citizens who had in some miraculous manner escaped serious injury; and for the following ten days and nights these men stayed at the post all day without thought of their own homes or dear ones, in many cases without sleep or a change of clothing, snatching a bite to eat, as the opportunity might occur, and working constantly organizing the various branches of Relief Work, cabling and telegraphing for assistance—supplying the destitute with housing accommodation, food and clothing and generally playing their part as heros in one of the greatest tragedies the world has ever known.

Halifax is a city built on the side of a steep hill. During the winter months it has not been the custom to use motor cars to any great extent, and with the blizzards that followed one on top of the other in swift succession, what cars were obtainable were one after the other frozen up and left in the gutters here and there in different parts of the city.

In spite of the almost insurmountable difficulties communication was kept up, however, and within the first twenty-four hours food depots established all over the City; clothing depots opened, emergency shelters were provided where thousands of destitute were housed. Hospitals with a normal capacity of hundreds were forced to extend their capacity to provide for thousands. At the end of the week a tremendous organization of voluntary workers, running with the smoothness of a well-oiled machine, were taking care of the various requirements of the situation as efficiently as if it had been in operation for years.

Relief came to the stricken city from all parts of the world,—our neighbours in the great nation to the South performing magnificent service by rushing doctors, nurses, surgical supplies, food, clothing and money to our assistance as fast as trains, steamships, and wire could be pressed into service. The great Commonwealth of Massachusetts is deserving of particular mention in this regard, since by Sunday morning, December 9, they had landed in Halifax a special train bringing nurses, doctors and hospital equipment galore. Subsequently they contributed in goods and money to the extent of more than three-quarters of a million dollars and have left no stone unturned to provide in every way possible for the comfort and assistance of those rendered homeless and destitute by the terrible disaster. But there—one could ramble on by the hour and still never touch on the one one-hundredth part of the awful things that happened, the marvellous work that was accomplished in rescue work, or the wonder of the way in which the situation was handled by men—many of whom were hitherto little known in the community in which they lived. Some day the story may be written, and when it is the outside world will perhaps get some little inkling of what will probably go down in history as one of the tragic happenings of the greatest war the world has ever known.

Some day I hope to have prepared a tabulated statement and figures that will better convey just what was accomplished by the Relief organization. When that time comes I will be only too happy to send you a copy. In the meantime believe me,

Sincerely yours,

RALPH P. BELL

Secretary Relief Commission.

PERSONAL NARRATIVE

W. B. Moore, M. D.,

Kentville, N. S.

When about to leave my office in Kentville to make
some calls on the forenoon of December 6th, I was informed by
from the D. A. R. office at Kentville of the Halifax
disaster, and was asked to go on special relief train, and to
ask nurses to go. At once I prepared to do as requested, and
was gratified shortly afterwards to find that willing response
had been made by all available medical men and nurses of the
town and vicinity, who were at the station and entrained for
Halifax. At Wolfville and Windsor there was the same gratify-
ing response to the appeal for aid and the valley contingent
represented the highest possibilities of the district, both in
quality and quantity. No realization of the extent and fright-
fulness of the tragedy was experienced until we reached Windsor
Junction where we found a trainload of terribly injured people
on their way to Truro. As they were in urgent need of more
help, one of our doctors and a nurse left us to assist them.
On reaching Bedford, the shattered appearance of the place gave
us the first real indication of the power of the explosion miles
distant. On reaching Rockingham we found innumerable masses
of ships' construction material, iron or steel, etc., over and
around the Railway, and many of our members collected what sou-

2.

venirs they could carry while we were detained there.   As we
neared the city, and viewed the desolate-looking little Africville and could even see the rolling whites of its denizens' *still stand-*
eyes as they wandered disconsolately around the ruins of their *ing*
little homes, and as we looked across the dismal green waters of
the Basin with its floating wreckage to the Dartmouth shore
and the destruction that was apparent even at that distance, we
were beginning to realize that we were approaching a scene, the
like of which probably none of us had ever witnessed, or scarcely heard of in the history of the world.   Approaching Richmond
              completeness
the ~~symptoms~~ of destruction was increasingly apparent,and when
we finally left our train to walk until we met faster means to
approach our destination, the City Hall where we were directed
to report for distribution, no word except "appalling" would
indicate the horrors of the scene.   To the writer it seemed
like an actual realization of the scene picture of Dante's
Inferno which he had witnessed at the moving picture theatre
some years ago.   The peculiar blackness of the whole devastated area lightened by lurid jets of flame springing from the
crater-like cellars of the ruins, with the fantastic shapes of
those around the destroyed homes, searching and probing vainly
for their lost ones, and springing back from the shooting flames,
like imps of Hades,and the blackened tree trunks in the region
standing gaunt and spectral like, as it were, the outpost senti-

ing
cture
Inferno

nels of their kingdom, with the rows of blackened and often
half naked and twisted bodies of the dead, through which we
picked our way, made a weird and desolate spectacle, the de-
pressing effects of which could only be understood by those
unfortunate enough to witness it.   One dramatic incident could
scarcely be duplicated in its tragic and pathetic features.   An
old man who a few hours before had left his wife and two beautiful daughters in their comfortable cottage in the destroyed area
and had gone into the south end of the city on business, returned
to find only the smoking ruins of his happy home, and after long
effort recovered all that was left of his wife and daughters, the
charred remnants of those he had parted from a few hours before
in the full enjoyment of life, happiness, and home.   Seeking in
vain in the destroyed region for any receptacle for the remains
he finally found on its outskirts an old oat sack.   Carrying it
back with him he nearly filled it with all that was left and
staggering under the weight of his burden and his sorrow, with
his back bent and his head bowed, he marched off, like Atlas of
old doomed to carry the load the fates had imposed, with nothing
else left of his little portion of earth, and heaven hidden from
his view.

A striking feature was the completeness of destruction
of nearly everything in the central area involved and this seemed
especially noticeable along the water front.   The greenish grey
of the water with its wreckage in the harbour and along the shore
was particularly gloomy, and with the occasional glimpse of some

108

4.

small craft, one was reminded of their Vergil of boyhood days,
and would scarcely have been surprised had old Neptune shown
his head above the waves after the wreck of the ships and ex-
claimed, "Rari nantes in gurgite vasto." It is safe to say
however, that neither Vergil nor the old sea god ever saw anything like the wreck in Halifax Harbour centuries later, and
it is probable that nothing in the world's history could com -
pare with its suddenness and completeness.

We were conveyed by autos to the City Hall where I
was surprised to find a better organization for application of
relief for sufferers than I anticipated, and the attempt to establish order out of chaos seemed fairly successful. We were
distributed by an efficient auto service to the various hospitals
where our services were most required, and it was my lot to be
sent to Camp Hill Military Hospital, with a number of other doctors and nurses of our party, where we at once went to work upon
the most urgent cases, whose name was legion. Many of us had
seen terrible sights of human tragedies and suffering but nothing
like this in the immensity of the number, and the frightful and
varied character of the injuries. Men, women, and children of
all sorts and classes were literally packed in the wards like
sardines in a box, the cots all occupied, and the floors covered
so that it was often difficult to step between them. The ghastly
appearance of so many, following the hemorrhage from innumerable
glass wounds disfiguring faces and destroying eyes, was really

quote

trying to the most experienced and strongest nerves, and some of the men who had been at the front in the war declared they had never witnessed anything so terrible.   Doubtless large numbers died from hemorrhage and shock before any help could be afforded, but I marvelled greatly at what had been accomplished in the way of relief by the city helpers before our arrival, with the limited number of physicians and trained nurses.   I am glad to refer to the fact for the honor of the profession to which I belong that its members have rarely, if ever, failed to respond efficiently when required to relieve suffering in any of the great tragedies of the world either in war or peace, and the Halifax civilian and military doctors must have done wonderful work in the first hours of the catastrophe, and certainly proved themselves able and willing to justify and continue the noblest and best traditions of the profession.   Without having any time to go through the different wards, I guessed that many hundreds must have been cared for in Camp Hill Hospital, but was somewhat surprised to be told later that it had sheltered and fed and cared for surgically and medically over fourteen hundreds in the first twenty-four hours.

The heroism and work of the girls and women of all ages to relieve suffering was worthy of the best traditions of the sex. Personally the admiration and respect which I have always felt for the finer types of girls and women, not alone for their physical charm but largely for their qualities of heart and mind, were

6.

intensified greatly by what I observed during the crucial test

of such an experience as that afforded by the victims of the

tragedy at this hospital.   Not only the **trained nurses,** who

showed their professional superiority, but other girl and woman

helpers and nurses, showed such a degree of coolness, combined

with acuteness of perception and rapidity of action as to con-

stitute a veritable godsend to the afflicted, and to the hard-

working surgeons, who could not but be grateful for such valu-

able help.   I am sure that the most hardened opponent of the

extension of the franchise to women would have been a convert

had he witnessed, as I did, their qualities of initiative, brains,

and efficiency, under such circumstances as would test to the

fullest degree such qualities in man.   I can only relate one in-

stance where activity greater than caution in one young amateur

nurse led to a mishap in which I suffered some loss.   While I

was working on the floor attending to the severe wounds of a suf-

fering woman, with my emergency bag and box and loose instruments

on a small table, the nurse in her hurry to make a little more

room for other patients under the table, suddenly upset it before

I could avert the calamity, and down went my possessions breaking

something most valuable which I could not easily replace.   I

know that my facial expression was instantly one of selfish rage

out of keeping with the terrible scenes around us at her blunder,

but glancing at her dilated eyes of horror and consternation fixed

upon the wreck, I did a lightning change artist act in facial

expression, and when she turned her eyes upon me with fear and

trembling, I met her gaze with a look of sympathy and understanding which made her realize that my regret for her misfor-
tune was greater than for my own, and with a charming blush she
helped me to restore things to order, and my loss was repaid.
Possibly the fact that she had a sweet face assisted me somewhat
but I think my vanity was more pleased at my successful effort
at facial gymnastics than anything else I accomplished during
my visit.

Considering the large number of all kinds of terrible
injuries in the ward in which I worked, I was much impressed with
the quiet that prevailed, only an occasional shriek from one or
two hysterical sufferers breaking the stillness.   The patients
as a rule seemed stoical and stunned with the severity of the
shock, few requiring anaesthetics for things that could not be
done in ordinary practice without them.   The nerve centres both
sensory and nemtal, seemed to be numbed, and while such a condition seemed to mitigate somewhat the horrors of acute suffering
yet it did not augur well for the future, and a larger mortality
rate, and slower recovery might be expected than from injuries
of similar extent under other conditions.   Glass wounds of all
degrees seemed to constitute the larger number of casualties, and
the face and especially the eye injuries were beyond anything
known in frequency and severity.   Fortunately, I think many
whose eyes were destroyed died from brain or other injuries

8.

inflicted at the same time, but large numbers will go sightless *40*

the rest of their days as a living illustration of the fact that

life isn't always better than death.   There were some horrible

cases of burns, and many fractures of all kinds.   As an illus-

trations of the irony of the application of "one being taken and

another left", I may relate the following incident.   While work-

ing on the floor with a poor woman covered with glass wounds, I

was hastily summoned by a nurse who had no doctor with her to the

other end of the ward to see the urgent cases just brought in on

one mattress.   Leaving my case with my own nurse, I went as quick-

ly as possible with the other, but of no avail.   When we reached

the mattress on the floor with its two occupants, the one to whom

I was summoned was lying peaceful and still in death, her clothing

nearly all torn off, one of the most perfect types of beautiful

young womanhood imaginable with scarcely a mark upon her, probably

dead from shock or internal injury, and the other possibly a

sister or stranger, with one eye gone, the other apparently hope-

lessly injured, her face terribly cut and torn, blinded and dis-

figured for life, and yet with a good pulse, plenty of vitality,

and would probably live, "The one being taken and the other left"

as my good friends would express it.   It is obvious that many

eye injuries resulted from the fire on the Mont Blanc preceding

the explosion, and the people at the north end looking out at

the burning ship, but when one observed the destructive effects

of the explosion on the glass all over the city and Dartmouth,

9.

their number is not surprising, as there must have been a light-ning-like hail of millions of particles of flying glass, much of it travelling with terrific velocity.   Leaving the hospital in the night to make my way over to Dartmouth where I had some relatives whose fate I did not know, and no autos being avail-able, a medical friend and muself stumbled over the darkened streets none too safe at best of times, on our way into the city, with the darkness intensified by the gathering blizzard.   Running the risk of breaking our legs or necks and not being provided with flashlights the use of which, by the way, may have been prohibited by the authorities as showing a Hun submarine commander our where-abouts, I could not refrain from expressing my views of the irony of the farce of so-called protective measures instituted by so-called authorities.   "Here", I said, "is a lamentable instance of 'straining at the gnat and swallowing the camel', and of a 'penny wise and pound foolish' policy of so-called protection I see in the Halifax papers where shop keepers are hauled before the tribunal of the Inquisition and fined for allowing some rays of light to escape from their premises, because of the alleged danger of the Huns off-shore locating the city, when it is well known that by necessary harbour lights, lighthouses, etc, and charts, etc, every Hun officer probably is better acquainted with the harbour approaches than the pilots seem to be and also knows the topography of the city, better than most of its citizens and could plant shells in it almost as accurately at midnight as at midday, yet we are in danger of serious injuries because of this

puerile regulation while engaged in doing what little we can
to mitigate the horrors of possibly the greatest catastrophe
the world has ever known, obviously the result of the most appalling negligence, ignorance, and inefficiency of the so-called
authorities ever known in the history of any port! Eventually
reaching the Ferry Slip for Dartmouth, and crossing on the boat
one was further reminded by the lurid flames in the distance
that the inferno at the north was still in action and that doubtless many poor victims pinned under the wreckage were being slowly
or rapidly consumed as the case might be, a conclusion, to those
who had time to think, as inevitable as it was tragic and tortur-
ing.   Dartmouthpresented as shattered an appearance as Halifax
and the casualties were terrible.   I was glad to find that my
relatives were more fortunate than most and although like all
suffering property loss, had escaped with minor injuries.   On
my return to Halifax I was requested to look after some victims
at the north end who had not been removed to hospital, and with
the excellent auto service I was soon taken from City Hall to the
injured in the desolate region of wrecked homes adjoining the
devastated area where only smouldering ruins could be seen.   Those
whose homes were not completely destroyed were trying to protect
themselves as best they could from the blizzard then raging, and
one could not but think of the even greater horrors and suffering
had the explosion occurred twenty-four hours later.   All that
many could do was to huddle together wounded and all in one room
with the windows covered with carpets or mats and boards to keep

11.

out the blizzard and exist as best they could.

I was impressed with some features of the catastrophe
with reference to the distant effects of the explosion.   Going
to Truro before my return home, I found at the Learment Hotel
where I stayed that glass had been broken to a considerable extent there and it was reported that a baby carriage had been
overturned on the streets and that horses had started and some
had run away,and that some bells inthe large buildings had been
rung.   At Windsor,however, nearer the explosion than Truro, and
at Kentville nothing was felt, but at North Alton on the mountain
a few miles from Kentville it was distinctly noticeable.   This
seemed quite explainable by the fact that no high ground existed
between Truro and Halifax while Windsor and Kentville, etc., were
sheltered by the high altitude of the Mount Uniacke region which
deflected the concussion waves upwards and,therefore, they were
duly felt on the high mountain top as experienced in the western
regions.   Of course, innumerable phenomena occurred which were the
natural result of perhaps the most powerful explosion the world
had ever experienced.   A great deal of skepticism has been expressed with regard to the statement of the man who said he was
carried from the deck of a ship on the harbour and deposited
without any clothes, but slightly injured, on the hill at Fort
Needham.   To the writer the story is not at all improbable as
to the facts.   Standing exactly in the centre of the terrific
cyclonic disturbance of the air around him which probably destroyed all outside of that centre within its influence, he

117

was compressed equally on all sides and carried by the whirl-
wind upwards until its force was exhausted, which luckily for
him, occurred on high ground, by which he escaped the destruction of a fall to a lower level.   Many incidents have occurred
in western cyclones where people and much heavier bodies have
been carried for miles, but the former seldom or never lived to
tell the tale because they were not released under such rarely
favorable circumstances as in the case of the Halifax man.

Doubtless innumerable phenomena have been observed
and recorded in connection with the tragedy to prove the Shake-
sperian truth that there is more in heaven and earth than dreamt
of in our philosophy, but we should pray that we may never see
it again demonstrated in the way that Halifax experienced it in
the terrible disaster of December 6, 1917.

Dr. Willis Bryant Moore died in 1939 in his 84th year. His obituary in The Nova Scotia Medical Bulletin described him as "a distinguished citizen and skillful physician . . . He was for many years a member of the Executive of the Medical Society of Nova Scotia and at one time he was president . . . He graduated from Halifax Medical College in 1879 . . . He studied in England for two years to further equip himself for his life work. After a short time as ship's surgeon on Atlantic liners and a three year internship as house surgeon in the Victoria General Hospital, he began his extensive practice at Kentville, the place of his birth . . . Dr. Moore was very versatile. He was a keen observer and student . . . It is to be regretted that a man of his talents was not persuaded to leave behind a record of the early years in medicine, dealing as it would with the important era of transition into antiseptic and aseptic surgery."

KNOWN DEAD AND MISSING

Male	933	Caucasian	1586	Single	820
		African	10	Married	571
Female	578	Mongolian	3	Widowed	64
	1611	Indian	11	Not Stated	156
		Malay	1		1611
			1611		

Church of England	437	Professional	13
Roman Catholic	538	Tradesmen	21
Presbyterian	194	Clerks	43
Methodist	121	Farmers	3
Baptist	60	Fishermen	1
Lutheran	9	Craftsmen	120
Congregational	2	Miners	1
Other Denominations	35	Laborers	165
Not stated	215	Railwaymen	39
	1611	Housewife	331
		Domestic	10
		Students	18
		Seamen	113
		Soldiers	21
		Miscellaneous	85
		No Occupation	627
			1611

	Male	Female
Under 1 year	36	31
One year	23	18
Two years	29	20
Three years	19	20
Four years	22	14
5 to 9 years	84	72
10 to 14	61	43
15 to 19	51	43
20 to 29	142	108
30 to 39	121	91
40 to 49	100	60
50 to 59	55	40
60 to 69	33	29
70 to 79	16	18
80 to 89	6	6
90 to 100	1	2
Not stated	134	83
	933	678

959   buried identified
242   "   unidentified

1201   Total buried

410   Bodies known to be missing.

1611   Total known dead.

74 known to be male	32 of the 242 unknown are known to be single.
26 known to be female	8 are known to be Roman Catholic
142 not known	91 are classed as Protestant
242	4 known to be seamen

Probable ages of some

	Male	Female
Under 1 year	1	1
2 years		2
4 years	1	
5 to 9 years	11	4
20 to 29	10	1
30 to 39	21	6
40 to 49	5	5
50 to 59	2	
60 to 69		2
Not stated	11	1

ADDITIONAL NUMBER OF KNOWN DEAD AND MISSING
December 5, 1918

Male	9	Caucasian 24	Single	15	Church of England	4
Female	15		Married	6	Roman Catholic	5
	24		Widowed	3	Presbyterian	6
				24	Baptist	1
					Methodist	3
					Not Stated	5
						24

			Male	Female
Craftsmen	2	Under 1 year	1	1
Laborers	1	One year	1	1
Housewives	6	Three years	2	3
No occupation	15	Four years	1	0
	24	5 to 9 years	1	1
		20 to 29 "	0	2
		30 to 39	1	0
		40 to 49	0	2
		50 to 59	1	1
		60 to 69	0	1
		70 to 79	1	0
		80 to 89	0	1
		Not stated	0	2
			9	15

Buried unidentified	1
Buried identified	12
Total buried	13
Bodies known to be missing	11
Total known dead	24

Unknown.
1 known to be male

Interim Report of Mortuary Committee, Halifax Relief, February 4th, 1918.

On the morning of December 7th, 1917, at the request of the Deputy Mayor, Alderman H. S. Colwell, I was asked in association with Alderman R. B. Colwell, to take charge of the Chebucto Mortuary, then established, and subsequently appointed by the Relief Committee to act as Chairman of the Mortuary Committee, with Alderman Colwell, Vice-Chairman, to arrange for the collection of the bodies from the devastated district and for the conduct of the Mortuary Chamber at Chebucto Road School. Alderman Colwell assumed direction of the gathering of bodies from the devastated district and despatched them as removed from the ruins or from the street to Chebucto Mortuary. On arrival at Chebucto School we found a number of bodies had already been received, while all the morgues connected with private undertaking establishments were filled to capacity. As soon as the basement of the school was in proper condition an order was issued for the despatch from the private morgues to the public mortuary chamber of all bodies not identified or claimed by relatives. At the Chebucto Mortuary a Committee was formed and helpers secured, who continued to aid in a voluntary capacity until shortly after the New Year at the school itself and subsequently continued the work at my office at 197 Hollis Street.

Attached is a list of the Committee of ladies and gentlemen who rendered such valuable and useful assistance in the respective capacities indicated.

As soon as I was requested to undertake this work I called upon Colonel Thompson, of Military Headquarters Staff, who agreed on behalf of the Militia to render all assistance possible. From that day until the present Headquarters have had at the Mortuary a number of men, reaching on some days as high as seventy, in addition to the supply of digging parties at the cemeteries and men engaged in clearing the ruins and searching for bodies. I cannot speak with too great praise of the manner in which the soldiers performed their trying duties under most difficult weather conditions.

It was necessary to place Chebucto School in habitable condition—first to make the basement snow and water tight. For this purpose the windows throughout the building had to be covered to prevent drifting snow from leaking through. All this repair work was done under the direction of the committee, by a company of the Royal Engineers. Owing to the cold weather it was impossible to use the ordinary heating apparatus of the school and stoves were placed in the building for this purpose. Two of the class rooms were put in fit condition for use of the office staff. After the arrival from Toronto of Messrs. R. N. Stone, Embalming Professor, and A. A. Schrieter, of Kitchener, sent by the City of Toronto to render Halifax assistance as undertaking experts, we appointed the one Mortuary Supervisor and the other his assistant. Professor Stone carried into effect plans he had previously formulated for proper arrangement and classification and convenience in identification of bodies. Suitable forms were made and as bodies were prepared for burial they were placed thereon. Before the arrival of Professor Stone the soldiers had washed all the faces of the bodies, carrying the water for the purpose from the homes of nearby residents, who in the early stages of the work rendered very valuable help to the Committee in this manner and in providing meals for some of the soldiers and the staff.

Under Professor Stone's direction bodies were washed, clothing removed and properly ticketed with a number corresponding to that on the body, the effects, such as rings, watches and money or small trinkets that would aid in identifying the bodies, were removed and placed in cotton bags with corresponding numbers. Descriptions of the bodies were taken on forms prepared therefor. All the bodies in the basement were covered with cotton in strips cut to size. Electric fixtures were installed in the basement so that identification could be carried on with equal facility by day or night and for this purpose the Mortuary was kept open until 10 p.m.

In order that the bodies might be retained for as long a time as possible about 200 were embalmed, including every child that it was at all possible to have embalmed. For this purpose a room was equipped with heating and other facilities to carry on the embalming processes.

After identification was established the statistical information was given at the office respecting each person, and no body issued from the Mortuary Chamber without a burial permit being first obtained.

The work of identification was, in many cases, made more difficult and in some cases impossible by the fact that the tickets placed on bodies, in the devastated district, were blown off before arrival at the Mortuary, or were in some cases sent there without indicating the place at which the body was found. This also applied to removals from some of the hospitals, no clothing or effects from the hospitals arriving with the bodies or forwarded to the Committee as belonging to any distinct body.

Contracts were made on behalf of the city with the Undertaking establishments for the burial of the unidentified bodies and such other identified bodies for whom there were no claimants or whose relatives were not in a position, owing to the disaster, to care for the expenses of burial. Under this over 375 bodies were buried at the charge of the Relief Committee. Contracts were also made with the Cemetery Companies for the burial of the unidentified and the identified who were accorded burial at the expense of the Relief Committee.

At all the cemeteries it was found necessary to supplement the ordinary labour employed, by military digging and covering in parties. These parties were given by the Military Headquarters, and from 25 to 50 men daily from the 10th of December to the 24th, and occasionally since, have been employed in this work. But for the assistance of the Military in this particular it would have been impossible to have buried our dead with the same expedition. Not only did the military dig and cover in the lots arranged for by the Committee, but also assisted the cemeteries in digging and covering in private lots.

All the unidentified are numbered, the number being placed inside the coffin, outside the coffin and on a slab at the head of the grave. A chart of the graves has been taken showing the position of the numbered bodies so that if identification is subsequently made we can indicate to relatives the exact position of the body sought.

I am not yet able to give a complete list of the dead from the disaster, as the work of identification is still proceeding, and of course we have not yet received from some of the Undertakers the full information with respect to the bodies they have buried. There are at this date about 400 positive identifications of bodies buried, charred remains, or of those who have presented facts undoubtedly establishing deaths. There are in addition to these 150 buried unidentified, and there are a number yet missing, particulars in regard to which I hope to have within a short time.

In making this interim report I desire to emphasize the very valuable aid that has been rendered by those who in a voluntary capacity have assisted in tabulating work, in the identification of the bodies from the effects and in the general office work connected with the Mortuary. There was little opportunity at the Chebucto Road School for them to go home for their meals, and after the work was well in hand provision was made, with the assistance of the Food Committee, and a military cook, for meals to be served to the staff. This also made possible continuous work and for three weeks the staff remained on duty from morning until nine and ten o'clock at night.

Very valuable assistance was rendered to Alderman Colwell in gathering the bodies by many of our citizens, by men from Bridgewater, from the Cook Construction Company and from the military forces. In the Mortuary Chamber itself truly heroic work was done by the soldiers without thought of emolument and in a manner which indicated that they were wholly imbued with the spirit of service. On the attached list of the committee I have indicated those who rendered specially praiseworthy service in their relative capacities.

ARTHUR S. BARNSTEAD, CHAIRMAN

PUBLIC ARCHIVES OF NOVA SCOTIA

December 17th. Public funeral of the majority of the unidentified dead from Chebucto morgue.

THE JAMES COLLECTION, CITY OF TORONTO ARCHIVES

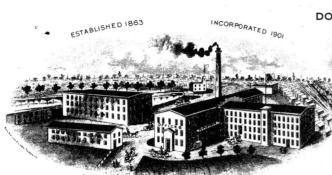

DOMINION MANUFACTURERS, LIMITED, OWNING AND OPERATING

ESTABLISHED 1863   INCORPORATED 1901

Christie Brothers & Co. Limited
Coffins & Caskets,
FUNERAL DIRECTORS' SUPPLIES, EMBALMING CASES,

AMHERST, N.S., April 26th, 1918
CANADA.

Mr. A.S. Barnstead,

Halifax, N.S.

Dear Sir:-   <u>CONFIDENTIAL</u>

Referring to our conversation re undertakers'
bills in Halifax for work done during the disaster, we
write to say that we fully intended to have written you
at once about the matter, but owing to press of business,
it was overlooked.

Regarding prices which we understand were agreed
upon early after the disaster, of $15.00, $20.00 and $30.00,
we write to say that as manufacturers we know those prices
are very low and that we cannot see how the undertakers
could come out with any profit after paying outside undertakers and their necessary extra help during such a time,
and unless the undertaker gets something better than the
above prices for part of his work, he will be very poorly
paid.

Writing from a manufacturer's point of view, we
may say that we did everything possible to supply the goods
required at enormous extra expense, having the Secretary-
Treasurer of our Head Office come all the way from Toronto
to look after the distribution of the goods, besides having
two men from our own factory down there. All these additional expenses cut out our legitimate profits on the goods
supplied.

Owing to the great uncertainty of the number of
caskets required, as the reports that came to us of the
dead were all the way from 2,000 to 4,000, we ordered from
other casket factory branches, a large number of caskets and
trimmings.

124

We may say that the transportation alone cost over $2,000 and for more than half of this amount we do not expect to get any returns, simply because we ordered the goods in to have them if needed and could not ask the undertakers to pay expressage on these goods since they did not personally order them.

This, in addition to the extra cost of our own Branch and to Mr. Andrews expenses from Toronto, gives you an idea of what the casket business did toward meeting the situation.

It would seem rather strange that since such large sums of money have been voted for Halifax that there should be any disposition on the part of the authorities to get the undertakers to work without compensation for their labor and all the unpleasantness connected with work of that nature. The Relief Fund was subscribed for legitimate purposes and we feel if there is a legitimate purpose more binding than another, it is the burial of the dead promptly to protect the living.

We may say that we have not been asked by anyone to write you in this respect but as we are in a position to know what the goods cost the undertakers, we are simply writing in justice to them.

Yours truly,

CHRISTIE BROS. & CO. LTD.

PER *JA Christie*

JAC/M

HALIFAX DISASTER

The beginning of our Red Cross year was marked by the terrible Halifax explosion by which 1635 persons lost their lives and 10,000 people were rendered homeless. Much generous help was received by the stricken City. Everyone knows the splendid aid sent by the American Red Cross, and the people and Government of the United States in despatching to Halifax train loads and boat loads of supplies, together with surgeons and nurses. Their neighbourly kindness will never be forgotten.

But the help rendered by our own Canadian Red Cross is perhaps not so widely known. The Chairman of the Executive in Toronto wired to the Shipping Agent in St. John to render every assistance possible in money and goods. The agent, Mr. Milburne, immediately requisitioned a special train, and brought with him all the Red Cross goods he had ready for shipment overseas, making two carloads in all. And this was the first assistance from outside the Province to reach Halifax. Hearing that some of the injured had been conveyed to Truro, Mr. Milburne put off cases of hospital necessaries for their use, at that station. A medical supply committee of the Canadian Red Cross Society was immediately formed with the sanction of the Halifax Relief Committee—Mr. Milburne being appointed Chairman, and Mrs. Sexton, vice-chairman, with a staff of forty-four voluntary workers. Twice daily all the Emergency Hospitals were visited, and their wants noted and supplied the same day. The number of these hospitals, dressing stations, etc., amounted to sixty-two.

At the same time, gifts of clothing, food and money, poured in from Red Cross Branches all over Canada. Ottawa Branch shipped in one day, eight carloads of clothing. The Nova Scotia Branch, under its President, Mrs. Dennis, cooperated heartily, practically every Branch and Auxiliary in the Province sending substantial and generous aid. [See also page 16].

Mr. Milburne speaks gratefully of the assistance given him by every one; of his entire staff of forty-four who remained on duty for the first seven days, on an average of twelve to fifteen hours a day; of Prof. Sexton who very kindly loaned the Technical College and also rendered valuable personal services; of a strong team of Commercial Travellers from St. John who did yeoman service; of Mr. Lewis sent by Sir John Eaton from Toronto with a gift of a splendid stock of drugs, who gave his valuable services for a fortnight; of the men who voluntarily ran motors loaded with hospital supplies till long past midnight night after night; of the Express Companies who did their best under great difficulties to expedite transportation. He thanks one and all who helped in this work.

When patients were able to leave hospital, a special committee of fifteen ladies with Mrs. Dennis as chairman, worked at the Technical College selecting suitable clothing for each case. Nothing but new clothing was handled; the

3

hospitals were furnished with Requisition Forms and were visited daily, the names and requirements of patients were taken, their parcels made up, marked with each one's name, and sent to the hospital to be in readiness when needed, eleven hospitals being thus supplied.

Pier No. II.

It was not until the month of March that the Red Cross was able to resume its work for returned invalided soliders. By that time the hospital on Pier 2, wrecked by the explosion, had been repaired. The hospital ships once more made their trips, and the Red Cross store-room on the Pier was re-stocked. Large requisitions were filled every month, sometimes only a few hours' notice was given to get these supplies on board— sometimes only a few minutes' notice, in the case of a hospital train. On one trip the ship docked in the morning, landed her men, and went out again with her new supplies in the afternoon. At another time 1400 ship-wrecked men from S. S. "City of Vienna" were visited and supplied with filled kit-bags, containing toilet necessaries, pipes and tobacco. Directly after, the Committee were called upon to minister to 300 Influenza contact cases. This necessitated our workers going into quarantine for two days, very busy days too, the telegrams alone requiring upwards of 300 telephone calls. The Y. M. C. A. and the Knights of Columbus Red Cross Musical Club were always at hand to cheer up men who were detained by the Medical Board, arranging for their benefit concerts, entertainments, motor drives, and teas at private houses.

The following is a complete list of the fifty-seven Hospitals and Dressing Stations supplied by the Red Cross:

A.O.H. Hall (Shelter).
Acadian Sugar Refinery.
Armouries.
Academy of Music.
Acadian Hotel.
Almon St. Dressing Station.
A.M.C. Training Depot.
Brandram-Henderson, Limited.
Dr. Bennet's Dressing Station.
Bellevue Hospital.
Cogswell St. Military Hospital.
Camp Hill Military Hospital.
Council House, Victorian Order of Nurses.
Chebucto Mortuary.
City Hall Relief Station.
Children's Hospital.
Convent of the Sacred Heart.
Central Relief Headquarters, Truro.

Dartmouth Relief Headquarters.
Dartmouth Oil Works.
Dressing Stations No. 1-3-4-5-6.
Emergency Shelter Committee.
Grafton St. Sunday School.
Hurley Crest Dressing Station.
Home of the Guardian Angel.
Halifax Dispensary.
Halifax Infirmary.
Halifax Infants' Home.
Hazelwood Hospital.
Imperial Oil Dressing Station.
Infectious Hospital, Dartmouth.
I.O.D.E. Home.
Jost Mission, Grafton Hall.
Knights of Columbus Shelter.
Dr. Little's Hospital.
Ladies College Hospital.

Mahons' Shelter.
Monastery of the Good Shepherd.
Mount St. Vincent Convent.
Medical Relief, McCurdy Bldg.
Nova Scotia Hospital, Dartmouth.
Nurses' Home.
"Old Colony" Hospital Ship.
Rosenburg Hospital, Dartmouth.
St. Paul's Hall.
St. Teresa's Home.
School for the Blind.
Salvation Army.
St. Mary's College.
Pine Hill Hospital.
Y.M.C.A. Hospital.
Victoria General Hospital.
Waegwoltic Hospital.

Some Notes on The Halifax Explosion

By HOWARD L. BRONSON, Ph.D., F.R.S.C.

(Read May Meeting, 1918.)

The explosion which wrecked Halifax on December 6, 1917, undoubtedly far surpassed all previous explosions both in its destructive effects and in the quantities of explosives involved. Although facts and figures concerning the explosion are necessarily incomplete and in many instances not very reliable, still it seems desirable to gather together and place on record such information as is available. The thermo-chemical and other theoretical and experimental data used in this article were obtained from Marshall's "Explosives," Brunswig's "Explosives," Molinari's "Chemistry," and from Mr. W. C. Cope, explosives chemist of the E. I. duPont-deNemours and Company. Mr. Cope was called to Halifax as the explosives expert at the investigation into the disaster, and was good enough to furnish me certain facts and figures.

The following is a brief account of the events leading up to the explosion. The munition ship *Mont Blanc*, loaded with some 2,500 tons of high explosives and with a deck load of monochlorbenzene, was about to enter the Narrows of Halifax Harbour when she collided with the *Imo* in such a way that the bow of the *Imo* was driven well into her side. The heat developed by the collision was sufficient to ignite either the monochlorbenzene or the picric acid, the latter being the more probable according to Mr. Cope. The fire burned for nearly 20 minutes, during which time the *Mont Blanc* drifted close to pier 6 on the Halifax side of the harbour and apparently grounded just before the explosion. During this time and previous to the final explosion there were at least three small explosions, apparently caused in the drums of monochlorbenzene.

Before describing or discussing the effects of the explosion, it would seem of interest to consider with some care the magnitude of the explosion in terms of the amount of energy liberated and the volume of gas formed, together with the probable temperature and pressure of the gas. In order to determine these various quantities the following assumptions have been made: (1) that the entire cargo of explosives entered into the detonation. This was evidently not the case, for it was burning 17 minutes previous to the explosion, and, as we shall see later, there is some evidence to indicate that part of the cargo sank without exploding. (2) That the products of detonation for this enormous unconfined mass of explosives are the same as those due to small masses in a bomb calorimeter. (3) That the specific heats of gases at high temperatures can be represented by the formula $C = A + Bt$.

The cargo of the *Mont Blanc* consisted of the following high explosives:

(1) 2,114,000 kilograms picric acid.

(2) 204,000 kilograms trinitrotoluene.

(3) 56,000 kilograms gun cotton,

The decomposition of these explosives is represented by the following equations:

(1) $2 C_6 H_2 (NO_2)_3 O H = 8 CO + 3 CO_2 + 3 H_2 + 3 N_2 + C.$

(2) $2 C_7 H_5 (NO_2)_3 = 12 CO + 5 H_2 + 3 N_2 + 2C.$

(3) $2 C_{24} H_{29} O_{20} (NO_2)_{11} = 24 C O + 24 CO_2 + 17 H_2 + 11 N_2 + 12 H_2 O.$

From these equations and thermo-chemical data from Marshall's "Explosives" the following approximate results can be obtained:

Substance	Vo	Q	t°	P
Picric Acid	828	875	2800	9640
Trinitrotoluene	983	680	2380	9870
Gun cotton	859	1045	2670	9570

Vo is the volume in liters, at 0° and 76 cm. pressure, of the gas liberated by 1 kg. of explosive. Q is the heat of explosion in large calories per kg. of explosive. P is the pressure in kg. per cm² developed by the explosion of 1 kg. in the volume of 1 liter. t° and P were calculated as follows:

$$t = \frac{Q}{C} \text{ where } C = A + B t \qquad P = \frac{1 \cdot 033 \times Vo \times (273 + t)}{273}$$

We thus see that the gases formed had a volume at N.T.P. of about 2×10^9 liters and that the total energy liberated was about $8 \cdot 7 \times 10^{11}$ kilogram-meters. This energy was at first stored in the gases at high temperatures and under enormous pressures. It distributed itself rapidly through the air, water and earth to the surrounding region. All the evidence points to the fact that the air was the principal factor in the transfer of this energy. Within a radius of four or five miles the earth wave was distinctly felt and was followed by the concussion of the air which caused all the damage. The experience of the writer confirms this point and indicates in a rough way the relative magnitudes of the earth and air shock. At the time of the explosion, I was standing in my laboratory on the second floor of the

Dalhousie University Science Building, about 3,500 meters from the explosion. I first felt a shaking of the building no greater than that caused by heavy blasting in the railroad cut, but it seemed to be directly under the building and I started for the boiler room, fearing an explosion there. I had gone less than 30 feet when the crash came which completely destroyed the windows and sashes on three sides of the building, broke heavy doors and locks, and even shifted partitions. The comparatively slight earth shock can be explained by the fact that the explosion was practically on the water, even though the ship was touching ground. Unfortunately I find it difficult to make any satisfactory estimate of the time between the arrival of the two shocks, but should estimate it between 6 and 10 seconds, which would not indicate a very high velocity for the air wave, or explosion impulse as it is generally called.

It is a well-established fact that the velocity of the explosion impulse is much greater than the normal velocity of sound. The wave probably starts out with about the same velocity as that of the detonation of the explosive, which may be above 5,000 meters per sec. The velocity decreases very rapidly with the distance, especially at first, and is said to reach the normal velocity of sound at about the distance that windows cease to be broken. The velocity at any distance apparently depends both on the quantity and nature of the explosive, though the initial velocity seems to be independent of the quantity. All three of the above explosives, and especially picric acid, have exceedingly high detonation velocities. The terrible destruction caused by the air concussion was undoubtedly due to this intense compression impulse travelling with high velocity.

Whether the above correctly interprets the phenomena or not, there is no question about the terrible destructive effect of the explosion impulse. In a general way it can be said that buildings within a radius of half a mile of the explosion were totally destroyed and that up to one mile they were very largely rendered uninhabitable and dangerous. No section of Halifax city escaped serious damage to doors, windows and plaster. The damage to the Dalhousie Science Building, already referred to, was quite characteristic of those sections of the city farthest from the explosion. More or less severe damage was caused as far away as Sackville and Windsor Junction, 9 or 10 miles N.E. of the explosion, and for a similar distance in the opposite direction. At Truro, 62 miles, and New Glasgow, 78 miles, the shock was sufficient to jar buildings very appreciably, and even to shake articles off from shelves. Even as far away as Charlottetown, 135 miles, and North Cape Breton, 225 miles, the explosion was distinctly felt or heard.

It is interesting to notice how closely the experience of this explosion, as regards the distance at which damage was done, fits in with the results of past explosions, and with experiments. If d is the maximum distance in meters from the explosion to points at which definite damage is done, and m is the mass of explosive in kilograms, then the expression $d = K\sqrt{m}$ has been found to agree pretty well with the observed facts. K is a constant which depends on the nature of the explosive and is about 10 in the case of high explosives. Applying this formula to the Halifax explosion, where m = 2,370,000 kg., d came out to be 15,400 meters. This distance is in satisfactory agreement with such information as I have thus far gathered regarding the maximum distances at which real damage was done.

It seems to be the generally accepted opinion that the intense compressional wave is followed by a wave of rarefaction of much less intensity. Whether this is the true explanation of the phenomena or not, it is certainly true that windows, doors and walls sometimes fell in toward the explosion though much more frequently away from it. One of the most interesting illustrations of this was seen about half a mile from the explosion on the Dartmouth side of the harbour. At a point nearly opposite the point of explosion, the highway was lined by a row of fir trees from six to twelve inches in diameter. These were uprooted and pointed away from the explosion centre where there was no obstruction between them and the explosion, but along that part of the road where there is a forest of these trees between the road and the harbour, the uprooted trees fell towards the explosion.

Further confirmation on this point, and other interesting information, was obtained from several barograph records, two of which the writer has in his possession. Both instruments were located near the centre of the city, about 3,000 meters from the explosion. The motion of the pens was so rapid and so great that there is uncertainty regarding the magnitude of the motion, and it seems quite possible that both pens went off the paper entirely. However, it can be safely said that the positive motion was much greater than the negative. The record from the Halifax Club shows at least a motion of $+1\cdot25$ in. and $-\cdot45$ in. and the one from the Halifax Nautical Instrument Co. shows at least $+\cdot75$ in. and $-\cdot45$ in. There were at least two other barograph records obtained in the city; one at the Dockyard within 300 meters of the explosion and the other on the cable ship *Minia*, about 3,000 meters from the explosion. The needle of the latter instrument went completely off the paper and did not return to its previous position. The record at the Dockyard has been lost, but the observer reports that the change in pressure was very small, not over an eighth of an inch. It seems probable that this must have been due to a failure to record.

There is another type of phenomenon, quite common within half a mile of the explosion, which deserves especial notice. The fact is thoroughly well-established that persons and many heavy objects were picked up from the ground and carried considerable distances. In one case a man was taken from the roof of a high building, about three-quarters of a mile from the explosion, and gently deposited on the ground. One of the best examples of this type of phenomenon occurred on the ship *Picton*, which was at its wharf about 250 meters from the explosion. A great boulder, weighing more than a ton, was picked up from somewhere and dropped on the ship. It crashed through the upper deck and still lies on the deck below. The surface of the boulder is worn smooth, suggesting that it must have come from the beach or the harbour bottom, but it was certainly not washed on board for no water came over the vessel. Such phenomena show that the air disturbance was something more than an intense compressional wave travelling out in a straight line. There must also have been some kind of vortex motion, such as occurs in cyclones.

The seismograph record of the explosion obtained at Dalhousie University is of more than passing interest, because three distinct shocks are recorded. The first occurred at about 9:05, the second five minutes later, and the third an hour after the first. The explosion was almost directly north of the instrument and unfortunately the N.-S. pendulum caught at the extremity of the first swing, which made it impossible to attempt any energy calculations from it. The E.-W. record is not purely seismic but exhibits oscillations of the pendulum. The three records on this component have much the same character and are of practically the same magnitude. The natural conclusion is that there must have been three explosions, though the two later ones were neither seen nor felt by the public. The only explanation so far suggested is that the entire mass of explosive was not detonated at first and that small quantities exploded later on the bottom of the harbour. In this case it must have been so confined as not to produce any air concussion and the slight motion of the earth might have escaped notice. This explanation has many serious objections and Mr. Cope considers it untenable.

The writer regrets the fragmentary nature of the data contained in this paper and hopes that it may be possible to supplement at it at some future time.

COURTESY ROYAL SOCIETY OF CANADA

Dr. LEWIS THOMAS, M. R. C. S. (Eng.) L. R. C. P. (Lon.)

OFFICE 299 BRUNSWICK STREET

Halifax, N.S., _____ March 20th 1919

This is to certify that Miss Mary
O   went insane in 1918
and died at the Nova Scotia
Hospital Nov. 18/1918
I first began to treat her in
Feb 6th for nervousness.
This nervousness gradually developed
into insanity.
I consider that the explosion of
Dec 6th 1917 had a good deal
to do in causing this mental
condition to develop.

Lewis Thomas M.D

134

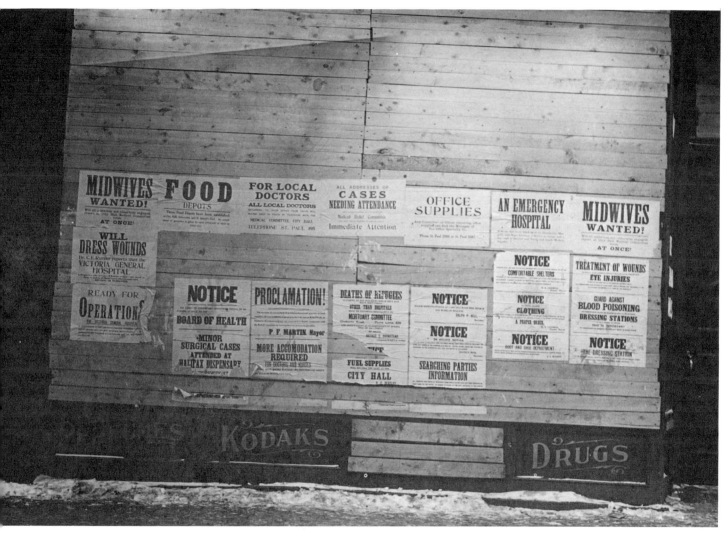

REPORT

OF THE

HALIFAX RELIEF EXPEDITION

December 6 to 15, 1917

BY

Hon. A. C. RATSHESKY, Commissioner-in-Charge

TO

SAMUEL WALKER McCALL

Governor of the Commonwealth of Massachusetts

Printed by an order of the Council dated June 12, 1918

WRIGHT AND POTTER PRINTING COMPANY, STATE PRINTERS
32 DERNE STREET, BOSTON

1918

REPORT OF THE HALIFAX RELIEF EXPEDITION.

His Excellency SAMUEL W. McCALL, *Governor of the Commonwealth of Massachusetts, State House, Boston, Massachusetts.*

YOUR EXCELLENCY: — I have the privilege to submit herewith a formal report on the Halifax Relief Expedition, of which you did me honor by placing me in charge, giving in detail the part the Commonwealth played in sending the Relief Expedition to Halifax, N. S.

The first news of the disaster was received at the State House at about 11 o'clock A.M. on December 6, 1917.

Immediately you sent a telegram to the Mayor of Halifax, offering the unlimited assistance of the Commonwealth, and called a meeting of the Massachusetts Public Safety Committee, composed of one hundred men, representing all parts of the State, for 2.30 o'clock that afternoon, to take action relative to handling the relief work. Although short notice was given, the meeting was largely attended.

Up to that time no answer had come to your telegram. Henry B. Endicott, Executive Manager of the Massachusetts Public Safety Committee, at your request, got into communication with the War and Navy Departments at Washington and learned that no news of the disaster had been received by them, and, as requested, wireless was dispatched along the coast, through the Navy, to the Mayor of Halifax, offering assistance from Massachusetts, but no reply was had that day.

Upon your request as to how soon and in what manner medical aid could be arranged, Colonel William A. Brooks, Acting Surgeon General of the Commonwealth, stated that if a special train could be had he would be able to dispatch a large corps of surgeons, doctors, nurses, and surgical and medical supplies in a few hours; and at your suggestion this plan was adopted by the committee, and James H. Hustis, receiver for the Boston

& Maine Railroad and a member of the committee, agreed to have a train ready by 10 o'clock that night. Mr. Endicott, acting for you, made all preparations for the train to proceed to Halifax, and at about 5.30 o'clock in the afternoon I received your commission to take full charge of the expedition, in accordance with the following letter from you to the Mayor of Halifax, N. S.: —

THE COMMONWEALTH OF MASSACHUSETTS,
EXECUTIVE DEPARTMENT, STATE HOUSE,
BOSTON, December 6, 1917.

To the Mayor, City of Halifax, N. S.

MY DEAR MR. MAYOR: — I am sending Hon. A. C. Ratshesky, of the Massachusetts Public Safety Committee, immediately to your city, with a corps of our best State surgeons and nurses, in the belief that they may be of service to you in this hour of need. I need hardly say to you that we have the strongest affection for the people of your city, and that we are anxious to do everything possible for their assistance at this time. Kindly express to the people of your city the very deep sympathy of the people of the Commonwealth of Massachusetts, and assure them that we are ready to answer any call that they may need to make upon us. Immediately upon hearing of the terrible blow dealt Halifax I sent the following telegram to you: —

Understand your city in danger from explosion and conflagration. Reports only fragmentary. Massachusetts stands ready to go the limit in rendering every assistance you may be in need of. Wire me immediately.

Upon being informed that the wires were out of commission, through the good offices of the Federal government at Washington this further telegram was sent you by wireless: —

Since sending my telegram this morning offering unlimited assistance, an important meeting of citizens has been held and Massachusetts stands ready to offer aid in any way you can avail yourself of it. We are prepared to send forward immediately a special train with surgeons, nurses and other medical assistance, but await advices from you.

Won't you please call upon Mr. Ratshesky for every help that you need. The Commonwealth of Massachusetts will stand back of Mr. Ratshesky in every way.

Respectfully yours,
SAMUEL W. McCALL,
Governor.

P. S. Realizing that time is of the utmost importance we have not waited for your answer but have dispatched the train.

At about 7 o'clock in the evening the American Red Cross asked permission to send five or six representatives of that body on our train, as otherwise they would be obliged to wait until 9 o'clock the next morning. To this I consented, without authority from you, knowing that it would meet with your hearty approval.

The train consisted of two Pullmans, one buffet car, one baggage car and an engine. Among the baggage were large quantities of surgical instruments, medicines, hospital supplies, blankets, sweaters, clothing, etc. Before leaving I had obtained letters or telegrams from a high official of each of the four railroads over which we were to travel to reach Halifax, giving the right of way for this special relief train.

The personnel of the expedition follows: —

SURGEONS AND DOCTORS (ALL MEMBERS OF THE MASSACHUSETTS STATE GUARD).

Major Harold G. Giddings (in command).
Major Edward A. Supple.
Major Donald V. Baker (Surgeon in Chief).
Major George W. Morse.
Major Peter Owen Shea.
Captain Edward F. Murphy (Adjutant).
Captain Thomas F. Harrington (Physician in Chief).
Captain John W. Dewis.
Captain Robert G. Loring (Ophthalmologist).
Captain DeWitt G. Wilcox.
Captain Nathaniel N. Morse (Anæsthetist).
Quartermasters Department, Captain Benjamin D. Hyde.
Quartermasters Department, Captain Henry G. Lapham.

RED CROSS REPRESENTATIVES.

John F. Moors, Chairman, Civilian Relief Committee (Metropolitan District).
C. C. Carsten, Secretary, Civilian Relief Committee (Metropolitan District).
Miss Katherine McMahon, Associate Director, Civilian Relief Committee (Metropolitan District).
J. Prentice Murphy, Secretary, Children's Aid Society.
Wm. H. Pear of the Boston Provident Association.
Miss Marion Rowe of the Boston Associated Charities.

6

NURSES.

Miss Elizabeth Peden (in charge).
Miss Charlotte Naismith.
Miss Marion Nevens.
Miss Mary A. Davidson.
Miss Caroline E. Carlton.
Miss Nellie P. Black.
Miss Edith F. Perkins.
Miss Elizabeth Choate.
Miss Jessie McInness.
Miss Florence B. McInness.

RAILROAD OFFICIALS.

G. V. Worthen, General Baggage Agent, Boston & Maine Railroad (going through to Halifax).

M. L. Harris, General Passenger Agent, Maine Central Railroad (left train at Portland).

E. F. S. Sturdee, General Agent, Canadian Pacific, Boston (through to Halifax).

C. K. Howard, General Agent, Canadian Government Railways, Boston (through to Halifax).

REPRESENTATIVES OF THE PRESS.

A. J. Philpott, Boston Globe.
R. W. Simpson, Associated Press.
Roy Atkinson, Boston Post.
Richard W. Sears, Boston American.
J. V. Keating, Boston Herald.

We left Boston at 10 o'clock on the evening of the disaster, and at Portland, Me., and at each station from there on until we reached St. John, N. B., the next morning, we wired continuously to the Mayor of Halifax, without receiving an answer.

At McAdam Junction we tried to get news from Halifax, but the most we obtained were rumors, and the more we received the worse they sounded. After consulting with Major Giddings, I called a meeting of the doctors, nurses and Red Cross workers, and requested that they take an inventory of the supplies, to learn if there were anything else they might need in such an emergency as I believed existed in Halifax, although we knew nothing definite.

After leaving McAdam Junction we were besieged at every stop with requests for accommodations on our train for workers going to Halifax in various capacities. I instructed those in

7

charge of the train to fill every available space, giving doctors and nurses the preference. Upon our arrival at St. John I instructed Captains Hyde and Lapham of the Quartermasters Department to secure additional drugs and supplies. They commandeered the services of King Kelly, Esq., a prominent lawyer of the city of St. John, who was waiting at the depot to go to Halifax as a member of the St. John unit. With his assistance we obtained large quantities of all kinds of medical supplies.

That we might definitely know just what supplies we had, I had an inventory made of those on board the train, including those belonging to the medical unit and those brought by the Red Cross, all of which had been turned over to this unit for use and distribution, and found we had the following: —

564 fracture pillows.
1,000 pillows.
1,368 muslin bandages.
53 splint straps.
330 gauze compresses, 9 by 9 inches.
4,000 gauze compresses, 4 by 4 inches.
432 flannel bandages.
1,196 bandages, 3 inches.
2,694 gauze bandages.
2,700 gauze compresses.
1,200 gauze sponges.
1,000 4-tail bandages.
1,720 gauze rolls.
204 flannel bandages.
890 slings.
8 Standard oil heaters.
4 boxes lanterns, glass.
21 pairs cotton blankets.
36 gray heavy army blankets.
6 litters.
3 bedpans.
4 urinals.

Red Cross Supplies.

498 sweaters.
226 flannel pajamas.
333 convalescent gowns.
8,300 gauze compresses, 4 inches.
9,354 bandages, 1 inch.
1 crate gauze sponges.
378 triangular bandages.
1 box miscellaneous.

Medical Supplies.

50 tubes morphine sulphate, $\frac{1}{8}$ grain, hypodermic.
5 tubes atropine, $\frac{1}{150}$ grain.
100 salt solution tablets.
1,000 aspirin tablets.
500 calomel, $\frac{1}{10}$-grain tablets.
500 cascara, 3-grain tablets.
9 pounds ether, $\frac{1}{4}$-pound cans.
6 pounds ether, $\frac{1}{2}$-pound cans.
10 gallons alcohol.
$\frac{1}{2}$ gallon tincture iodine.
100 corrosive tablets.
1 pint carbolic acid, 95 per cent. solution.
1 quart boracic acid, 4 per cent. solution.

And we purchased the following to add to our supplies: —

10 gallons alcohol.
1 gallon tincture iodine.
5 pounds cotton.
5 pounds boric ointment.
30 pounds vaseline.
8 ounces tincture digitalis.
500 caps camphor in oil.
1 gallon aromatic spirits of ammonia.
1 gross assorted catgut in tubes.
11 skeins No. 1 white twisted silk.
8 ounces 4 per cent. cocaine.
4 ounces 1 per cent. atropine.
1 pint olive oil.
12 pairs dressing scissors.
12 pairs dressing forceps.
1 dozen 4-ounce tins.
$1\frac{1}{2}$ dozen glass stoppered bottles (empty).
2 dozen rolls adhesive 7 by 36 inches.
4 dozen rolls adhesive 2 by 60 inches.
4 pints brandy.
1 gross safety pins.

While at St. John we received the first intimation of the awfulness of the disaster, together with the information that all telegraph and telephone wires were down and that no word had been received from Halifax, except in a roundabout way, — by relay, — of what had happened. I immediately

wired Mr. Endicott to forward at once a trainload of glass, putty and building materials of all kinds.

At St. John we encountered a heavy snowstorm, one of the severest of the winter, accompanied by a gale of terrible velocity. The snow was piling up and progress was difficult. We lost considerable time between St. John and Moncton. At this point, to insure getting through to Halifax, a large freight engine was attached to the train. Beyond Truro and Moncton the storm increased and was a veritable blizzard. We were also delayed several hours while our engine, which had broken down, was repaired. The climax was reached when we came up Folleigh Mountain, and the conductor in charge, C. H. Trueman, accompanied by C. K. Howard, General Agent, Canadian Government Railways, stated that, as an enormous snowdrift lay across the track, it was impossible to proceed farther. I then showed them the telegram from the official of the railroad, in which orders were given for the right of way to the special train. I pleaded with them to do everything in their power known to railroad men to clear the track. Under general conditions no attempt would have been made to keep the train moving, but the need was tremendously urgent. The men realizing this, and knowing that every moment was precious, worked like Trojans. Within an hour, by hard shoveling, the use of steam and ramming, and amid great cheers from all on board, we went through the drift, which extended higher than the door of the baggage car. We succeeded in reaching Truro, and found another engine and crew waiting for the final haul to Halifax.

We reached Halifax about 3 o'clock in the morning of December 8, with about sixty-five passengers, which included those taken on board at Fredericton Junction for Halifax. On account of the destruction of the depot at Halifax we were obliged to make a detour around the city. This was accomplished on tracks which, fortunately, had been prepared to connect with the new deep-water terminus, then in process of construction.

We landed at Rockingham Junction, which is six miles from the terminus. Mr. Howard and I had remained up all night. We got out of the train, but, as none of the officials connected with the affairs of the city were near, we returned and were obliged to wait about three hours for the snowplough to clear the line to the terminus. We aroused all who had retired and ordered an early breakfast.

We arrived at the terminus about 7 o'clock. Mr. Howard and I left the train, and, as well as we could, proceeded up the main road to the building which had been taken by the Canadian Government Railways for temporary headquarters. It was our good fortune to find there C. A. Hayes, General Manager of the Canadian Government Railways, — the first man we met in Halifax, and to whom I showed your letter to the Mayor. He was so affected that tears streamed down his cheeks. He arose and greeted me with: "Just like the people of good old Massachusetts. I am proud of them. I was born in that State, having formerly been a resident of West Springfield," and added that anything he or his railroad could do was at our service. I asked him for the service of Mr. Howard during my stay in Halifax, which he gladly granted. He gave us the use of his temporary wires, which had been connected with City Hall, and informed us that the private car of Sir Robert L. Borden, Premier of Canada, was on the tracks very near to ours.

Accompanied by Mr. Hayes we went back to the road, near our car, and Mr. Hayes dispatched a message to the Premier, with the suggestion that members of the relief party from Massachusetts would be very glad to call upon him in his car as soon as possible. His answer came most informally. He joined us in person in a very few minutes, expressing to us in appropriate words his profound appreciation of the quick action on the part of the Commonwealth of Massachusetts, and stating that this was the first relief to arrive in Halifax. He asked us to join him in proceeding to City Hall in order to present your letter to the Mayor and to learn what disposition we should make of our party and supplies. I requested Mr. John F. Moors of the Red Cross, Major Giddings of the medical unit, Mr. Hayes, General Manager of the Canadian Government Railways, and Mr. Howard to accompany us.

The conveyance that we took, we were informed, had been used day and night in carrying the wounded to hospitals,

and the dead to the morgue. The young man driver had lost all the members of his family, consisting of his wife and four children. It was a gruesome start. Débris had not been removed from the streets, and after a great deal of difficulty we arrived, at about 9 o'clock, at City Hall, which is located in the center of the city. An awful sight presented itself, — buildings shattered on all sides; chaos apparent; no order existed.

We were ushered into the office of the Mayor and introduced by Premier Borden to His Honor Governor McCullum Grant of Nova Scotia, General Benson, Military Commandant of the District, Admiral Chambers, Naval Commandant of the District, Colonel McKelvie Bell, Military Medical Officer, Chief Justice Harris of the Supreme Court of Nova Scotia, Chairman R. T. MacIlreith and members of the temporary relief committee.

The Mayor's secretary informed us that the Mayor was out of the city, and that Colonel McKelvie Bell and his committee were in full charge of the medical relief of the entire city. In this room, which was about 12 by 20, were assembled men and women trying to organize different departments of relief, while the other rooms were filled to their utmost capacity with people pleading for doctors, nurses, food and clothing for themselves and members of their family. Everything was in a turmoil, and apparently the first necessity was organization.

In conference with Premier Borden, Colonel Bell, Major Giddings, Mr. Moors, Mr. Hayes and Judge Harris, we decided that organization was our first duty, but it was necessary to broach the subject very carefully, as the situation was delicate and we did not wish to appear as intruders. We suggested that a building away from City Hall should be secured for headquarters for the relief committee, and as a result the City Club house, centrally located, was selected.

The above-named conference committee then proceeded to the City Club, where they held a conference with other citizens in relation to the appointing of committees and to properly organizing for relief work. From the time of the conference I was requested to join in the organization of different committees, to run the departments of the city and for relief. The immediate need was a Transportation Committee, on account of the large number of people coming to the city for relief work and the arrival of great quantities of food, clothing and supplies which were being forwarded from all parts of Canada and the United States; a Committee on Supplies, to take charge of supplies of all kinds coming into the city, divided into food and clothing; a Finance Committee, to take charge of all moneys that were being sent in from all parts of the world; a Committee on Construction, to take charge of buildings that were partially destroyed, that either had to be demolished or that could be temporarily repaired, and to get building supplies and labor from Canada and the United States; a Relief Committee, in which the members of the Red Cross, headed by Mr. Moors, took an active part, and to which they, with their experience, were particularly adapted; a Housing Committee, to care for those whose homes had been entirely destroyed or which could not be repaired, and whose efforts must be directed to caring for the large number of people entering the city from Canada and the United States; a Medical Department, to divide up the work of the surgeons, doctors, nurses and assistants; a Warehouse Department, to properly sort, store and distribute all the supplies being rushed into the city.

We then found that there was a great demand for doctors and nurses, which demand was partly filled by sending the members of our unit to different quarters of the city, with instructions to leave addresses so that all members of the unit could be readily gathered together that night, my opinion being that the greatest good could be done in keeping the unit working together and in establishing a hospital at the earliest possible moment.

Major Giddings and Colonel McKelvie Bell, acting at my request, in company with leading doctors of the city, found a large building near the center of the city known as the Bellevue Building and used as the Officers Club house. The building was turned over to us in very bad condition, — not a door or window remaining whole, and water and ice on the floor of every room. Apparently, under ordinary circumstances, it would have been impossible to have put it into shape for a long time. But by 12.30 o'clock, on the first day of our

arrival, Major Giddings with his quartermasters, ably assisted by about fifty of the crew of the United States training ship "Old Colony," who had arrived under an officer in charge with orders to report to me for service in any way required, together with a company of Canadian soldiers, ordered by General Benson, immediately set to work cleaning the rooms, covering the windows with paper and boards, as best they could, washing floors and woodwork, and removing all furniture to the upper part of the building. By 6 o'clock that night we had installed an operating room and had fitted up wards with one hundred beds and medical supplies taken from our relief train. On account of the urgency of the situation we received about sixty patients at 9 o'clock that night, and by noon the next day after our arrival the fully equipped American Bellevue Hospital, flying the American flag, was caring for one hundred patients and in full running order. This hospital received the worst cases from the different hospitals, which had become so overcrowded that proper attention could not be given them. This was especially true of the Military Camp Hill Hospital, which ordinarily could care for only three hundred patients but which was now caring for approximately sixteen hundred. Such equipment as was required in the nature of bedside tables, rubber sheets, dishes and silverware was furnished from the British Medical Stores Depot. The British authorities also furnished us with cooks, kitchen detail, and, from their commissary, supplied the hospital with food. They also detailed us a corps of trained clerks and orderlies.

On the day of our arrival we were entertained by Premier Sir Robert Borden at the Halifax Club, where the Premier made arrangements for the housing of the doctors of the unit, the Red Cross people, the newspaper men and myself. The club ordinarily has no sleeping facilities, and I am told that it is the first time in its history that beds have been set up. The nurses were quartered at private homes near the hospital, four of them being entertained at Government House, which is the Governor's private residence.

In order to give you a report on the medical aspect of the mission on which you sent me I am herewith including in my report to you the report of one of my assistants, Major Harold

G. Giddings, to the Acting Surgeon General. I wish also to note that the following nurses, in addition to those who came with us, worked with our unit, and to whom great credit is due: —

Miss Phillips.	Mrs. Davidson.
Miss Chambers.	Mrs. Brock.
Mrs. Leonard Tilley.	Mrs. McIntyre.
Mrs. Allison.	Miss Harrington.
Mrs. Bowman.	Miss Donville.

Major Giddings in his report says: —

We took formal possession of the Bellevue Military Hospital on the morning of December 9. That afternoon the hospital was officially visited by Sir Robert Borden, Premier of Canada. After his inspection His Excellency issued the following statement: "This afternoon I visited the hospital established at Bellevue by the Massachusetts hospital unit. They took possession yesterday afternoon at 2 o'clock, and within a few hours had every arrangement made for receiving patients, of whom nearly seventy-five are now being accommodated. All the arrangements were wonderfully planned considering the shortness of the time and difficulties that had to be overcome. The hospital is a triumph of organizing ability."

On the evening of December 9 the commanding officer attended by request a meeting of Red Cross representatives, — Lieutenant-Colonel F. McKelvie Bell, Mr. Ratshesky and representatives of the Boston Red Cross unit, which with the independent contingent of Dr. E. A. Codman had reached Halifax that morning. Dr. Codman was also present at this conference. That day a Medical Relief Committee had been appointed, with Lieutenant-Colonel F. McK. Bell as chairman. Among other things discussed at the meeting were ways and means of best caring for the sick and wounded of the city. As a result of observations made on the 8th by various members of this unit, who had visited many people in their homes, we were able to suggest the mapping of the city into districts, with the recommendation that a house-to-house canvass be made, first, by the social worker, who would report as to whether medical or surgical help was needed, the case then to

be seen by a doctor or nurse. This suggestion was made because our doctors found that large numbers of injured people requiring surgical aid had sought the shelter of buildings near the devastated area, where they were content to stay. So dazed were they by the disaster that they did not realize that help would come to them for the asking. Also, the members of our staff had found that many people could not leave their places of refuge for dressings because they had literally lost all their clothing.

Another observation made by our doctors was that contagious diseases would be likely to make an early appearance, due to the complete destruction of toilet facilities, the huddling together of large numbers in small quarters and the general physical demoralization. Because of these conditions we recommended the immediate establishment of a contagious hospital. That our surmise of early contagion was correct was proved by the fact that on December 12 three cases of throat infection, cultures of which immediately were made, were proved to be diphtheritic.

Our suggestions, as above indicated, were both accepted, the house-to-house canvass being made by members of the United States medical units, which went to the aid of the city between the time of their arrival in the city and the establishment of their respective hospitals. While doing this work their headquarters were at City Hall.

The morning of December 10 saw the Stars and Stripes flying over the hospital, the first time they had appeared in the city following the disaster. The flag was secured for us by Mr. Ratshesky. It is fitting here to record an incident in connection with the flag. It was brought to our attention that at the Camp Hill Hospital there was a woman from Lowell, Mass., Miss Martha Manter, so far as we know, with one exception, the only Massachusetts person injured in the disaster. Captain Harrington, whose home was formerly in Lowell, obtained permission to have Miss Manter transferred to Bellevue. After a good deal of effort the transfer was officially made. A laundry sleigh was commandeered, as all ambulances were engaged. As the patient was removed from the sleigh and carried into the hospital she broke down and cried.

When she finally gained control of herself, Captain Harrington, who thought perhaps the jarring of the sleigh had caused her pain, asked her what was the matter. Her reply was, "The sight of the American flag was too much for me, and I could not control myself. It looked so good to me."

On this same day we received an official visit from Samuel Wolcott and Dr. W. E. Ladd, the respective civil and medical heads of the Massachusetts Red Cross unit, who were establishing a hospital and were anxious to learn how we had proceeded. We supplied them with copies of all our orders, which they very much appreciated, and explained to them in detail the workings of our hospital, of which they made a complete inspection.

On the afternoon of December 11 the volume of work had become so great that additional nurses were required. We notified medical headquarters of this fact and they detailed to us the following ladies, all from St. John, and all, with one exception, graduate nurses: Miss Chambers of St. Luke's Hospital, New York; Miss Phillips, V.A.D., two years, England; Miss Donville, Newport Hospital, Rhode Island; Miss Harrington, Newport Hospital, Rhode Island; Mrs. Tilley, Royal Victoria Hospital, Montreal; Mrs. Allison, Newton Hospital; Newton; Mrs. Bowman, Waltham Hospital, Waltham; Mrs. Davidson and Mrs. Brock, Royal Victoria Hospital, Montreal; and Mrs. McIntyre, Massachusetts General Hospital, Massachusetts. These ladies remained with us until we surrendered control of the hospital, and did very valuable work.

A pleasing incident occurring this same day was a request from Colonel Bell that the commanding officer personally visit at Government House, the official residence of the Lieutenant-Governor, the son of Admiral Charles E. Kingsmill, who had been injured at the time of the explosion. The lad was more or less cut about the face, but fortunately was not seriously injured, and was taken to Ottawa the next afternoon by his father.

Another pleasant occurrence on the 11th was the arrival of Mrs. Wendell Barrett from Boston, who brought a considerable quantity of clothing for distribution, and certain needed hospital supplies, the gift of Mrs. Charles D. Sias of Boston.

Mrs. Barrett was met at the train by Dr. Dewis, who brought her and Mrs. Archibald, a prominent Halifax lady, to the hospital, where we were able to offer certain suggestions toward the accomplishment of the work they had in mind.

On the morning of the 12th there came to the hospital a sailor from the Norwegian boat concerned in the collision. He walked lame and one eye was injured. Examination failed to disclose any serious trouble, but for the purpose of observation it was decided to keep him in the hospital twenty-four hours. Late that afternoon, during the confusion incidental to the inspection of the hospital by the Rhode Island contingent, to whom the plant was to be turned over that evening, Johnson was observed limping toward the stairway from the top floor. He was sent back to his ward by our medical officer. Later in the evening he offered $25 to one of our volunteer nurses if she would allow him to go home. She informed Captain Lapham of this, who then placed a guard over the man and immediately notified the provost marshal of the man's actions, with the result that his arrest was ordered, and the man is now in custody awaiting the result of the inquiry. On being searched a letter written in German, badly incriminating the man, was found on his person, also many notes concerning the catastrophe.

On the morning of December 12, after a conference with Mr. Ratshesky, it seemed that the situation as regards medical aid was so well in hand that our unit might with propriety withdraw. In addition to the Massachusetts and Rhode Island Red Cross divisions, already referred to, there had arrived in the city a large number of doctors and nurses from Maine, prepared to establish a hospital. Other doctors had come independently, and altogether there was an abundance of professional help at hand.

After this conference we held another, attended by Colonel Potter, Medical Department and Staff Officer from Ottawa, Colonel F. McK. Bell and Major Garry DeN. Hough, commanding the Rhode Island division of the Red Cross. At this latter conference both Colonel Potter and Colonel Bell agreed that even without the aid of Massachusetts there were doctors enough to cope with the situation. Major Hough also expressed

---

* The sailor was later identified as Norwegian citizen Johan Johansen. The letter, in no way incriminating, was written in Norwegian, not German as originally claimed. J. C. Burchell, K.C., the counsel for the IMO's owners secured Johansen's release after several days of argument with military intelligence.

The spy scare and anti-German feeling were aggravated considerably by the irresponsible and inflammatory journalism of the Halifax Herald.

"We know now, too, that the prime responsibility for this, as for every other catastrophe which has afflicted the peoples of the earth as a by-product of the war, rests with that close co-partner, that arch fiend, the Emperor of the Germans; neither are we disposed

to hold the German peoples entirely free of direct responsibility for this catastrophe; the cause is obscure; but it is certain that there are in Halifax today certain people of German extraction and birth whose citizenship in the Dominion has been respected since the war began, who have been allowed full freedom in our community to buy and sell, and to pursue their normal occupations. WHO HAVE REPAID US WITHIN THE LAST FEW DAYS BY LAUGHING AT OUR DISTRESS AND MOCKING OUR SORROW . . . so long as there are people in Halifax who remember this past week, or whose children remember it, so long will the name of Germany be a name for loathing and disgust." Editorial, Halifax Herald, December 12, 1917.

his willingness to take over the command of Bellevue. That this arrangement might be official, I sent the following letter to Colonel Bell:—

BELLEVUE MILITARY HOSPITAL,
HALIFAX, N. S., December 12, 1917.

Lieutenant-Colonel F. McKELVIE BELL.

The medical unit of the Massachusetts State Guard came to Halifax at the time of the disaster as a relief expedition to help until the relief work could be thoroughly organized and until sufficient surgical help had been obtained to take care of the situation.

Since there are at the present time sufficient civilian doctors and nurses in the city to cope with the situation, and because of the serious conditions in Massachusetts requiring the presence of the unit there, the commanding officer of the Massachusetts State Guard unit respectfully requests permission to withdraw from Bellevue Military Hospital and to transfer said hospital to the Rhode Island Red Cross division, which has signified its willingness to take over the work of the hospital.

Since the above was dictated, I am in receipt of a telegram from Colonel Brooks stating: "It is very important that you and others of the State Guard unit return as soon as Mr. Ratshesky is willing, and you can get proper accommodations."

HAROLD G. GIDDINGS,
Major, M. C., M. S. G., Commanding.

Very shortly afterward there came the following reply from Colonel Bell:—

HALIFAX, N. S., December 12, 1917.

Major H. G. GIDDINGS, *M. C., M. S. G., Officer commanding Bellevue Hospital, Halifax.*

SIR:— I have the honor to acknowledge receipt of your communication of December 12, 1917, informing me that it is necessary for your unit to return at the earliest possible date to take up your military work in Massachusetts.

As the Rhode Island Red Cross division will be able to replace your unit at Bellevue Hospital, it will be quite satisfactory for your unit to transfer the hospital to them on the 12th instant.

Permit me to assure you and the other members of your unit that the city of Halifax is profoundly grateful for the valuable assistance which you have rendered during this crisis. Would you kindly convey to Colonel Brooks our heartfelt thanks for sending us a unit which was most capable and efficient in every branch of the medical work, and whose organization was perfect. It is with great regret that we see your unit leaving us, but we realize that the emergency is now over, and your services are needed at home.

Again thanking you on behalf of the Medical Relief Committee and the Department of Militia and Defence for your excellent services, I have the honor to be, sir,

Your obedient servant,
F. McK. BELL, *Lieutenant-Colonel,*
Assistant Director Medical Services, Medical District No. 6.

In reply to this letter from Colonel Bell I sent the following, with a copy of my report to you dated December 10. The report was forwarded with the letter, at Colonel Bell's request.

BELLEVUE MILITARY HOSPITAL,
HALIFAX, N. S., December 12, 1917.

Colonel McK. BELL, *Church of England Institute, Halifax, N. S.*

MY DEAR COLONEL BELL:— I am enclosing a copy of my initial report to Colonel Brooks. I wish also to take this opportunity to express to you, on behalf of the Massachusetts State Guard medical unit, the profound thanks of each and every member of the organization for the many courtesies and very great help which you have extended. Had you not come to our aid as you did when we arrived here ready for work, it would have been quite impossible for us to have accomplished our modest contribution in relief work. I would make special mention of the services rendered, if I may so term them, by Captain Barrett. His tireless energy, his thorough knowledge of military hospital organization, and his unfailing courtesy were indeed a bright spot.

I would also take this occasion to acknowledge with deep thanks your very courteous letter authorizing me to hand the command of the hospital to the Rhode Island division of the Red Cross.

With sincere regards, believe me,
Most cordially yours,
HAROLD G. GIDDINGS,
Major, M. C., M. S. G.

P. S. I am very sure that Colonel Brooks would sanction in any way that you see fit the use of the enclosed report.

Arrangements were then made between Major Hough and your representative for the transfer of the hospital to the Rhode Island contingent at 7 o'clock that evening. During the afternoon the doctors and nurses from Rhode Island visited Bellevue, and we pointed out to them its organization and plan of operation. At 7 that evening the transfer was formally made.

20

On the afternoon of the 12th there came a request from Mr. Ratshesky that the commanding officer visit Miss Helen Graham, daughter of George E. Graham, General Manager of the Dominion & Atlantic Railways. Miss Graham had a septic hand, which had been neglected, the result of being cut by flying glass at the time of the explosion. It was necessary to open the hand, and that she might have suitable care after our unit left Halifax, we were able to have her admitted to the Red Cross Hospital under Dr. W. E. Ladd of Boston.

The general character of the wounds treated at the hospital is of interest. They were very largely injuries of the face caused by flying glass, and included many injuries to the eyes. In fact, there were more of these than of any others. The explanation of this is as follows. Two explosions occurred; one was a comparatively minor affair, but was sufficiently severe to bring people to their windows to see what had happened; then came the terrific explosion which razed the city and created so much havoc. It was at this time that so many people were injured by the glass.

A number of cases of insanity were reported following the disaster, but at Bellevue we had only one such. This was a woman who finally created so much disturbance that it became necessary to transfer her to the Hospital for Insane across the harbor, at Dartmouth. Cases of mild shell shock, while not officially appearing on the hospital records, were not infrequent. This type of case was well illustrated by a stenographer who came to work at the hospital. At the time of the accident she was but a short distance beyond the more severely affected district. After working part of the morning of the 12th (the explosion having occurred on the 6th) she was in such a nervous state, trembling, occasionally crying and utterly unable to concentrate or to manipulate the typewriter, that it became necessary to send her home and to bed.

There were certain bright spots in all the suffering which we saw at Bellevue. Social workers, mostly from the Red Cross, were constantly coming to the hospital, distributing dainties to the children and clothing to all who needed it; and the need was surely very great.

During our first twenty-four hours in the hospital there came

to us many people who were but slightly injured but who had no homes. Of course all such were taken in, accorded every attention, and kept at the hospital until the Housing Committee had made arrangements to supply them with clothing and with accommodations.

One patient we had in the hospital was a little girl of four years who was the only existing member of her family, and who could not understand why her calls for "Grannie" were unheeded.

Another pathetic instance was the following. A little child of about three years had had both eyes removed. When she recovered from the ether she clapped her hands and gleefully remarked to the nurse, "Oh, Nursie, it's night, isn't it?"

Also among our patients was Corporal Combeau of the Canadian Army, who at the time of the disaster was corporal of the guard at one of the piers. When he saw the munition ship in flames he turned out the guard. As the guard came down the pier the explosion occurred, and every man except Combeau was killed. He himself was blown in a cloud of débris a distance of fully one-half mile. When he came to us we found that he had a fracture of the right thigh, and a ragged piece of steel was embedded in his left shin; in addition, there was a lacerated wound of the left elbow.

The work of no individual member of the unit stands out pre-eminently. Perhaps the one surgeon whose services were of the most help was Captain Loring. This was because of the great number of eye injuries, already referred to. Captain Loring was called upon to do work not only at Bellevue but at the Military Hospital, the Halifax Infirmary and at Camp Hill Hospital, where he saw, at the request of Lieutenant-Governor Calvin Coolidge of Massachusetts, Miss Bertha Ferguson, an American girl of Boston. Dr. Loring's presence was most urgently needed when we arrived, and his work received much favorable comment.

Arrangements had been made for the care of the hospital at night by one medical and one surgical officer. The work was done voluntarily throughout our time of occupation by Dr. Harrington and Dr. Shea.

On the afternoon before we left Halifax, Major Baker, Captain Nathaniel Morse and Captain Lapham assumed the role of Santa Claus and carried to the children in the hospital a generous contribution of toys.

The day of December 13 was given over to visiting various parts of the city and in general getting ready for our departure for home on the morning of the 14th. Up to this time several members of the party had not had the opportunity to see the devastated area. Through the courtesy of the provost marshal of the city, Major Edward Mooney, a most charming and genial officer, we were supplied with automobiles and drivers to take us through the district, which was, of course, a trip of the greatest interest. That evening His Honor Lieutenant-Governor and Mrs. F. McCullum Grant, of the Province of Nova Scotia, gave to our party a delightful and informal dinner, which was in the nature of an official recognition of the work the unit had done. Lacking other means of conveyance to the Governor's home, the doctors were carried in one of the new automobile trucks, the gift of our State, which that day had reached Halifax from Boston.

In addition to the members of our own party there were present at the dinner General Benson, commanding the Military District of Halifax, Admiral Chambers, representing the Naval Forces there, Colonel F. McKelvie Bell, from the Medical Department of the Dominion, the Hon. R. T. MacIlreith, Chairman of the Halifax Relief Committee, Mr. John F. Moors, of the American Red Cross, and Colonel Edmund Billings, who had arrived at Halifax on the "Calvin Austin" the night before. Speeches were made by all of the above-mentioned guests, and in addition Captain Harrington and your representative were called upon. The occasion, at which cordiality was the keynote, was a most delightful one. Besides the speaking already alluded to, a toast was proposed by His Honor the Governor to "The President and the King," and both the British and the American national anthems were sung. Thus the event assumed certain international significance. In fact, Governor Grant during the course of his remarks expressed what we all felt, namely, that, lamentable as the disaster was, it had undoubtedly furthered the cordial relations between Canada and the United States.

At the dinner Mr. MacIlreith read the following letter, which he afterwards presented to the commanding officer of the unit: —

HALIFAX, N. S., December 13, 1917.

H. G. GIDDINGS, *Major, Medical Corps, State of Massachusetts, Halifax, N. S.*

DEAR MAJOR GIDDINGS: — At a meeting of the Executive of the Relief Committee, held this afternoon, it was the earnest desire of all the members that before the Medical Corps of the State of Massachusetts took its departure from Halifax a formal minute should be placed on our records, which in the future will be the basis of the official history of the Halifax disaster, expressing the committee's deep appreciation of the prompt and humane action of the authorities in Boston in dispatching your corps to Halifax, and of the professional efficiency and noble spirit which you and all members of your unit have exhibited since coming to our stricken city. We shall always bear you in grateful remembrance, and wish you a safe journey home.

Yours truly,

R. T. MACILREITH,
Chairman, Relief Committee.

Major Giddings concludes his report with the following summary of the work done by the unit: —

Total out-patients treated,	167
Visits in homes,	53
Hours spent in advisory capacity,	23
Combined surgical and medical service: —	
Total house admissions,	75
Total operations done (exclusive of eye service),	10
Total discharges,	17
Total ethers,	46
Total ether used (pounds),	3½
Total cases turned over to Rhode Island unit,	58

Eye service, Dr. Loring: —		
Total cases seen at Bellevue,	27	
Total cases seen at Cogswell Street Military Hospital,	85	
Total cases seen at Halifax Infirmary,	10	
		122
Total operations at Bellevue,	18	
Total operations at Cogswell Street Military Hospital,	15	
Total operations at Halifax Infirmary,	2	
		35

In addition to these, 68 others were admitted, of whom no clinical records were kept.

MASSACHUSSETTS HALIFAX RELIEF COMMITTEE.

Halifax Branch: 1918-19

[Letter to Henry B. Endicott from
G. Fred Pearson, January Eighth, 1918, and
reply to the same, concerning
work of the committee, Jan. 18, 1918.]

H. B. Endicott, Esq.,

    Massachussetts Relief Committee,

        State House - Boston.

Dear Mr. Endicott:-

        The Committee appointed by you and the gentlemen

accompanying you as representatives of the Massachussetts Halifax

Relief Committee to act for that Committee in Halifax, met this

morning, all the members being present and I was directed to

advise you as to the matters discussed.

        An attempt was made to frame a tentative immediate

policy.

TENTATIVE IMMEDIATE POLICY.

        There are two classes of people in Halifax who will

require to be helped to make a new start in life.

        First.   Those families whose homes and furnishings
                 have been wholly destroyed and,

        Second. Those families who are still living in
                 a portion of their homes and who have
                 suffered a partial loss of furnishings.

        For the first class, temporary housing is now

being provided by the Reconstruction Committee.

        The second class are now housed in their own

homes and have the furnishings which they had before the

disaster.   It is true that in most cases they are living in

                    [1918]
                     915.

H. B. E...........2

one or two rooms, but generally speaking, the house has been made weather-proof, and with the exception of minor things in the way of furnishings, this class of people are now fairly comfortable. When the Reconstruction Committee finally repairs the houses, so as to make the entire house fit for occupancy, it will undoubtedly be discovered that much of the furniture has been injured or destroyed, and this Committee, subject to your direction, might very well undertake to supply the deficiencies.

It seemed to the members of the Committee present that the first problem was to carry out your wishes with respect to the first class of people above noted. This class could roughly be divided into two sub-divisions. First, those families who will be provided by the Rehabilitation Committee with a standard outfit, which outfit will equal, and in many cases exceed the outfit which the family had previous to the disaster. Let us say for the moment, that there will be 500 of these cases. That leaves roughly 500 cases or homes which could not be reinstated in the enjoyment of their former comforts by the outfit proposed to be given by the Rehabilitation Committee. It is proposed to have access to all the information which the Rahabilitation Committee has collected and to endeavour, as far as possible, from this information, to segregate the cases mentioned above.

It is further proposed to investigate these

cases, first endeavouring to get all the information available from the friends or acquaintances of the family, in order to arrive at some independent opinion of their necessities, and finally to visit the family and from the standpoint of a friend, offer them assistance in the fitting out of their new home.

It seemed to the Committee that certain of the essentials proposed to be provided by the Rehabilitation Committee would be common to all homes. As an illustration, - bed-springs and a kitchen table. Steps are now being taken to ascertain what these uniform essentials are *and* of what quality and type the Rehabilitation Committee propose to provide.

I should like to make it plain to you that the opinion of the Committee was that only a portion of the standard equipment provided by the Rehabilitation Committee would, in any case, be used, because it fully shares your views that there should be variety, and not uniformity, in these new homes, but at the same time it was felt that if some of the essentials proposed to be furnished by the Rehabilitation Committee could be used without violating the policy so well expressed by your Mr. Russell, that, to *that* some extent, *it* would conserve the Massachussetts funds.

PURCHASING SUPPLIES.

       The Committee then considered the question
of where the furnishings which it is to provide could best
be purchased. In this connection, it was felt to be highly
desirable if the housewife could be given an opportunity,
within reasonable limits, of selecting the articles which she
would prefer. The suggestion was made that a warehouse
should be established in Halifax, containing samples of the
articles which the Committee would furnish. Having in view
your request that there should be variety, instead of uniformity, in which view the Committee fully concurs, it was pointed
out that this would require a very large warehouse, which
would involve a considerable expenditure for rent, light, heat
and labor. The suggestion was then made that the same
object of giving the recipient an opportunity of selecting
the articles, might be served by the preparation of an
illustrated catalogue. A suggestion was then made that this
object could be accomplished in one of two ways, either by
your Committee in Boston making arrangements with a responsible
house-furnishing firm There to purchase the articles required from
that firm, in which case a representative of the firm might
very well be asked to visit Halifax, see the type of houses,
to get an idea by personal touch with this Committee of its
proposed plan of operation. On his return, either the

existing catalogue of the firm could be availed of, or
possibly a new one might be made, selecting the cuts of
the articles from such existing catalogue. This, it seemed
to the Committee, would not involve a great deal of expense.
In the alternative, a sub-Committee of your Boston Committee
might be appointed as sort of a purchasing Committee in Boston
and that Committee itself might issue a catalogue and carry a
stock in Boston.

The idea of the Halifax Committee would be to
send any orders for articles as nearly as might be, in carload
lots, but have the articles packed, tagged and addressed to
the person in Halifax to whom they are to be given. This
procedure, if it commends itself to your judgment, would give
the beneficiary in Halifax the opportunity of exercising his
or her own judgment, and also the personal touch of goods
being shipped direct from the good people of Massachussetts
for the assistance of their friends in Halifax.

METHOD OF SHIPMENT.

We are taking the question of shipping the
supplies up with the Dominion Atlantic Railway and will advise
you later as to the result. Our present thought is that
goods would arrive more expeditiously if shipped by boat to
Yarmouth and thence by rail to Halifax, and if that line

could guarantee ∦ quick despatch and closest rates, it
seems to us at the moment that this would be the best way
to ship goods.

PURCHASES IN HALIFAX.

The Committee is of the opinion that from time
to time it may be necessary to purchase articles in Halifax
for emergency purposes.   In the present view of the
Committee, these purchases would not be large or numerous,
but in order to quickly fill a need, it is probable that
we shall have to make certain purchases here.   In this
connection, would you be good enough to advise how these purchases shall be paid for; that is to say, whether you would
care to establish a credit here for the Halifax Committee,
subject to weekly audited reports as to its expenditure, or
would you prefer that bills should be sent to Boston for
payment?

ORGANIZATION.

For the present, the view of the Halifax Committee is
that it should secure the services of a competent stenographer
who could act as assistant to the Honorary Secretary, take
charge of all the correspondence, filing, tabulation of
reports for the information of the Boston Committee and
kindred clerical duties.   In view of the great demand in
Halifax for persons of this class in connection with the

various Relief Committees, it is not thought possible to quickly procure an efficient male or female for this purpose.   Do you think it possible for you to select a competent person in Boston and arrange that he or she should come to Halifax to undertake these duties?

The Committee is also of the opinion that it should have the services of a capable office manager and book-keeper to take charge of the office, to receive and check up shipments of goods, see that they are delivered as instructed by the Committee and obtain receipts from the persons to whom they have been delivered. We think we can find such a man here.

REPORTS.

It was felt by the Committee that the Minutes of all its meetings should be kept in duplicate and one copy forwarded to you, to be inserted in a Minute Book in Boston, so that you would be kept in daily touch with matters that come before our Committee for decision, and you would, in this way, be enabled to indicate to us from time to time your wishes with regard to any particular matter.   It is also the opinion of the Committee that weekly reports, or if you prefer it, semi-weekly reports, should be made to you on the progress of the work, in as ~~its~~

complete detail as reports are expected to be made
to your Halifax Committee.

OTHER WORK.

It was felt that an effort should be
made at once to ascertain the needs of the class of
persons, such for instance, as the clergyman referred
to by your Mr. Russell, who met with such a heavy loss,
and deal with each case of that character along the lines
suggested by you.   For that purpose we are endeavouring to secure the services of a corps of investigators
whose services will be given voluntarily, and of a type
and character to be relied upon.   The people who lived
in the devastated area and adjacent thereto have been
investigated and investigated until they are sick of the
thought of investigation.   The investigation in all cases
has not been carried on by sympathetic and mature people,
and it is our desire to be very careful as to the class
of people whose assistance we shall ask to gather for us
the information for the above purpose.

You will quite understand that we have not
yet had an opportunity of properly organizing our work,
and it is with the hope that you will be good enough
to peruse this lengthy letter and give us the benefit

H. B. E.........9

of your valuable judgment in connection with this
matter that this letter is written.

Will you, in your reply, also indicate
to whom and where we shall address our future
correspondence intended for the consideration
of your Committee.

Yours very truly,

G. Fred Pearson

Chairman

January 18, 1918.

Mr. G. Fred Pearson, Chairman,
Massachusetts-Halifax Relief Committee,
Halifax, Nova Scotia.

My dear Mr. Pearson:

This will acknowledge receipt of your letter of January 8th and supplement my letter to you of January 9th.

We have read your letter carefully, and at the outset must say that you and your Committee in Halifax, representing the Massachusetts-Halifax Relief Committee here, have grasped fully our intentions regarding the disbursement of the Massachusetts Fund.

Replying to your first inquiry,-

TENTATIVE IMMEDIATE POLICY: We would say, by all means take care of those who have lost everything. Then as funds will permit take care of those whose furniture was only partially destroyed. As we have already written you, we will have at least $500,000 for this work.

We agree with you that it may be that in certain essentials, such might have to be common to all homes,—that is, such things as kitchen tables, kitchen utensils, bed springs, mattresses, sheets, pillows and slips, towels, table cloths, etc. We see no reason why some of the essentials proposed to be furnished by the Rehabilitation Committee could not be used; in fact, we would fully approve of using them, and it would in no way violate the policy suggested by us, and as you well say, would conserve the Massachusetts Funds that the work may be extended further, but even in this it may be that your Committee may see its way clear to have some variety without much difference in cost.

PURCHASING SUPPLIES: We think the catalogue suggestion (from which to choose) would be the least expensive, and for your purposes fully as comprehensive. We hope to get in touch with one of the large dealers today and have them assign to us a man who would be capable of working up such a catalogue, and will forward one to you as soon as possible.

Regarding your suggestion to send the articles in car load lots, but marked direct to the person in Halifax to whom they are to be given, we doubt the feasibility from our end. We think these things should go forward in car load lots, but we believe that your committee could very much better allot them to the respective families. We are inclined to think that the shipping of the goods should be made direct by boat to Yarmouth. We have taken this matter up with the Eastern Steamship Company today and found that their boat, which is the only boat running between Boston and Yarmouth, has been taken off and sent to dry dock at New York. The Boston office will not know much before Tuesday when this trip can be resumed, but we will let you know as early as possible. The Eastern Steamship Company connects at Yarmouth with the Dominion Atlantic Railway. If it is not going to be possible to send goods by boat, then we shall have to send them all rail.

PURCHASES IN HALIFAX: You will probably find it necessary to make purchases in Halifax, and in this connection we think the most advisable way to handle such purchases would be for our Committee to establish in Halifax credit for the use of your Committee. This can be arranged by our making a deposit subject to your order at some Halifax bank which you may designate, and payments against this account might be made along the lines suggested in our letter of January 9th.

ORGANIZATION: We, of course, expect that you will establish a proper organization for the conduct of your work, such organization to be comprised of the number and kind of employees that you think would be necessary. We think that it would be better for you to employ Halifax people rather than for us to send anybody from here, as we feel that they would more fully and thoroughly understand their work and appreciate your situation.

REPORTS: We agree with you that it would be well to keep minutes of meetings in duplicate,—one copy to be retained by you, and one to be sent forward to us. We would prefer weekly reports to semi-weekly reports, as this would entail less work at your end, and will answer our purposes fully as well.

OTHER WORK: We fully approve of the manner in which your propose obtaining information regarding those who should be rehabilitated and the purposes thereof. In this connection, we repeat that you apparently fully comprehend just how we wish Massachusetts money to be spent, as you have outlined it quite clearly under the heading, "OTHER WORK."

We have no suggestions to make to you at this time, but should any develop from time to time, we will certainly forward them to you. Meanwhile, please address all communications as follows:

Henry B. Endicott, Chairman,
   Massachusetts-Halifax Relief Committee,
      State House, Boston, Mass.

Will you kindly accept and convey again to the members of your committee the thanks of my colleagues and myself for your splendid co-operation in this work.

Yours very truly,

HENRY B. ENDICOTT

CHAIRMAN,
MASSACHUSETTS-HALIFAX RELIEF COMMITTEE

GAUVIN & GENTZEL PHOTO, PUBLIC ARCHIVES OF NOVA SCOTIA

Gov. McCall Apartments, Exhibition Grounds, October 9, 1918.

RECONSTRUCTION COMMITTEE HALIFAX.   FEBRUARY 11th, 1918.

Type	Reconstruction Committee Design
Location	Exhibition Grounds
Number	40. 102 x 25 ft. 2 stories high
	320 houses; 4 rooms and bathroom
Equipment:	Range, boiler, bath, closet and sink; hot and cold water.
Accommodation.	320 families averaging 6 members to a family.
Total capacity	1,920 to 2,240 persons.
Contractor.	Reconstruction Committee.
Rent.	$12.00 per month.

"With splendid heart and quick efficiency the State of Massachusetts sent by sea a complete relief expedition—food, clothing, bedding, medical supplies, doctors, nurses, trained welfare workers, together with a fleet of motor trucks complete with drivers and gasoline and loaded with carefully selected supplies—all ready to move off as soon as the ship came alongside. It was a perfect example of American generosity and quick-wittedness, and the city greeted it with a gasp of relief. And this was only the beginning. Financed entirely by American funds, the Massachusetts. Relief Commission continued its clinics and its housing and welfare work in Halifax long after the disaster, a memory cherished by Haligonians to this day."

FROM *HALIFAX: WARDEN OF THE NORTH* BY THOMAS H. RADDALL. REPRINTED BY PERMISSION OF THE CANADIAN PUBLISHERS, McCLELLAND AND STEWART LIMITED, TORONTO.

"Halifax and Dartmouth stand face to face with one of the biggest problems which has ever confronted any community this side of the Atlantic. Nothing can restore the lives lost or eliminate the serious physical and mental injuries sustained by thousands. The work of restoring the homes, the places of business, the churches, and the schools is a colossal one, while the work of rehabilitating those who had lost all or part of their worldly possessions is perhaps greater."

CANON C. W. VERNON, *CHURCH WORK*, JANUARY 10, 1918

BUILDING MATERIAL USED BY RECONSTRUCTION COMMITTEE TO THIS DATE.

Material	Quantity	No. of Carloads.
Lumber	7,500,000 ft.	525
Beaver board and wall board	2,419,000 "	62
Roofing paper	41,000 rolls	46
Tar paper	5,600 "	5½
Nails	2,500 kegs	7
Shingles	168,000	1
Lath	91,000	1
Glass	2,347,000 ft.	78
Putty	45,510 lbs.	1
Brick	662,000	33
Cement	159,000 lbs.	5
Lime	80,000 "	2
Sand	1,140 tons	19
C. I. Pipe	14,915 ft	3
W. I. "	7,496 "	3
Tile pipe	16,058 "	5
		796

NOTE: 22 trains of 36 cars each, covering about 6 miles of track,
or enough to encircle the City.

11/2/18
McR/HJB

76 brick

REPORT OF TEMPORARY REPAIR WORK UP TO FEBRUARY 11TH,1918.

Number of requests made for General Repairs	5,258
Number of Building Reports handed in by the District Building Inspectors.	1,426
Number of buildings temporarily completed so far reported	3,894
Temporary Repairs completed to Soldiers' Homes by the 1st. C.C....	50
Temporary Repairs completed to the Soldiers' Homes by the Military Housing Committee	7
Number of public institutions and other buildings fitted up for Relief Purposes.	68
Number of Barns and Stables repairs completed	68
Dwellings reported by City Engineer and put in hand for Permanent Repairs	645
Dwellings reported on by City Engineer upon which no repairs are to be made	555
Number of Chimney Repair Requests	2,624
Number of Chimneys Inspected by District Chimney Inspectors and found O.K.	1,268
Number of Chimney Repairs completed	1,867
Number of Sanitary Repair requests	1,940
Number of Sanitary House Inspections by City Health Board	848
Number of Sanitary Repairs completed so far reported	1,276
Total Number of men registered (Reconstruction Committee	5,114
Total Number of men registered (Bate, McMahon & Co.)	645
Total number of men registered (Cavicchi & Pagana)	1,000

Total number of men working February 11th.

Reconstruction Committee	3,052	
Cavicchi & Pagana- clearing devastated area	704	
Bate & McMahon, Contractors- building temporary dwellings	420	
Eastern Investment Corporation- building temporary dwellings	138	
Falconer & MacDonald, Contractors- building temporary dwellings.	146	
Dartmouth Relief	65	
Webbey-Smith, Contractors, Dartmouth- building temporary dwellings	20	
Fairview to Bedford Relief	17	4,562

Total number of teams working February 11th:

29 double)		
22 single)		51
Total number of transports (motor trucks) February 5th.		30
Total number of passenger cars February 5th.		21

24/2/18- C J.

In conversation with my friend, Fred Longland, I discovered he had been an eye-witness of the dreadful explosion at Halifax, Nova Scotia, on 6th December, 1917   **Norman F. Ellison**

In due course I found myself back in Halifax at the end of October 1917, reporting to the NIOBE for draft again. I think it was the end of November 1917 that "Seagull Patrol" was moved to Sydney, Cape Breton, to deal with the German submarines very active outside this port and Louisbourg and all along that coast up to the French Islands of St. Pierre and Miquelon.

So here I was back again on the old NIOBE reporting to the Drafting Officer. "Chippy" Carpenter was an old shipmate of mine and the next few minutes were happily spent in reminiscences and light-hearted conversation. Happening to glance through a porthole, I noticed a ship inbound for the anchorage at Bedford Basin, and remarked to "Chippy": "There's no doubt about the nationality of that vessel; look at the size of her flag." I left him and found my way up to the boat deck to take another look at the ship with the large flag at her stern. She was MONT BLANC, a French vessel arriving from Galveston, Texas, with a load of explosives, 3,500 tons of T.N.T. and 3,000 tons of Lyddite, as well as a deck cargo of benzol contained in steel drums, a very dangerous cargo. By this time I had returned to the upper deck to take another look and found MONT BLANC well advanced towards the Narrows, the entrance to Bedford Basin, and at the same time a Belgian Relief ship in ballast outward bound was coming out. Maybe it was due to the latter being in ballast and so not answering her helm, but she appeared to lose steerage-way, and I could see at once, unless some miracle intervened, there would be a collision, and so it happened. This was serious, and I moved to the forecastle deck for a better view. The next thing was a series of minor explosions as the benzol drums ignited and exploded. By this time the fire had begun to get a serious hold, and a large column of black smoke rose from the deck of the stricken ship. I stepped on a bollard and placed my hands on the shoulders of a chief petty officer to steady myself.

Practically the whole ship's company had assembled on the forecastle as the word "ship on fire" got around, and I thought, "There's going to be trouble here before long unless I am very much mistaken." I turned to Jock standing next to me and said, "They'll never put that fire out," and I had hardly spoken the words when there was a blinding flash, an awful shudder and a bang which made me think it was the end of the world. I felt as though I had been hit in the face with a big flat board. There was a momentary stillness, and then boiler tubes, rivets and jagged steel plate from the hull were flying all around us. I saw a large piece hit the foremost funnel of our ship and completely flatten it; flying debris destroyed our other three funnels. It was imperative to take cover quickly but I could find none as the crowd on the forecastle deck must have thought the same. Every conceivable hole and corner was occupied; some were even hanging down ventilators. There was nothing else for me to do but to run the whole length of the deck to reach the after companion-way when I would be behind armour and safe. But the explosion had caused a large tidal wave to sweep across the harbour lifting our ship to an acute angle and throwing me down violently on the steel deck. I had to crawl the rest of the way and thankfully reached the shelter of the after deck badly bruised.

What an unholy mess the main deck was in; 19 men lay dead without a mark of any kind on them and the wounded crowded the sick bay for attention. One poor fellow was bleeding to death and nothing could save him. It seems he suffered from that condition known as haemophilia when even a cut finger can be serious. By noon the ship was on an even keel out adrift from her moorings. Willing hands rectified this, and a little order began to appear out of complete chaos. The scene in the harbour was unbelievable. Cargo ships partially wrecked, drifted about out of control; the Belgian Relief ship IMO involved in the collision, had been flung so far up on the Dartmouth beach that it took expert engineering to get her back in the sea again. A large tug-boat was reposing on No. 2 Pier dropped there by the tidal wave. Four large cargo ships were complete wrecks with their middles cut out as though by a giant scythe.

I was detailed now to take a platoon and look for dead sailors on the streets, and in the schools which had been turned into morgues. The bodies just as they were picked up, were in the boy's side of the school, and when cleaned up a bit were laid out in the girl's side for identification. It was my job to go into the streets and wherever I saw a pair of bell-bottomed pants, to heave out the remainder and lay it on one side.

At the end of this gruesome task, I returned to the ship and had a much needed brandy in the wrecked wardroom. Then in walked a commander who said, "Does anyone know of an officer called Longland?" I stood up and said, "Yes, sir. That is my name." Then he said, "There is a man in Victoria Hospital Emergency ward, badly hurt, and in his extremity keeps on calling out your name. Have you any idea who it is?" I replied, "No, sir, but I will go along and see." On reaching the hospital I was taken to where this man lay but could not recognize him at all. He was pitted all over with what looked like bits of cinder and was a nasty yellow colour. I was very puzzled when he started repeating my name, and could not make head or tail of it and had to go away. For three weeks he was in a state of coma, but when he became conscious, the hospital advised me and I went down there again. He was sitting up in bed and nearly normal. He said to me, "Hello, Fred," and I found him to be a youthful friend of mine, the son of the postmaster at Waterloo. He had remembered where I was serving and in his extremity had called my name. This man caused a real sensation in Halifax. He was the chief officer of the cargo ship just moored ahead of us but I had no idea at all he was anywhere near, else I would have gone to see him. The force of the explosion disembowelled his ship, killed most of the crew and the captain and blew him 150 yards on to a grass plot in the dockyard, where he landed naked except for one boot and sock.

On my way back to the ship I was hailed by an undertaker and asked if I could identify an officer he had collected on the road. I found it was Rod Burnett, the carpenter, without a mark of any kind on him. It seems that concussion of this kind causes a bubble to form in the blood stream with fatal consequences.

I had hardly returned to the ship, when news was received that the ammunition dump in the dockyard was ringed with fire and in great danger. Volunteers were called for and practically everyone who could respond, including myself, did so, and all the ammunition was removed by hand to safety.

By now it was evening and the sky looked overcast and ominous. Soon it began to snow, becoming worse as the wind rose to a gale. By the time it was dark, we were in the middle of the worst gale I have ever lived through, a real Canadian blizzard. There was further danger now in the harbour. Ships out of control were drifting about with the ebb and flow of the tide; I have never experienced anything like it. Halifax has a large harbour and now it was just like a wild sea. Particularly dangerous were two partially wrecked vessels on fire, one with a cargo of black gunpowder. We simply had to secure this ship, wandering up and down and from side to side in the middle of the harbour, as there was the possibility of another explosion. In such a crowded area it would have been another disaster. Eventually she was secured. When we went aboard, we found that only one bulkhead door separated the fire from the explosive cargo.

The cruiser HIGHFLYER anchored in the middle of the harbour and just back from convoy escort, was in a bad way. Her funnels and part of the upper deck were stove in and her casualties were 25 men killed and many wounded. The lieutenant-commander was on the bridge watching MONT BLANC burning when the explosion happened and was decapitated. The lower part of his body was shielded by armour but his head was exposed to the blast. Her picket boat carrying fire-fighting apparatus must have reached the doomed ship just as the explosion occurred. Our own picket boat under Boatswain Mattison left with the same object in view; both have never been seen since. The two crews were awarded posthumously Royal Albert Medals.

The French 75mm gun on the stern of MONT BLANC was found six miles away, on the other side of the North West Arm, and the anchor three miles away.

So ends an episode in my life I will never forget. I re-visited Halifax in 1932. Richmond on the side of the hill had been rebuilt but the marks of the disaster were still obvious. At the time of the explosion Richmond was a small suburb composed mostly of wooden frame houses. Overturned by the force of the blast, the stoves set fire to them and many people were trapped by falling timbers and roasted alive. Many had been at their windows watching the burning ships and were blinded by glass splinters.

When the hard weather set in, stray dogs became a problem which the naval patrol keeping order in the ravaged city had to tackle. The dogs were living on human carrion and were as savage as wolves. Volunteers to shoot them were called for and many were destroyed. My ship NIOBE was a complete wreck and I was transferred to Esquimalt, B.C., where I was commissioned to H.M.C.S. RAINBOW. I finished the rest of the war in her patrolling the Pacific.

FROM A COPY OF THE ACCOUNT PRESENTED TO THE PUBLIC ARCHIVES OF CANADA BY NORMAN F. ELLISON

163

7 January, 1963

Dear Cousin Kate,

I want to tell you of an astonishing experience I've just had, and because I think Uncle Allan will be interested too, I'm making a carbon copy of this letter to send to him. It is about a book I just read, The Town That Died, by Michael Bird, an English author. Johnny has ordered copies for each of you and will send them along, but if you're squeamish, don't open the covers.

I asked Johnny (who works evenings in an English bookshop) to watch out for publication. Just after Christmas and a few days before I had an announcement from the publishers, Putnam, about the book, Johnny gave me a copy. I skipped through it idly whilst coming home in the bus, saw a picture of my alma mater (Saint Joseph's), read about our old church (Saint Mark's), and then my eye caught the opening lines of a chapter beginning on page 109 of the American edition.

Try and imagine my surprise to read of Mrs. Clark and her daughter—without any doubt at all, our Mrs. Clark!

Reading further, and going back to the beginning, I realized that the Mr. Fowlie whom the author had met and evidently stayed with in Halifax, and who gave him much material about that day in 1917, was the very young cable man whom Grandmother and Hoodie had rescued that morning: the same young man who wanted them to get out safely and leave him to die! There's positively no doubt in my mind: each detail (save one) of his story matches exactly the particulars I heard recited many times afterwards. The one detail which is different is the story of the teapot. I think that probably she had gone back for that after gathering up the other things.

It is strange to have this all brought back to me. Grandmother picking up the four corners of the tablecloth (after sweeping onto it what she could from the sideboard) and tying it up like a knapsack. It was there beside the flagpole when I was placed there to await the carts. Remember the flagpole halfway down the garden toward the Wellington Barracks fence? I wonder how she and Hoodie carried that bundle around town all day, in and out of hospitals and things, looking for me? Perhaps they had been able to leave it at the Hillises.

In the photograph of Saint Joseph's I can see the window from which I jumped, and in my mind's eye I can see the grand piano in the hall, its legs through the floor so that the top of the piano was just a step-height and easy to get on to and run across to the window . . .

Because I was an Anglican I was excused from morning prayers and due at school at five after nine each day. I had just walked past the piano, hung up my coat and hat and taken my seat beside Frances Hayes—in the front row of the classroom.

In Bird's book I learned that there would seem to have been some question as to whether there was one explosion or two. There were two. The first produced semi-darkness and a great rumble, rather like thunder that was taking place alongside of you instead of up in the sky somewhere. With it I saw the windowpanes blow inward, like a sail. I will never forget such an unbelievable sight, but indeed that is what happened. Even at my tender age, I knew they would burst, and instinctively I ducked my head—which is why the stilettos of glass the author writes of hit my forehead instead of my eyes!

When the incredible noise of the main explosion occurred immediately after, I ran for the door. The ceiling above gave way at one corner and down two sides of the room, hanging like the flap of a great envelope and spilling out children from the room above. It was pitch dark in a minute. Sister had hold of my wrist and that of Frances Hayes with a regular death grip, ordering us to get down and pray. I could see the white marble of the big statue of the Virgin swaying out in the blackness of the hall, and instinctively again, decided to get out first and pray afterwards. I clutched madly at her habit and beads, and she let go. After that, over the piano and out. I landed in a little heap of old snow in the corner by the steps and there I stayed a little while.

There was a little girl named Bently in my class. Lying in the heap of now red snow, I saw her run down the steps to the street, and then run back into the building screaming about the coat she had left inside.

I may have half-fainted or something after that because when I realized that some men were shouting and walking about I tried to call them but couldn't speak well. I raised my arm and one of them walked over to me and helped me up. My leg pained but I could stand on it, and when they were satisfied about that, they left me to fend for myself.

The raising of my arm was another instinctive gesture almost. Many times in my life I have marvelled at the human animal, its instinct for self-preservation. Certainly I was too young to have had much experience, too young to reason—but so many times that day I seemed to know just what to do to save my life. Walking toward the gate I prayed like anything, wondering all the while whether it would be best to say the Lord's Prayer which I didn't quite know by heart, or Now I Lay Me, which I did know. I settled for what

I knew of the Lord's Prayer, saying it over and over and yearning for Dad, because, of course, I thought Kentville was on fire, too. In Bird's book I read that others did the same things I did, like raising an arm to let someone know they were alive, like praying over and over . . .

There was a little street linking Kaye and Russell Streets through which I walked each morning, running my pencil along the rounded white pickets of a fence that flanked the whole length of the street. (Wonder who lived in a house there with such a big garden?)

Going along it now I noticed the fence was lying on the ground—which was a fine thing, because its familiar white pickets were all I could see from the peep-hole of vision I had; all else seemed darkness. I didn't realize, of course, that my eyes were almost covered with caked blood from my forehead. Once along that street to the corner, I knew where I was, could feel the cobbles of Russell Street under my feet. (One funny thing is that I can't remember being cold or anything like that, though it was winter and I had no coat on). I heard some deep, long cry coming toward me and I scratched at my eyes till I could see.

I don't remember being at all surprised or shocked to see a naked man coming up the hill just in front of me. I remember very well, however, the sight of the iodine-coloured curls of skin all over him like the curls of wood a plane makes on a board, except for the colour. He was feathered with these curls, and the white flesh showed through wherever there was not a curl. He asked for directions to some street I didn't know, and then went on up the hill, still crying aloud, and I descended to Grandmother's gate. Watching for me, she recognized the bright red plaid hair ribbon which Mother had sent in her last letter from Boston.

She led me to the lawn and put me down by the flagpole, by the knapsack of dishes, and in a little while the coal cart came. It was two-wheeled and drawn by a horse. It was painted green and had big white letters on its side, spelling C O A L. Grandmother came for me and helped me to it and I was lifted in—on top of layers of others. From then on she lost track of me for some time.

As I write this many things come back to me. Do you recall a family just up the hill next door—a large family in which each child had carrot coloured hair? I watched that house while I lay beside the flagpole. It was burning furiously, and from one of the windows I saw one of those red-haired children waving and screaming . . .

I remember so many things, since reading that book. Some of the things he speaks of at Camp Hill are before my eyes again. I have often thought that what went on there that day, and the blizzard next day, deserved a book by themselves.

But how lucky I was to have a father who was a druggist. I can imagine Dad now, emptying his shelves of all the drugs in the store, and then slipping that little phial of chloroform into his pocket!

I fear I must be boring you dreadfully; and probably you cannot be as amazed as I to hear of Grandmother and Hilda being put down in a book about the Explosion. ....

Love

Helen Clark Gucker

COURTESY OF HELEN CLARK GUCKER, WOLFVILLE, N.S.

Repercussions

After the first traumatic days of rescue there was a growing demand for an enquiry to place the blame. The German people and the Kaiser were thought the real culprits. In a wave of anti-German feelings, fanned by the Halifax Herald, many Halifax residents of German extraction were attacked, abused and finally arrested. However, even the most gullible of Haligonians soon came to their senses. Espionage or sabotage were never seriously suspected, except briefly in the case of Johan Johansen.

On December 13th an investigation was opened before the Wreck Commissioners in the old Court House on Spring Garden Road. The Hon. Judge Arthur Drysdale, Chairman of the Commission, appears from the outset to have been biased towards the owners of the IMO, represented by C. J. Burchell, K.C. Burchell's aggressive courtroom tactics and his browbeating of witnesses went unchecked until the Hon. W. A. Henry, K.C., representing the Dominion Government at the enquiry, felt obliged to intervene: "My Lord, I object to council speaking of shifting responsibility; it is high time I said something. My learned friend [C. J. Burchell], from the first, with regard to the evidence of any witness which did not suit him, has persistently abused and used language in regard to these witnesses which I do not think should be allowed."

The hearing revolved mainly around the testimony of Captain Aimé Le Medec, skipper of the MONT BLANC, Francis Mackey, the Halifax pilot on the MONT BLANC, and Commander Frederick Wyatt, Chief Examining Officer responsible for the movements of all large vessels in harbour.

In his cross-examination of Captain Le Medec, Burchell attempted to cast doubt upon his account of the sequence of movements of the vessels and the signals given, but Pilot Mackey confirmed Le Medec's testimony. Burchell accused Mackey, who naturally had left the burning MONT BLANC when the Captain and crew abandoned ship, of saving his own skin at the expense of thousands of lives and of being a heavy drinker. He implied laxity on the part of Commander Wyatt in carrying out his duties, lack of cooperation between the pilots and the port authorities, and with no apparent evidence he suggested that Wyatt ordered rescue workers out of the Dockyard because of the second explosion scare.

Judge Drysdale's findings, serving perhaps the quest for scapegoats, condemned the Pilot and Captain of the MONT BLANC and Commander Wyatt:

Halifax, N.S.
4 February, 1918

Sir,
Having been directed by the Honourable Minister of Marine to hold a formal enquiry into the cause of the explosion on the S.S. MONT BLANC on 6 December, 1917, I have to report as follows:

That as directed I had associated with me as Nautical Assessors, Captain Demers of Ottawa, Dominion Wreck Commissioner, and Captain Walter Hose, R.C.N. of the City of Halifax. I began the enquiry on the 13th day of December, A.D. 1917, and having heard all the witnesses that could throw any light on the situation, and having conferred with the Nautical Assessors, I have reached the following conclusions and desire to report as follows:

1. The explosion on the S.S. MONT BLANC on 6 December was entirely the result of a collision in the harbour between S.S. MONT BLANC and the S.S. IMO.

2. Such collision was caused by violation of the rules of Navigation.

3. That the Pilot and Master of the S.S. MONT BLANC were wholly responsible for violating the rules of the road.

4. That Pilot Mackey by reason of his gross negligence should be forthwith dismissed by the Pilotage Authorities and his licence cancelled.

5. In view of the gross neglect of the rules of Navigation by Pilot Mackey, the attention of the Law Officers of the Crown should be called to the evidence taken at this investigation with a view to a criminal prosecution of such pilot.

6. We recommend to the French Authorities such evidence with a view to having Captain Le Medec's licence calcelled and such captain dealt with according to the law of his country.

7. That it appearing that the Pilotage Authorities in Halifax have been permitting Pilot Mackey to pilot ships since the investigation commenced and since the collision above referred to, we think the Authorities, i.e. Pilotage Authorities, deserving of censure. In our opinion the Authorities, should have promptly suspended such pilot.

8. The Master and Pilot of the MONT BLANC are guilty of neglect of the public safety in not taking proper steps to warn the inhabitants of the city of a probable explosion.

9. Commander Wyatt is guilty of neglect in performing his duty as C.X.O. in not taking proper steps to ensure the regulations being carried out and especially in not keeping himself fully acquainted with the movements and intended movements of vessels in the harbour.

10. In dealing with the C.X.O.'s negligence in not ensuring the efficient carrying out of traffic regulations by the pilots we have to report that the evidence is far from satisfactory that he ever took any efficient steps to bring to the notice of the Captain Superintendent neglect on the part of the pilots.

11. In view of the allegations of disobedience of the C.X.O.'s orders by pilots, we do not consider such disobedience was the proximate cause of the collision.

12. It would seem that the pilots of Halifax attempt to vary the well known Rules of the Road, and, in this connection, we think Pilot Renner, in charge of an American tramp steamer on the morning of the collision, deserving of censure.

13. The regulations governing the traffic in Halifax harbour in force since the war were prepared by the competent Naval Authorities; that such traffic regulations do not satisfactorily deal with the handling of ships laden with explosives

and we have to recommend that such competent Authority forthwith take up and make satisfactory regulations dealing with such subject; we realise that whilst war goes on under present conditions explosives must move but, in view of what has happened, we strongly recommend that the subject be dealt with satisfactorily by the proper Authorities.

Given under my hand at the City of Halifax this Fourth day of February, 1918.   The Hon Judge. Arthur Drysdale

Captain Le Medec, Pilot Mackey and Commander Wyatt were arrested and accused of manslaughter, but these charges were dropped in a matter of weeks. A Royal Commission recommended changes in the organization of the Halifax Pilotage Commission. On January 11, the owners of the MONT BLANC had filed suit against the owners of the IMO claiming $2,000,000 damages. The IMO owners had counterclaimed for the same amount. The action was tried in the Exchequer Court before Justice Drysdale who stood by his earlier judgment. The MONT BLANC owners appealed to the Supreme Court of Canada.

The Supreme Court found both ships equally liable. The IMO owners appealed to the Privy Council in London, who ruled as follows:

Their Lordships have thus examined critically and at great length the evidence bearing upon the points in issue in the action. They have upon the whole come to the following conclusions:

First, that the MONT BLANC, from the time she passed the HIGHFLYER till she starboarded her helm in the agony of the collision, never left her own water, though she may, no doubt, before she was actually struck, have forged ahead so as to cross the middle line of the channel.

Second, that as she steamed up through her own waters her speed was not immoderate.

Third, that the IMO in order to inflict the injury to the MONT BLANC, which it is proved she did inflict must have struck that ship with more force and at a higher rate of speed than her witnesses admit.

Fourth, that the MONT BLANC must at the time of the collision have had little, if any, way on her, else the stem of the IMO would have been twisted to some extent, which it was not.

Fifth, that the inclination of their Lordships' opinion is that the IMO could, when she first reversed her engines, have crossed into and remained in her own water, as she was bound to do, but never did.

It is not necessary, however, absolutely to decide this last point, because in the case of both ships, it is clear that their navigators allowed them to approach within 400 feet of each other on practically opposite courses, thus incurring the risk of collision, and indeed practically bringing about the collision, instead of reversing their engines and going astern, as our assessors advise us, they, as a matter of good seamanship, could and should have done, long before the ships came so close together. This actually led to the collision. The manoeuvre of the MONT BLANC, in the agony of the collision, may not have been the best manoeuvre to adopt, and yet, in the circumstances, was excusable. But their Lordships are clearly of opinion that both ships are to blame for their reciprocal neglect above-mentioned to have reversed and gone astern earlier than they did.

They are therefore of opinion that the appeal and cross-appeal both fail, that the judgment appealed from should be affirmed, and they will humbly advise His Majesty accordingly.

Pilot Mackey, who following the report of Justice Drysdale's enquiry, had been suspended, was reinstated as a pilot. Captain Le Medec went on to serve the MONT BLANC owners until 1922. In 1931 upon retirement he was promoted Chevalier de la Légion d'Honneur. Commander Wyatt was cleared of the manslaughter charge that was brought against him but was transferred away from the port. His treatment caused much ill feeling in naval circles.

No one will ever know how many perished or were injured in the disaster. The Halifax Relief Commission listed 1,963 killed, 9,000 injured, 199 blinded; these figures are generally considered conservative. F. C. MacGillivray pointed out that he had to provide more than 3,000 grave markers. It is uncertain whether the Commission took fatalities on board ships into consideration and the hundreds of people who completely disappeared.

Over 25,000 people were left without adequate shelter and 6,000 lost their homes altogether. Within a 16 mile radius, 1,630 buildings were totally destroyed and 12,000 damaged. An estimate of total loss and cost of repairs was $35,000,000.

Halifax received relief from all over the world. Australia sent $250,000; Britain $5,000,000; New Zealand $50,000; the Canadian Government voted $19,000,000. Altogether contributions amounted to $30,000,000. Special thanks went to the New England States for the promptness and generosity of their response.

This account relies heavily on Michael Bird's THE TOWN THAT DIED, which includes a fuller account of the legal repercussions of the disaster.

An early photograph of reconstruction in the Richmond district.

The Hydrostone Neighbourhood

Ernest Clarke, M.R.A.I.C., M.C.I.P.

The explosion of December 6, 1917, literally flattened whole areas of Halifax. It is well to remember that this devastating action was matched by an equally strong reaction—the will and determination of Haligonians to rebuild their city. The clearest manifestation of this reaction is the Hydrostone neighbourhood, one of the largest enterprises of its kind ever undertaken in Canada.

A relief commission was formed within hours of the explosion and the commitment to rebuild came early and was total. Not only did the city resolve to rebuild quickly but, to its credit, it resolved to rebuild better. The process that followed constitutes one of the most outstanding events in the history of Canadian town planning.

The housing shortage resulting from the explosion was calculated to be 5000 homes with the North End being the hardest hit area. The relief commission was granted sweeping powers to prepare town planning schemes, make by-laws, alter streets and divert public sewers and water lines. "It is seldom," said one official, "that an old established city can offer unrestricted latitude to the ideas of the experts in town planning."

The objectives of the relief commission in replanning the devastated area were high minded indeed: "We are hoping for Halifax, clean, smooth streets, beautiful and commodious homes, adequate public buildings; in short, a city constructed in such a way as to harmonize with its beautiful situation and surroundings." It was left to the town planners' report to introduce sober practicality: "This is not a time, nor are the conditions in Halifax such, that the occasion is opportune for spending money on purely ornamental purposes. Nothing will be included in these schemes unless for some useful purpose connected with the economic development of the land or for protecting the health and well-being of the inhabitants."

Thomas Adams, town planning advisor to the Canadian Government, was engaged to prepare a plan for the portion of the city's North End which had received the full force of the explosion and suffered the worst devastation. The area generally runs north along Gottingen Street from Kaye Street. Quick recognition was given in his report to the natural advantages of the district: "As a residential district this portion of Halifax is unsurpassed, having a wonderful outlook over the harbour, the Narrows and Bedford Basin with the hills of Dartmouth in the background."

Thomas Adam's plan consisted of three main elements: (1) restructuring of the street pattern to obtain bet-ter grades—"an opportunity afforded by the disaster of December 6"—to quote his report; (2) creation of a large public park on the site of historic Fort Needham; and (3) construction of 324 homes plus local shops. And indeed, as one views the completed project now after nearly 60 years, it is the combination of these three elements—the boulevarded wide streets creating a tree-lined commons in every block, the compactness and architectural homogeneity of the housing, and the lofty expanse of Fort Needham hill—which gives the area its unique character within the city of Halifax.

In their design of the new residential street pattern, the planners neatly confined service traffic, utilities and storage to rear lanes while locating large tree-lined boulevards in front. These boulevards are 80 feet in width and create formal streetscapes for the housing blocks. But the planners were also concerned with through traffic and future traffic flows in and out of this part of the peninsula. They laid out several streets with wide rights-of-way to "provide the devastated area with an excellent system of main arteries." Some of their traffic projections may have been a little too optimistic such as their prediction that "at no distant date, a bridge will be built across the Narrows to Dartmouth somewhere in the region of Leeds Street."

The planners realized the need for open space in their residential design and recognized as well the potential and historic significance of the hill adjacent to the housing development. At Fort Needham, there is a high knoll which is one of the highest points in the city, commanding an extensive view of the water and surrounding country. It is proposed to develop this into a park. This park together with the boulevards in each block make the Hydrostone neighbourhood one of the most well endowed residential areas of the city with respect to open space and recreation amenity. This was an important innovation at the time.

The Montreal architectural firm of Ross and MacDonald was engaged to design the housing and by the middle of 1918 construction was well under way. Halifax was and is a city of wooden buildings but the town planners specified fire proof materials for this district. Consequently concrete block construction was used, in itself a sharp contrast to other residential areas of the city. The blocks were made from wet concrete subjected to enormous pressure and a stucco-like finish was given to the exterior face. Manufacture occurred in a plant built specifically for this purpose near Halifax and used a unique process developed by the Hydro-Stone Company of Chicago. Henceforth, the local name of the neighbourhood has been simply "The Hydro-Stone."

The architectural style used is vaguely Tudor but the scale is firmly domestic with a consistent plan pattern for the housing blocks. Complex roof slopes and sensitive detailing of windows and entrance ways establish the architectural quality of the project. The Hydrostone is a classic example of modern planning objectives such as low rise, high density and mixed uses. Its importance in residential planning terms derives from its successful mixture of small shops and offices, public parks, semi-detached houses, townhouses, quadraplexes, and apartments at an overall gross density (including the boulevarded streets) of 50 persons per acre. This is an incredibly high density considering the low-rise, spacious quality of the area. The high quality of architectural design served the planning requirements very well by minimizing any adverse effects of higher density and the accommodation of commercial development.

The houses got built at an estimated cost of $1,800 for a four-room house and bath and $2,500 for a detached house; but not without an agreement among construction companies to a fixed maximum fee schedule to prevent raiding in a tight labour market brought on by the general reconstruction. Interior house plans were generous for the times and boasted a clothes closet for each bedroom, at least one window in every room, porches, storage areas and pantries, and hot air central heating systems. The houses were rented until the 1950's when they were gradually transferred to individual freehold ownership. Market values have since appreciated steadily and the neighbourhood retains its attraction in the residential marketplace.

The strength of its original planning concept and its architectural quality have enabled the Hydrostone to age gracefully and to successfully withstand the impact of a half century of use and change. The planning approach was far from grandiose and here the planner's report can be quoted. ''The necessity of preparing schemes that are practical, both from a financial and from an engineering point of view, is not solely due to the need for economy. One must be practical in method to get a thing done at all—and it is waste of time to set up idealistic utopias of what we would like to do but cannot do. The Halifax schemes will be prepared on lines that can be carried out and enforced, however far short they may be of the ideal one would like to attain.'' However, modest and rooted in practicality, this approach has ultimately led to a model of planned housing development in Canada.

Ernest Clarke is Director of Planning for the Nova Scotia Housing Commission. His special interest is the design and construction of a bicycle pathway system around Nova Scotia.

Chronology

December 1st, 1917
S.S. MONT BLANC sails from New York

December 6th, 1917—Thursday
7:30 a.m. MONT BLANC enters the harbour.
IMO weighs anchor in Bedford Basin.
8:30 a.m. The vessels sight each other.
8:45 a.m. The Collision.
Alarm sent into West Street Engine House.
9:06 a.m. Explosion.
Rescue work begins.
PICTON cut loose.
10:00 a.m. Second alarm and panic.
10:30 a.m. Truro sends aid.
11:30 a.m. Relief train leaves Kentville
Emergency meeting at City Hall.
12:00 noon Relief train leaves New Glasgow.
1:00 p.m. All available troops reach the North End.
Train of wounded leaves for Truro.
3:00 p.m. The City Council meets.
3:45 p.m. D.A.R. relief train arrives.
4:00 p.m. Train of wounded reach Truro where hospitals are ready.
6:00 p.m. New Glasgow relief train arrives.
U.S. hospital ship, OLD COLONY, opens as a hospital.
6:00 p.m. Morgue and various shelters open.
7:30 p.m. First American relief leaves Boston.
9:00 p.m. Tent city on Common completed.
Aid arrives from Amherst.
11:00 p.m. Aid arrives from Moncton.

December 7th, 1917—Friday
a.m. The blizzard begins.
11:00 a.m. Meeting at the City Hall.
12:00 noon St. John's Ambulance Brigade inaugurates organized relief, district visiting, etc. with headquarters at the City Hall.
Automobiles commandeered.
The Blind School opens as a hospital.
2:00 p.m. Green Lantern Clothing Depot opened.
School teachers organize for relief.
5:00 p.m. Aid arrives from Charlottetown.
Premier Borden arrives in Halifax.

December 8th, 1917—Saturday
a.m. Boston Relief train with Hon. A. C. Ratschesky arrives staying until January 5th.
The Salvation Army cooperate with workers at the City Hall.
Four food depots are established.
The U.S. Government offers $5,000,000.
3:00 p.m. Relief Committee meet with Premier Borden and U.S. representatives at the City Club.
7:00 p.m. Relief train arrives from Montreal.

December 9th, 1917—Sunday
2:00 a.m. Storm begins.
Dr. Codman and nurses arrive from Boston.
Y.M.C.A. building converted into a hospital.
Relief Ship CALVIN AUSTEN leaves Boston.
Maine Relief Unit arrives.
Stores open all day.
Sunday papers.
Maine Unit occupies Ladies College.
The Halifax Herald demands that blame be fixed.
Church services at St. Paul's.
Aliens are interned.
St. Mary's College Hospital opened.
Fire on the PICTON at Eastern Passage extinguished by four soldiers and one civilian.

December 10th, 1917—Monday
Relief train arrives from Toronto
The Mayors of Halifax and Dartmouth publish an appeal for aid.
Non-residents are requested to leave city by a civic proclamation.
The Christian Science Relief arrives.
4:00 p.m. Rhode Island Unit arrives.
3:00 p.m. Patients taken to New Glasgow.
Queen Alexandra cables her sympathy.
The Canadian Red Cross open a dispensary at the Technical College.
Canadian Government grants $1,000,000.
Clergymen organize for relief.
The Relief Executive is transferred from the City Hall to the City Club.
Severe snow storm in the afternoon.

December 11th, 1917—Tuesday
Train service at North Street Station resumed with departure of Ocean Limited.
Relief Offices moved from City Hall.
Relief Ship NORTHLAND leaves Boston.
The Relief Committee tenders thanks to Massachusetts.
A trainload of artisans arrives from Sydney.

December 12th, 1917—Wednesday
First published list of unidentified dead in morgue.
Relief Ship CALVIN AUSTEN arrives.
Cable of sympathy from King George.
The British Relief Fund is begun.
The Inquiry into the explosion is postponed.
The V.O.N. establishes 8 dressing stations.
3:00 p.m. Meeting of the City Council.
A mounted guard is placed over the devastated district.
Meeting of the Clerical Relief.
Free cables offered to men at the front by Musgrave & Co.
Living man exhumed from the ruins.
Military search parties continue in devastated area until January 11th.

December 13th, 1917—Thursday
The Court of Inquiry is opened.
A Commission of Inquiry is appointed on January 15th.
Relief Steamer NORTHLAND arrives from Massachusetts.
Helmsman Johannsen of the IMO is arrested.
Notice of the burial of the unidentified dead.
A maternity hospital is opened at the Y.M.C.A.

December 14th, 1917—Friday
A severe storm.
The Massachusetts S.P.C. arrives.
The election is postponed.
The Inquiry is continued.
A proclamation that no credence should be given to rumours of danger of a second explosion.
Proclamation calls upon all men to work.

December 15th, 1917—Saturday
The Board of Trade asks for a conference.

December 16th, 1917—Sunday
The OLD COLONY hospital ship is evacuated.
Services in the various unde-molished churches.

December 17th, 1917—Monday
A Commission is proposed.
The Inquiry is continued.
Public funeral of the majority of the unidentified dead from Chebucto morgue.
Systematic districts for relief visiting are created.
The gas is turned on for the first time.
The merchants have com-pletely resumed trade with the rural districts.
Civic activities have been completely resumed.
Halifax Disaster Record Of-fice officially inaugurated.

December 18th, 1917—Tuesday
Sufferers register for Relief at St. Mary's Army and Navy Club.
Messrs. Carstens and Moore of the American Red Cross leave.
The Canadian Club of New York makes a contribution for the children affected.
The Inquiry is continued.
An infectious hospital is opened at Oxford Street School.
A nursery for blind babies is established at the Blind School.

December 21st, 1917—Friday
The visit of the Duke and Du-chess of Devonshire.
A visit from Mr. Adams, Do-minion town planning expert.
Fixing of rents advocated.

December 23rd, 1917
The Rhode Island Unit leaves Halifax.
The State of Maine Unit leaves Halifax.

December 24th, 1917
The Waegwoltic Convale-scent Hospital is opened.

December 25th, 1917
Christmas celebrations in the hospitals and shelters.

December 27th, 1917
Halifax thanks the American Red Cross.

December 28th, 1917
The Clerical Committee urges a permanent commission.

December 29th, 1917
Conference of sub-committee of Federal Ministers.
Ballantyne's statement as to need for more port control.
11:00 a.m. Meeting in Legislature.

January 1st, 1918
Memorial services held in the churches.

January 3rd, 1918
Ladies College evacuated.

January 4th, 1918
Statement published as to what relief committee will supply.
Ward Six Depot established.

WOMAN

Well, it affected me. To this day I'm very sensitive to noise and I have a great fear of fire. I've never been even to a movie after that without looking where the exit was. It was always on my mind—how to get out. I get claustrophobia in a crowd.

MAN

I was very nervous for a long time, very nervous of plate glass. Mind you, I've seen some dreadful things. Windows that have come in and cut people all to pieces.

WOMAN

I wasn't proud of myself after the explosion. I had to cover my face if anyone looked at me. Felt terrible, you know. At seventeen you're just starting to get, well, cute, if you want to call it that, starting to grow up—and it gave me a complex.

MAN

I don't like boasting that we've got a bigger thing than this and a bigger thing than the other, but the number of people killed in the Halifax Explosion was, oh, about eight times the number of people that perished in the Chicago fire, and about four times the number of people that died in the 'Frisco earthquake. It was really pretty terrific.

WOMAN

About 24 of my family, counting my father's, my aunts and my uncles, you know . . . in all the family about 24 were killed. Yes, my best friend—up until we were seventeen, we went to school together, we went everywhere together—the only friend I had, and she was killed.

MAN

If you'd been here and had seen what I saw, you would hate all thoughts of war and that sort of thing.

WOMAN

No, we didn't forget it, we didn't forget it, but you know what life is, you have to live.

FROM SOUND RECORDINGS BY PAT KIPPING

DATE DUE

MAY 29 1996	
APR 0 7 1999	
Mar. 23/99	
BRODART	Cat. No. 23-221